EXPATRIATE IDENTITIES IN POSTCOLONIAL ORGANIZATIONS

Studies in Migration and Diaspora

Series Editor:
Anne J. Kershen, Queen Mary College, University of London, UK

Studies in Migration and Diaspora is a series designed to showcase the interdisciplinary and multidisciplinary nature of research in this important field. Volumes in the series cover local, national and global issues and engage with both historical and contemporary events. The books will appeal to scholars, students and all those engaged in the study of migration and diaspora. Amongst the topics covered are minority ethnic relations, transnational movements and the cultural, social and political implications of moving from 'over there', to 'over here'.

Also in the series:

Multifaceted Identity of Interethnic Young People
Chameleon Identities
Sultana Choudhry
ISBN 978-0-7546-7860-1

The Invisible Empire
White Discourse, Tolerance and Belonging
Georgie Wemyss
ISBN 978-0-7546-7347-7

Lifestyle Migration
Expectations, Aspirations and Experiences
Edited by Michaela Benson and Karen O'Reilly
ISBN 978-0-7546-7567-9

International Migration and Rural Areas
Cross-National Comparative Perspectives
Edited by Birgit Jentsch and Myriam Simard
ISBN 978-0-7546-7484-9

Accession and Migration
Changing Policy, Society, and Culture in an Enlarged Europe
Edited by John Eade and Yordanka Valkanova
ISBN 978-0-7546-7503-7

Expatriate Identities in Postcolonial Organizations
Working Whiteness

PAULINE LEONARD
University of Southampton, UK

ASHGATE

Published by
Ashgate Publishing Limited
Wey Court East
Union Road
Farnham
Surrey, GU9 7PT
England

Ashgate Publishing Company
Suite 420
101 Cherry Street
Burlington
VT 05401-4405
USA

www.ashgate.com

British Library Cataloguing in Publication Data
Leonard, Pauline, 1957-
 Expatriate identities in postcolonial organizations :
 working whiteness. -- (Studies in migration and diaspora)
 1. Postcolonialism--Social aspects. 2. Organizational
 sociology. 3. Foreign workers--China--Hong Kong--Social
 conditions. 4. Whites--Employment--China--Hong Kong.
 5. Whites--Race identity--China--Hong Kong.
 I. Title II. Series
 331.6'217409-dc22

Library of Congress Cataloging-in-Publication Data
Leonard, Pauline, 1957-
 Expatriate identities in postcolonial organizations : working whiteness / by Pauline
Leonard.
   p. cm. -- (Studies in migration and diaspora)
 Includes bibliographical references and index.
 ISBN 978-0-7546-7365-1 (hardback) -- ISBN 978-0-7546-9156-3 (ebook)
1. Whites--Race identity. 2. Aliens. 3. Postcolonialism. 4. Organizational change. I.
Title.
 HT1575.L46 2010
 305.9'0691--dc22

                                                                      2010004777

ISBN 9780754673651 (hbk)
ISBN 9780754691563 (ebk)

Mixed Sources
Product group from well-managed
forests and other controlled sources
www.fsc.org Cert no. SGS-COC-2482
© 1996 Forest Stewardship Council
FSC

Printed and bound in Great Britain by
TJ International Ltd, Padstow, Cornwall

Contents

Series Editor's Preface

In recent decades the image of the immigrant has been one of negativity; of poverty and threat; of individuals migrating due to necessity rather than desire. In contrast, British expatriates are perceived as privileged – middle or upper class – individuals who, whilst living overseas, continue to retain their national identity and separation from the mainstream; inhabiting a notional, or actual, ring-fenced community of whiteness within which the 'organization' (employer) and the Club are the focal points of expatriate life. It is the acting out of the role of the working expatriate through the intersection of race, gender, class and nationality that Pauline Leonard explores in this thought provoking volume which centres on her empirical research amongst British expatriates in Hong Kong. Using a poststructuralist methodology grounded in theoretical strands which are indebted to, amongst others, Foucault and Derrida, Leonard highlights the way in which whiteness is central to the construction and maintenance of expatriate identity, behaviour, and control.

Expatriates fall into two main categories: retirees and those whose employment by multi-national organizations or government bodies has taken them overseas. In this book Leonard focuses on working expatriates, the majority of whom began their employment before the handover to China. By so doing she has enabled the reader to evaluate the way in which the transition from British expatriate in a British colony to British worker in an Asian country impacts on self, and outsider, perceptions of identity. Unlike the often harsh and exploited immigrant experience, expat life in Hong Kong – even after the handover – is shown to be well paid, luxuriously accommodated and protected; as one interviewee explains, '... it was fantastic'. In the workplace, racial and managerial superiority endowed workers with a possessiveness that distanced them from their indigenous colleagues.

The traditional perception of expatriate life has been viewed through a gendered lens. In the colonial era the expatriate worker was male and middle class, his wife the 'trailing spouse', her role played out in strictly domestic and social territories. Even in the twenty-first century employment opportunities for expatriate wives within the expatriate community remain limited. Those wives that want to occupy themselves beyond the social spaces are often forced to position themselves on the margins in order to carry out voluntary or paid work; either of which is perceived as despoiling the purity of the expatriate image. Yet, changes are taking place. In the global world single women are becoming independent expatriates, though, as the author illustrates, rarely at the same level as their male counterparts. However, whilst the gender expatriate balance is changing and new blood is entering the arena, others who appear in this volume are considering retirement. Significantly

Leonard found amongst those she interviewed that their British identity had begun to fade; having become disillusioned with the nation's politics and lifestyle, not all would be retiring home to the United Kingdom. Some were considering staying on, others looking at pastures new. For those that do return, resettlement will demand a renegotiation of identity. Whiteness, gender and work will play different roles, while the organization, if present at all, will take a minor part.

The expatriate experience is shown to be a very different one to that of the independent immigrant. Whilst the latter has to make his or her own way, integrating to a greater or larger extent with the mainstream, the expatriate leads a sheltered and nurtured existence. To fully appreciate the nuances that separate the two, a reading of this book is a priority.

Anne J. Kershen
Queen Mary University of London
Spring 2010

Acknowledgements

I am very grateful to the University of Southampton for funding aspects of this research which made this book possible. Thanks also go to colleagues at the various conferences and workshops on whiteness, professional migration and expatriate life who provided me with invaluable and insightful feedback on earlier stages of this research and Caroline Knowles who was a co-researcher and travelling companion at early stages of the project. Many thanks to all colleagues at Southampton for support of various kinds: in particular Susan Halford, Bernard Harris and Derek McGhee; and family and friends Guy, Will, Frances, Ed, Emily, Molly, Guinness, Gill, Murphy, Annabel and Nell.

Chapter 1

Introduction

'*Expatriates*' – the very word conjures up images of lavish lifestyles, hedonistic pleasures and social irresponsibility. Contemporary representations of expatriates in the media often focus on the derogatory: unfortunate entanglements with the legal systems of host countries, often as a result of conflicting attitudes on sex, alcohol or drugs; or the nationalism and parochialism of the downshifters who, whilst seeking to escape the materialistic and climatic pressures of urbanization and dreary winters, only recreate the banalities of their native culture in some rural or sunny idyll (Billig 1995, O'Reilly 2000). However alongside these more salacious or humorous examples of activity exists an ever more routine reality of contemporary working life: from bankers to builders, planners to plumbers, increasing numbers of workers of all backgrounds and skills are now becoming caught up in the busy cycle of packing up and leaving homes and lives for a term of employment overseas. In spite of breathtaking developments in information and communication technology, physical movement by air, land or sea is still a feature of today's global labour markets, and one which now touches all occupational sectors.

Yet there is something distinctive, not to say contentious, about the word 'expatriate', as well as the people to which it refers, which raises some interesting questions about labour migration and difference. The term 'expatriate' is baggage-laden, particularly when used in a work context: connoting not only *the West*, as it is most commonly used in reference to people living overseas who originate from Europe, North America and the Antipodes; but also *privilege* – as it is usually used to refer to well paid members of the professional middle classes; and *whiteness*, as it is rare to hear the term used in relation to people who are, for example, natives of the Caribbean or South Asia. The rootedness of this term in the classed whiteness of the West is underpinned by its historical and literary connections, for it was often used to describe communities such as the American writers living on the left bank in Paris in the 1920s, the Australian artists in London at the turn of the century, as well as the dissolute lives of colonial administrators and their wives in Kenya or Malaysia, such as those depicted in the novels of Doris Lessing, Somerset Maugham and Joseph Conrad (see also Fechter 2007). It is today still a regularly used term; drawn upon principally by white Western professional expatriates themselves – both in their talk, as well as on the Internet. Here numerous 'expat' sites offer all sorts of advice on housing, leisure, food and cultural norms to Westerners living in a range of countries overseas. It also appears in the management and human resources literature which focuses on the international needs and programmes of multinational corporations. And increasingly, it is making an appearance in sociological and geographical debates on mobile professionals, albeit in far more self conscious terms (Fechter 2007, Leonard 2008, Coles and Fechter 2008).

It is therefore in many ways an exclusionary term. It has connotations of classed Western whiteness, as well as, in its use in working contexts, middle class professionalism, and this means that it 'Others' other migrants, differentiating expatriates by virtue of their race, class, nationalities, occupations and education. This sense of difference between migrants is also reflected in other broader and more contemporary terms, such as 'lifestyle migrants', 'privileged migrants' and 'mobile professionals', which are all increasingly being used to refer to those already relatively affluent (and usually white) individuals who move overseas in order to improve their quality of life. Diverse groups such as the retired British in Spain, Northern European families in France, Italians in East Africa, gap year students, young European travellers in South East Asia, and Australians and South Africans in London – these are all clearly dramatically different forms of movement than that of those fleeing from conflict and political persecution, famine, war or poverty. Thus whilst the term 'lifestyle migrant' more specifically tends to be used to refer to those who are seeking satisfaction from aspects *other* than work: good weather and food, better housing, new spiritual or cultural experiences, or a more relaxed, less materialistic culture, it is acknowledged that many skilled labour migrants are *also* seeking more than economic return alone: for many mobile professionals, migration offers *multiple* attractions, in terms of career enhancement, upward social mobility for themselves and their families, as well as the opportunity of travel and experiencing other cultures.

The word *opportunity* is important here. Clearly these sorts of migrants-lifestyle, privileged and/or professional, are all seen to be able to take up new opportunities in mobility offered by economic globalization with a degree of agency which is quite different from that possessed by other labour or political migrants. Restrictions on their rights of settlement and citizenship are usually made, and felt, with a somewhat lighter touch, and as such the consequences of their displacement in terms of inclusion and exclusion are far more ambiguous. These political differences are played out in the social through the broad diversity of the ways that different sorts of migrants are able to live their new lives, and the new identities they are able to construct for themselves. Due to this enormous range of experiences and circumstances in migration there is a growing recognition therefore that research should broaden its focus to include privileged migrants from the industrialized West, traditionally a somewhat invisible category (e.g. O'Reilly 2000, Walsh 2006, Fechter 2007, Coles and Fechter 2008, Willis and Yeoh 2002). This new research is interdisciplinary, and insights from sociology, anthropology, geography and cultural studies are now revealing the complexity of issues in the study of expatriate lives. Much of this research takes the form of ethnography, often drawing on a mixed methods approach which may include unstructured interviews, observation, visual methods, mapping and textual analysis to produce rich qualitative data which complements more quantitative analyses of skilled labour markets. Of particular interest here has been the impact of migration in the construction of *identity*, especially through the lenses of gender, family life, community, personal and social relationships and the making of new homes (e.g. Callan and Ardener 1984, Coles and Fechter 2008).

However, to date, there are two key aspects which are less commonly approached in these analyses. First is the importance of the world of *work* as a key site for the construction and performance of new identities and lives. Whilst there is some rich and thoughtful literature on the place of work in the lives of unskilled labour migration (e.g. Sørensen and Olwig 2002, Westwood and Phizacklea 2000), qualitative research into the work contexts of skilled migrant labour is unusual. What does exist in the broader field of 'expatriates and work' tends to be in the management and human resources literature, and adopts a positivist, non-theoretical approach that focuses on organizational issues such as recruitment and selection, turnover and career management rather than people themselves. Much of this literature also assumes that the expatriate worker is male, and as such ignores the increasing entry of highly skilled women into the expatriate labour force (Kofman and Parvati 2006).

The second aspect which has not always been made central is the place of *race and ethnicity* in the making of expatriate identities and lives. Yet for many expatriates, race and ethnicity, in combination with nationality, class and gender, can operate in their new lives with a particular salience. As such it should not be underplayed in the analysis of expatriates' lives if we are to understand better the differences between labour migrants and their place in the global order. For most expatriates, whilst there may be a whole host of complex social and personal reasons behind the decision to migrate, it is *work* which will provide the *where*, *the how* and *the who*. Occupational sectors are geographically specific, such that the chemical engineer is more likely to go to America or Europe, the construction manager to Africa or the Middle East, and the banker to New York or Hong Kong. The 'how' will include the ease with which multinational corporations can engineer the 'where' for their (white) expatriate employees: the management of flights, visas and accommodation as well as the organizationally framed lifestyles that await them. It will also include how expatriates understand themselves in their new lives – *who* they will be. Work will often therefore be the first point of entry to the new life – the context through which the newly arrived expatriate at first negotiates the people and places of their new home. Analysis must therefore acknowledge the *power* of work and organizations in people's lives: not only to exercise control over daily routines, but also in the shaping of their social and personal relations and identities:

> Indeed it is in the very nature of organizations that they attempt to systemise power relations between members, bestowing official rights of power to certain individuals over others, validating certain cultural and/or normative beliefs or discourses and not others (Halford and Leonard 2001: 26).

Organizational sociology has shown us how the principles of differentiation and inequality are embedded within organizational practices through the intersections of race, gender and class. However, whilst some exciting research is emerging analysing these issues of workplace diversity, this is concentrated in the main in Western organizations (e.g. Konrad et al. 2006). Yet, in this age of global migration, it is important to ask what happens to organizations *outside the West* when (white) Westerners arrive to them? How are the ascriptions of race, gender, class (and nationality) configured and reconfigured through the processes which accompany migration and displacement, at both the level of the organization and the individual?

The starting point for this book was thus a desire to contribute to three strands of research and debate. First, the book aims to contribute to the opening up of the ethnographic research on labour migration to include a focus on white, privileged labour migrants. Second, it aims to broaden the ethnographic literature on expatriates and identity-making to include a focus on work and organizational contexts, and the place of race within these. Third, it aims to open up the research on workplace diversity to include an exploration of the impact of migration on race- (specifically whiteness-) making (Proudford and Nkomo 2006). The book seeks therefore to centralize questions of race and ethnicity, and look at the resonance of whiteness in expatriate lives. Situating this exploration in the workplace not only provides a material context in which to explore racial difference, but also a political one: for it is in the workplace that racism and racial discrimination can thrive. With the expanding global economy and increasing mobility and movement of workers, it is no longer acceptable to retain these explorations with national boundaries: just as transnational organizations are mushrooming, so are the transnational productions and performances of difference.

I approach this exploration by examining the practices, identities and lifestyles of expatriates working in a range of organizational contexts. These are investigated primarily through a poststructuralist approach to analysis, which is a model particularly suited to looking at the ways in which identities and experiences are produced in specific social and interactional contexts. Broadly, this perspective considers that institutional discourses work to position people within different sets of power relations, which can be shaped and reshaped by individual acts of support or resistance (Baxter 2008). This is therefore particularly useful in the study of the ways in which the institutions of work position their employees. Drawing on emerging empirical research on expatriates as well as my own research conducted with white British expatriates in Hong Kong, I analyse the discursive, as well as the material and spatial contexts of their working lives. I trace the contours of race, in intersection with gender, class and nationality, and explore how these position expatriates in migratory workplaces. At the same time I aim to explore how expatriates position *themselves* in relation to these configurations, and, in these practices, contribute to the making and remaking of racialized organizations and work relations. My aim is to explore these processes in fine detail in order to offer a point of access to understanding the complexity and diversity of skilled migrants' working identities as they are negotiated in the new social and organizational contexts of migration.

This first chapter lays out this theoretical and methodological basis for the book further. To put this in context, I do this by presenting a brief introduction to the key contemporary debates on expatriates and outlining my position within these. First, I review how *globalization* theory conceives of skilled migrants. Many globalization theorists claim that a new highly mobile and disembedded 'transnational capitalist class' (Sklair 2001) now exists which transcends bordered connections with the national and the local. This new 'cosmopolitan' class is said to express both 'nationalitylessness' and 'placelessness' through their 'consciousness of the world as a single place' (Robertson 1992: 132). However, my argument is that a more detailed analysis of the voices and everyday lives of these people would appear to challenge this conception (Deutsche 1996). A more grounded methodological approach reveals how those who work in the upper echelons of global corporations *do* maintain strong cultural connections and placed allegiances with their home countries. Further, the detail provided by such an approach reveals diversities and fluidities within this group of people, throwing into question the very existence of a 'class' as such.

In the second section therefore I expand on this grounded methodological approach through a discussion of the ways in which the theoretical and methodological ideas associated with *transnationalism* can provide a productive way through the questions raised by globalization theory. By focusing on the *discursive*, *material* and *spatial* practices of social actors, and the ways in which these make connections across and between societies, transnational approaches reveal how integral place and local context are to the making of migrant identities and lives.

In the third section I introduce recent developments in migration research which focus on the lives of expatriates/mobile professionals. As with the transnationalism literature, these also aim to challenge the notion of a free flowing global movement of a class of skilled elite workers who are disembedded from their home nations. Rather, this research argues that nation, together with race and gender, are regularly drawn upon in the construction and performance of migrant lives and identities, albeit in uneven and fragmented ways. The extent and manner to which this activity is bound up with the contexts of work is the key focus of this book.

In the final section I introduce the theoretical and methodological approach of this book, which is subsequently developed and expanded through the chapters that follow.

Skilled Migration in a Globalizing World

It is now well recognized that dramatic economic, political and cultural changes have reshaped the world in the latter decades of the twentieth century – globalizing changes that go far beyond the individual systems of nation states (Sklair 2001). These changes have emerged from powerful transnational forces, processes and institutions which cross national borders and as such have reshaped patterns of capitalism, consumerism, communication, culture and labour markets. As the world is becoming more and more interconnected and 'globalized', new mobilities are created in terms of where we may work and live, what jobs we may do and who are colleagues are.

Integral to the process of globalization, then, is international migration. Economic and political explanations for this focus on the fact that, since the 1970s, a series of globalizing practices have led to the expansion of capitalism and the creation of new labour markets, mushrooming 'flows' of international population movements across the globe. These were to serve the new rise of free market capitalism which followed the collapse of socialist politics and the decline of labour movements in both the East and the West (Bauman 1989). The intervening years have seen rounds of economic restructuring, privatization, state deregulation, increases in the power of large transnational corporations and the proliferation of new technologies: and all these are seen to have facilitated a new connectivity and new social relations based on global 'flows' (Savage 2005). As Hannerz (1992) argued:

> the traditional picture of human cultures as forming a global mosaic – of cultures as plural, bounded, pure, integrated, cohesive, distinctive, place-rooted and mapped in space-must now be complemented by a picture of "cultural flows in space" and by a global ecumene (Rapport and Dawson 1998: 25).

However if the aim of 'globalization' is the establishment of a 'borderless global economy, the complete denationalization of all corporate procedures and activities, and the eradication of economic nationalism' (Sklair 2001: 3) such that we may all have seamless rights to 'flow' across the globe (Appadurai 1996), then we are still far from this. Contradictions exist between the levels of the global market and the nation state: many people live and work in countries where they cannot become citizens, whilst others are denied rights of entry completely. Many migrants are so poorly paid that they have little choice as consumers. At the same time other labour migrants, the 'expatriates' or skilled professionals, are accorded opportunities to bypass immigration regulations and work almost wherever they may choose, often being highly rewarded to boot. Migration thus 'reveals much about the dialectic of inclusion and exclusion' which is so typical of the new global (dis)order (Castells 2000: 12).

Global Systems Theory maintains the key drivers of these inegalitarian processes have been transnational corporations. In the last 20 years, these have gained dramatically in number, size and strength in the quest for profit maximization and development of the global economy (Sklair 2001). In order to function effectively across national boundaries, these corporations have particular organizational requirements which demand highly skilled support (Sassen 2002).

These are professional services such as legal, financial, accounting, managerial, executive, planning, advertising and marketing, all of which have increased exponentially as multinational contexts have grown in complexity, specialism and competition. Transnational corporations need to be adept at handling these functions across national boundaries, whilst at the same time keeping abreast of the rapid innovations which are constantly developing. Increasingly this means that these services will be bought in, and thus in every global city there now exists a proliferation of service organizations. These not only represent a strategic factor in the organization of the global economy, but also the rationale for maintaining the need for worldwide mobile professional labour (Sassen 2002). In addition, the formation of explicitly global institutions and processes such as The World Trade Organization, The World Health Organization, The International Monetary Fund, The United Nations, The World Bank, and war trade tribunals (Sassen 2007) also demands that professionals are willing to be posted overseas. As such, highly skilled migration represents an increasingly large component of global migration streams, and we can see that 'the operation of the professions has become a transnational matter' (Iredale 2001: 7).

Some theorists argue that mobile professionals such as these: corporate executives, globalizing bureaucrats, knowledge workers, politicians and professionals are part of global class formations which are creating a new privileged transnational elite. Dubbed the 'transnational capitalist class', this group of people is seen to be located at the top of the global hierarchy, and it is they who are more or less in control of globalization (Sklair 2001, Friedmann 1997). Whilst Hannerz (1992) argues that this class possess 'decontextualized cultural capital': cultural capital which is recognized across nations (Weiss 2005), closer analysis quickly reveals that the cultural capital these people possess is in fact very much *contextualized* in the Anglo-American/western world. Its inclusion of such attributes as attendance at Western expensive fee-paying schools and 'old' universities, proficiency in (expensive) sports such as sailing, skiing, rowing, rugby, or horse riding, membership of exclusive clubs, and familiarity with global cities such as London, Hong Kong and New York, mean that these are the

> sort of people who attend business-school weddings around the world, fill up the business-class lounges at international airports, provide the officer ranks of most of the world's companies and international institutions and through their collective efforts, probably do more than anyone else to make the world seem smaller (Mickelthwait and Wooldridge 2000: 229).

In addition, they

> can afford advanced technologies of transport and communication. Their social autonomy is ensured by the acquisition of several citizenships or a well accepted one. They are educated in global and prestigious places and take care that their children incorporate dominant (western) *habitus* (Ong 1999). In most cases they

will be white or be accepted as white by their peers. Being able to move and to possibly spread different aspects of their lives across the globe is a result of wealth and enhances it at the same time (Weiss 2005: 714).

However it would be quite wrong to situate all expatriates, privileged as they are, with the sort of classed status and privilege which Mickelthwait and Wooldridge (2002) encapsulate in their term 'cosmocrats'. We need to acknowledge the *diversity* of the expatriate experience. First, expatriates work in widely differing contexts, and not all of them are invested with the power of transnational corporations: aid organizations, educational organizations, health care services, construction, small size businesses, entertainment and so on can all be quite local and small in scale. Second, gender is critical in the ways it diversifies experiences, yet this is ignored by these abstract approaches to globalization. Third, for many, the period of their expatriation may be quite temporary, perhaps only for one or two years. This fluidity in the expatriate experience means that a stepping *into* the privileges of the transnational classes may be offset by the experience of being thrown *out* again at the other end: suddenly the school fees cease and it is back to 'economy' flights. This scenario is illustrated by an example from my own research in Hong Kong.

Colleen and Connor were posted to Hong Kong five years ago by the multinational bank at which Connor worked as an actuary. Having already migrated to England from Northern Ireland, they were at the time living in a modest house on a housing estate on the outskirts of London. Their four children attended local state schools, and although Colleen aspired to send them to fee paying secondary schools, it was unlikely that they could afford it. Out of the blue a posting to Hong Kong was offered, which Connor was very keen to accept as it represented a step up the career ladder and the opportunity to add 'overseas experience' to his CV. School fees came as a standard part of the package: as did a large apartment in the expatriate enclave of 'The Peak': a prestigious area of Hong Kong. The three older boys aged 8, 10 and 12 were dispatched to an English boarding school of some substance and off they went. Once in Hong Kong they joined the banking elite: club membership at one of the prestigious sailing clubs was automatic and soon their weekends were spent sailing in the waters of the South China Sea, at Christmas they were skiing in Whisper, in the summer they travelled between London and Hong Kong. Colleen had a 'helper' to look after the youngest child and was relieved of all housework. The children's boarding school friends were on the same circuit: indeed their headmaster visited Hong Kong regularly as part of his recruitment tour. They all got used to this global life: hopping on and off planes, access to an international group of contacts and a sense of boundless opportunity. However 'the tour' came to an end – one request for an additional year was granted, but then it was time to move on. Back in England, bad timing in terms of the 2008 'credit crunch' meant that demotion awaited: there was no longer any question of help with either the school fees or the cleaning. Indeed Connor's job lasted a mere three months before he was made redundant.

Thus whilst it is useful to draw attention to the power and privileges enjoyed by certain expatriates, it is clear that fixed theoretical concepts such as the 'transnational capitalist class' fail to account for the detail, diversity, fluidity and even fragmentation of the expatriate experience as a whole. The same criticism could be levelled at the macro-level theoretical approaches such as Globalization and Global Systems Theory which, whilst offering explanations for global migratory patterns and flows based on larger understandings of power and domination, fail to account for the multifaceted nature of labour migration, and the simultaneity of a whole range of smaller scale social, political and personal activities that may either promote or challenge globalizing agendas at the local and individual levels. In order to gain a richer understanding of migration, and its relationship to globalization, we need therefore to embrace *both* the macro and the micro to explore the ways in which the economic/social levels inter-relate with the individual, and are played out at the local level. The study of expatriates forms an essential part of this endeavour, for it is this elite group who are frequently seen less as pawns in a globalizing project over which they have no control and more in terms of being somehow bound up in the implementation of it. To what extent is this the case? How much power, privilege and control do they actually have, and how coherently can they use this? In order to answer such questions, we need to know so very much more about them.

This book is at once therefore about the inter-relationship of the large and the small: the way in which large, abstract categories such as 'labour migrants', 'transnational capitalist class' and 'expatriates' are clearly at the same time referring to individual people, whose lives will have all the humdrum complexity and ambiguity that most of us have to deal with as we go about our everyday routines. The fact that at one level someone may have migrated in order to carry out the broader agenda of the multinational corporation for whom they work does not give us any real insight into the extent to which or how their movement may *actually* further the globalizing aims of that corporation. Indeed, something else altogether may be a key personal motivation and this may be drawn upon to mediate or upset the onward march of the corporation (Achbar et al.'s film *The Corporation* 2004 shows an interesting analysis of this). Indeed, motivations are likely to be complex, and 'work' may be just one of the reasons someone may give for their migration. Displacement and settlement are difficult processes and survival strategies may involve 'separate, sometimes parallel, sometimes competing, projects at all levels of the global system' (Guarnizo and Smith 1998: 6).

For example, in my new research in South Africa, I have met a couple with complex relationships to both the organization they work for as well as the nation-state. Hugh is a highly motivated and ambitious project manager who has been accompanied to Johannesburg by his partner Hazel. Hazel herself had been very reluctant to make the move for all sorts of personal reasons: health problems, the giving up of her own career, and the leaving of family. Consequently she found it hard to settle. She found the deeply entrenched racial divisions in the country very difficult to handle, as well as the gendered divisions within the corporation which positioned her in the role of the 'expatriate wife' whose primary occupation was to lunch with the other wives. She also found it difficult to adjust to the lack of personal freedom allowed to her in the advice by other whites that that she should not walk around the city on her own. She had a great deal of unfilled time on her hands. The way forward for her was to become involved in a day nursery in one of the townships: visiting regularly, working with the children and helping with fundraising activities. This is very important to the nursery which, like most in Soweto, relies totally on donations to provide care for young children whose mothers have died from AIDS. Hazel, a qualified Marketing Consultant, began to lobby the corporation for the finance needed to build an extension: in her view the company has a responsibility to the local community, and as such should endeavour to 'put something back'. She has also arranged for her friends at home to send all their unwanted children's clothes, books and toys to the company's London HQ, from whence their courier system transports the goods free of charge to the nursery. Her marketing and lobbying abilities were recognized by the company who then offered her consultancy work to manage their own Public Relations in South Africa.

This story illustrates the multiple and simultaneous roles men and women can play, as well as the way in which power cannot be understood as a uni-directional flow, a top down process from the powerful agents of globalization to the powerless individual on the ground. Yes: on the one hand Hazel is in the disempowered position of the trailing spouse who has given up her life in her native country to fulfil the demands of her partner and the corporation. However at the same time she is able to draw on this relationship to contribute both to the local community *and* to the globalizing aims of the corporation, whilst also utilizing her transnational connections. The multiple layers of this story raise the question as the extent to which the activities of expatriates can be read off as merely an articulation of the domination of the transnational capitalist corporation. It is clear that in order to understand the texture of the connection between the expatriate and globalization we need to ask a broad range of sub-questions. We need to know the strength of the relationship with the politics of work – that is, what is the place of work and/or the organization in the construction of the expatriate's work and personal performances and identities? This will involve *inter alia* understanding the motivations for migrating and exploring the detail of the social and personal processes which accompany the leaving of the old and the arrival at the new. What are the social and political connections between the old spaces of home and the new spaces of migration which are maintained, and how is this done? In addition, given the hegemony of Western social characteristics in multinational and transnational corporations, to what extent are the key social resources of this dominance: those of race, gender, class and nationality, drawn upon on in the performance of work and life by expatriates in the new migratory context? How effective are these in the procurement of privilege at the individual level? Or are they also used to disperse privilege and challenge traditional boundaries? In sum, to what extent do changes in the places of work and home bring about changes in, and new forms of, identity and social and political relations?

It is through asking questions such as these that the multiplicity and complexity of the relationship between globalization and expatriates can be approached. We therefore need a conceptual framework beyond the macro-level approaches of globalization theories which enables analysis to be done with more nuance, and at a range of scales.

Transnationalism

Current developments in *transnational* migration research, which acknowledge migration as a multi-faceted process operating at multiple scales, are of particular value here. Transnationalism seeks to counterbalance the macro-level approaches which explain labour market migration in terms of the globalization of capitalism, the agendas of multinational corporations or technological revolutions in transport and communication by enquiring how these processes are experienced and activated at the micro-level of local communities and individual people. As Guarnizo and Smith (1998) argue: 'it is the everyday practices of migrants that provide a structure of meaning to the acts of crossing borders ... and reproducing transnational social relations' (pp. 18–19).

Transnational studies have therefore been concerned to develop an analytical approach which explores the *multidimensionality* of the migration experience, and, more specifically, the ways in which power can be seen to operate at multiple levels of social organization. On one level, the enquiry of transnational research is similar to that of globalization in that they both explore the ways in which social, economic, cultural and demographic processes that take place *within* nations *also* transcend them. However, transnationalism takes a self consciously more *grounded* approach in that it looks at the ways in which these processes can be seen empirically to be activated in and between nation states rather than at some more abstract or theoretical level of 'global space' (Mahler 2006, Kearney 1995). More critically, it strives to include the 'local' as well as the 'global' in its analysis – not in a frame based on any sense of binary opposition, but through a bifocal lens which views the nation-state and transnational practices as mutually constitutive (Yeoh et al. 2001; Smith 2001: 3–4). The emphasis is therefore on the *material* and *spatial* practices of social actors: both men *and* women, and the ways in which they make (in particular gendered) connections across and between societies, revealing the interplay of both the 'here' and the 'there'. This includes an interest in practices both at the macro level of powerful elites – often termed 'transnationalism from above' – as well as those which are 'grounded in the daily lives, activities and social relationships of quotidian actors' (Glick Schiller et al. 1992: 5): 'transnationalism from below' (Guarnizo and Smith 1998).

The basic concept of 'transnationalism from above' has some similarities with Sklair's (2001) notion of the transnational capitalist class, in that the focus at this level is also on powerful elites. Multinational corporations, the media, global financiers, technocrats and so on transcend national borders in their quest for political, economic and social dominance (Mahler 2006). A common illustration here are the practices of the American junk food giant McDonalds, whose quest is to serve standard menus of beefburgers across the globe. Such activity is seen to represent all that is worst in the homogenizing forces of 'transnationalism from above' (Mahler 2006): 'big, brutal unethical business, US imperialism, environmental despoliation, loss of jobs and local identity, the rape of the familiar *terroir*' (Patten 2008). A central recognition in transnationalism however is that in spite of the power*ful* range of resources, and the 'specialized flexibilty' (Smith 1990) of transnational corporations' activities, which enable them to present imagery and information on a global scale, thereby threatening to swamp the cultural networks and individualities of local communities, their power is in practice uneven and these aims are not always achieved. This is because they are integrally connected to the local level, and this is never totally power*less*. In Rome, for example, the city has decreed that the 'golden arches' of McDonald's iconic logo are painted black, and their shop windows are small, making it difficult to pick these restaurants out from amongst the other, more attractive, street furniture and local eating places.

By contrast, a key focus of interest in 'transnationalism from below' is the exploration of the migration experience at the level of individual and the local. Today's migrants are transnational in that they are able to continue their connections with their country of origin whilst at the same time building a new life elsewhere. Technological developments in transport and communication mean that experiences and lives are no longer sharply segmented between home and host communities, but are fluid and continuous as multi-stranded connections are maintained. These strands include the familial, economic, social, organizational, religious and political experiences and relationships that span nations (Basch et al. 1994). For Basch et al. the essential elements of transnationalism therefore are the *multiplicity* and *simultaneity* of involvements that transmigrants sustain. These mean that 'transmigrants take actions, make decisions, and develop subjectivities and identities' which are embedded in the networks of relationships that connect them with two or more nation states (1994: 7). More critically however they argue that this conceptual framework also enables us to see 'the ways transmigrants are *transformed by* their transnational practices and how these practices *affect* the nation-nation-states of the transmigrants' origin and settlement' (Basch et al. 1994: 8, my emphasis). Taking this a step further, Smith argues that 'the ways that the everyday practices of ordinary people, their feelings and understandings of existence, often modify those very conditions and thereby shape rather than reflect new modes of urban culture' (1992: 493–494). The key point here is that transnational migrants can create change and contest hegemonic power relations at the level of the *local*. They can develop 'creole identities and agencies that challenge multiple levels of structural control: local, regional, national and global' (Mahler 2006: 68). It is in such quotidian actions that the ambivalence and dynamism of the power relationships which bind the global and the local can be seen (Urry 2002).

The chief focus of research within the 'transnationalism from below' approach has been, by definition, on migrants leaving poorer countries to seek work in the West. Newly emerging however are debates about whether and how these perspectives articulate through the activities of other transnational migrants working at different 'levels' of the labour market (Beaverstock 1996, Findlay, Li, Jowett and Skeldon 1996, Willis and Yeoh 2000). Where should 'expatriates' be placed: above or below? Some scholars, particularly those examining the growth of what they describe as 'a transnational group of globetrotting, highly skilled, highly paid professional, managerial and entrepreneurial elites who circulate in a series of career or business moves from one city to another in response to global competition for skilled labour' (Yeoh et al. 2003: 209) would seem to place them in 'the transnationalism from above' category. Others, exploring the lives of those such as the middle class professionals who take time out to work overseas – in jobs for which they might be overskilled – refer to a 'muddle in the middle' (Conradson and Latham 2005a, Smith 2005, Scott 2006). However this ambiguity is useful, forcing recognition of the diversity between expatriates and which encourages a useful move *beyond* the above/below dualism.

To what extent can the arguments about transnationalism, change and creolization be contained within communities of unskilled workers, or do they extend to expatriates? Can *expatriates* be seen to be transformed by their transnational activities, developing creole/hybrid identities and contesting hegemonic power relations within the social and political context of the new host society? Or should they be seen merely as agents of the 'homogenizing forces of multinational elites'? Clearly to answer these questions we need to know more about *who expatriates are* at the individual level. And, as Smith reminds us, we need to take diversities based on race, class, gender and nationality into account:

> the unbridled celebration of the "hybridity" of transnational subjects serves to erase the fact that no matter how much spatial mobility or border crossing may characterise transnational actors' household, community and place-making practices, the actors are still classed, raced and gendered bodies in motion in specific historical contexts, within certain political formations and spaces (2005: 238).

A transnational approach to migration is inspirational for this enquiry therefore in that questions of identity formation and identity politics in transnational spaces have been keen areas of scholarship. These recognize that migration involves multiple and complex processes of identity and relationship construction as individual migrants move across the new spaces of their lives (Li et al. 1995; Song 2005; Yeoh et al. 2003). The fact that transnational subjects live in, and connect with, several communities simultaneously, both at 'home' and 'away', means that their identities and performances are not limited by location, and that in the interplay of the multiple sites of migrants' lives, fluid subject positions and states of 'between-ness' may be created (Lawson 2000). Far from conceptualizing identity as fixed and immutable therefore, this analytic frame acknowledges this fluidity of identities and meanings, 'highlighting the notion that identities are constantly (re)worked, not in a freewheeling manner but through simultaneous embeddedness in more than one society' (Yeoh et al. 2003: 213).

Going one step further Yeoh et al. (2003) argue against the notion that identities, whether ethnic, racial, social or national, are 'localized' or derived in relation to the specific context of a particular space. They claim that transnational subjects 'obviously play by a different set of rules since they live in, or connect with, several communities simultaneously' (p. 213). This means that identities, behaviour and values are not limited by location, but that instead transnational subjects construct and utilize *flexible* personal and national identities (see also Ong 1999). This leads on to the argument that transmigrants formulate transnational identities that both draw on and contest national identities, and which collapse the 'isomorphism of citizenship with cultural identity, of work with kinship, of territory with soil or of residence with national identification' (Appadurai 1998: 449). As a result of these discrepancies between citizenship and locality, transnational identities may also be associated with a sense of 'placelessness.'

However, I would argue that we need to be cautious about transporting abstract terms such as 'flexible identities' and 'transnational placeless subjects' wholesale to white, privileged expatriates. To do so would be in some danger of reiterating the essentialisms about placelessness and identity made by globalization theorists. We need specific, empirical research to uncover the extent to which *these* migrants *do* develop new identities built on weakened and more flexible notions of place and national identity. Yes, some are given citizenship in the new country of residence, but to what extent does this mean that they do this through a sense of 'placelessness' or declining national identity with the country of home? Or to what extent are their senses of place and nationality maintained and utilized as resources?

This book will explore these questions. Transnational approaches thus make useful connections with broader debates on migrants, and in particular with the debates about the extent and scale to which *place* and *space* are implicated in migrant identity making; whether in terms of a theoretical 'absence', of 'place*lessness*', or whether in terms of presence, of the importance of the local and its interplay with global/transnational/home spaces in the production of 'new' identities. Whilst, as we have seen, the former conceptualization is most often proposed by economic globalization theorists, ongoing debates within contemporary cultural geography join those in transnational studies to lend support to the latter. These show how the constructions and performances of our identities are *always* in some way spatialized, embedded as they are in the places and spaces of our lives (Lefebvre 1991, Cresswell 2004, Massey 2005), and that subjects are made, *not* in aspatialized abstract, but through the multiple and powerful ways that the spatial contexts of our lives mould and shape our senses of self (Pratt 1992, Valentine 2001). In contrast to the Euclidean underpinnings of globalization theory therefore, transnational approaches stress the *importance* of place: both the places of home, in terms of both memory and ongoing material links, as well as the social and political particularities of the places of migration in the construction of new lives and identities (Fortier 2000, Westwood and Phizacklea 2000). This is a concern which is shared by this book.

Expatriates

In recent years there has been a growing academic interest in the lives of expatriates. In common with transnationalism, much of this work challenges some of the macro-level notions central to globalization theories: particularly the ideas of free and mobile flows of movement by workers across the globe, a declining interest in borders and nationality harbingering a detachment from place, the existence of a transnational elite class and a 'global ecumene' (Hannerz 1992: 34). These are thrown into question by a micro-level interest on the detail of expatriate lives. Fechter (2007), for example, challenges the notion that privileged migrants lead fluid and unbounded lives, or are members of a flowing, elite class of cosmopolitans. Rather, she argues, the notion of '*boundaries*' is key to understanding the lives of expatriates – wherever they are, whatever they are doing, their lives are marked by boundaries. In her research on Western expatriates living in Indonesia she found that boundaries were constructed across the spaces of their lives:

> there were boundaries between the orderly insides of their houses and the chaotic streets, between Western food served at home and street vendors' fare outside, and between the cocooned Western expatriate and a sprawling third-world city which surrounded them (2007: vi).

The construction of such boundaries becomes apparent through the domains of race and gender, the body, the use of space and the social lives of expatriates. Fechter's (2007) ethnographic analysis shows how many of the expatriates in Indonesia construct their identities through the act of differentiating themselves from others – other white Europeans as well as other Indonesians – and retreating to live in an 'expatriate bubble'. Thus although being largely disembedded from the local communities, the German and British expatriates constructed habitae based on essentialized forms of national identity. In addition, the spatially and temporally contingent nature of their lives makes it clear that any elite status is only ever situational – in keeping with my story of Connor, membership of the social elite is unlikely to be held before migration, and is usually quickly lost on return.

The ongoing salience of nationality (as well as race and gender) in expatriate lives is also revealed in Walsh's research on 'ordinary' British expatriates in Dubai (2005). She demonstrates the importance of a sense of *belonging* in expatriate lives, and argues that everyday practices of domesticity and intimacy show how belonging is lived and understood in emotional, material and embodied ways.

Broader terms such as national identities, as well as transnational identities, can only be understood through more 'localized' scales of belonging. From the 'Great British Day' in which supposedly national customs are sweated out in the heat of the Dubai sun, to the 'banal' practices (Billig 1995) of everyday habits and routines of home life, the construction of expatriate identities in Dubai reinforce the persistence of Britishness as a form of bounded and collective belonging as well as a form of 'imperial capital' (Parker 2000) which can be drawn upon in the negotiation of identity.

Important diversities *between* expatriates' senses of nationality and ethnicity are revealed in O'Reilly's (2000) ethnography of British residents on Spain's Costa del Sol. Whilst these Britons have not integrated into their host communities, they are far from a powerful unified group colonizing a foreign land that cling proudly to their 'Britishness'. Rather, nationality is used more as a 'we' identification with other Britons than a 'they' identification against the Spanish. Further, rather than a seamless 'class' of 'expats', O'Reilly (2000) found that important distinctions existed between 'full residents', 'returning residents', 'seasonal visitors' and 'peripatetic visitors'. These different groups had different orientations towards both Spain and Britain, with perhaps only the former looking to Spain to provide a version of community felt to be lost in contemporary Britain.

Whilst ethnographic studies such as these have established the ongoing importance of nationality, race and gender in the construction of expatriate lives, their primary focus is on familial and domestic contexts rather than those of work and organizations. Yet work is a primary context of expatriate life. However, detailed in-depth ethnographies of life *within* organizations are still rather thin on the ground, particularly those that give attention to the racialized nature of everyday life and routines, and the extent to which boundaries based on race and nationality are constructed within working life and relations. Exceptions include Meier's (2006, 2007) research with German expatriates in Singapore and London in which, in keeping with the work on expatriates discussed above, he argues that whiteness and nationality continue to shape the ways in which expatriates position themselves in international contexts. Leggett's research (2005) in Indonesia also reveals how race and nationality conjoin to form a division between East and West in corporate space. Whilst not looking at whiteness so explicitly, the importance of nationality in expatriate identities is supported in Moore's (2005) study of German expatriates based in a German bank in the City of London.

Emerging studies such as these show that whilst contexts of work and organization are critical in the formation of identities, lives and relations, this is not through dramatic proclamations of explicit racist identities, but rather through subtle methods of maintaining silent and unmarked practices which serve to marginalize others. These practices are critical to the construction of the white cosmopolitian subject as normative (Byrne 2006). This book builds on this research to offer a timely and contemporary discussion of the role of work and organizations in maintaining or challenging structures and cultures based on racism and discrimination as well as an international extension to emerging debates on the meanings of contemporary whiteness and nationality.

Theoretical Approach and Summary of the Book

This book is about white expatriates and their working lives. It is an exploration of the salience of race, intersecting with ethnicity, gender, class and nationality, in the making of new lives in migratory work contexts. It looks at the ways in which expatriates draw on these as resources in the negotiation of their new lives and identities, as well as the ways in which organizations use these to position their expatriate employees in particular ways. Whilst the different places, spaces and times of different contexts offer distinctive opportunities and constraints in the making of different lives and subjectivities (Hacking 1986, Halford and Leonard 2006), at the same time the social structures and discourses forged through race offer some consistency to the experiences of white expatriates across the diverse spaces and times of migration. Work, and work organizations, have long drawn on race as a way of differentiating workers, to such an extent that the doing of particular sorts of work is part and parcel of the doing of whiteness.

The project of this book is therefore one of deconstruction (Derrida 1978), and this clearly accords with my theoretical position of poststructuralism. I will be drawing on this in the chapters that follow and discussing how the insights offered by Derrida and Foucault (1972, 1980) in particular offer a valuable way of analysing the ways in which expatriates construct their racialized and gendered identities in their new lives. My key task is to deconstruct the working and organizational contexts of migration, as I recognize these as critical sites in the organization of the workforce along social axes such as race, in intersection with other aspects of identity such as gender, class and nationality. Through the contexts of work, employees are differentially located as either being central or peripheral, and whiteness is a key aspect of this structuring process. I start in the next chapter by taking an historical approach to show how work has long been a critical context in defining what whiteness is, as well as a means by which diverse groups of people have been able to 'achieve' whiteness and consequent status. However exploring the relationship between work and whiteness in different times and spaces also reveals the ways in which whiteness is an unstable concept which varies between contexts, and that it is mediated by other aspects of identity such as class, gender and nationality. The worlds of work and organization help to reveal the differences which exist not only between whites and non-whites but between whites themselves. The starting point of Chapter 3 is an acceptance that researching whiteness and expatriate identities – who they are, and how they use race – requires a range of research methods which can access detail and difference. However, researching race and identity is always complex and researching whiteness in particular may involve power differentials which may be of an alternate patterning to other forms of research. This chapter reviews the research methodologies in use for empirical studies of race, whiteness and expatriates to explore the complexities which may be involved. Chapter 4 commences the detailed focus on white expatriates with an exploration of the multifaceted processes involved in 'becoming an expatriate' and the ways in which these are inflected by race and gender. I show how (white) expatriates must be seen as a highly diverse social group, differentiated by not only by gender, but also by the duration of their migration, the places to which they migrate and the types of work they do. These diversities may be augmented by the powerful role that some organizations play in organizing the migration experience, as well as the raced and gendered identities of their employees. The discussion of the power of organizations is continued in Chapter 5. This chapter explores the construction of expatriate identities within a variety of organizational contexts, looking at the diverse ways in which different organizations, though their processes and routines, draw upon attributes of whiteness and masculinity in their expectations of their male employees. This opportunity is exploited to differing degrees by expatriates in the negotiation of their identities. The discussion is extended in Chapter 6 with a look at the work experiences of expatriate women and the extent to which feminine subjectivities, intersecting with whiteness, can in some ways be seen to be more enabling in challenging hegemonic identities and power relationships. However, these compete with powerful discourses of home and domesticity which also work to position women in expatriate contexts. Chapter 7 turns to explore the critical importance of place and space in expatriate lives, and draws on geographical debates to explore how expatriates use place as a resource at a range of spatial scales in the construction and negotiation of their racialized selves.

Chapter 8 begins with the discussion of returning home, and how thoughts of return impact on the way in which expatriate men and women consider their position in the world (Mills 2005). I then turn to draw the debates of the book together through a concluding discussion of ways in which a poststructural approach can offer a fruitful way of understanding the power, performances and identities of expatriates as well as their relationship to place.

Chapter 2
Contextualizing Whiteness and Work

When white people migrate, their race and ethnicity can take on new meanings. For some, race may become visibly significant for the first time; whilst others may be aware of more subtle shifts in the raced aspects of their lives, brought about as a result of their displacement to a new and different context. The extent to which race offers a useful or powerful resource through which to construct and perform identities in the new community will vary however, for whiteness is far from stable or predictable, interplaying critically with time and space. In postcolonial and settler contexts, whiteness (together with nationality and gender) will have a particular historically-based relationship to power, and an ongoing and dynamic connection will exist between this and more contemporary versions. The new iterations of race, identity and relations which emerge do not simply erase and replace previous ones, but are constructed through and alongside them. Spatial configurations will also contribute to this mix, as race is worked out in different ways in different locales. Within these landscapes, the contexts of work will both reflect and contribute to the texture of race making, but, for most labour migrants, it will certainly be one of the most critical sites in which this is done.

This approach to understanding whiteness has clear connections with what Levine-Rasky has termed the *contextual* perspective (2002: 320). Levine-Rasky usefully categorizes the literature which has burgeoned on whiteness since the early 1990s into three key approaches: critical, relational and contextual. This is a working categorization, because the boundaries between each perspective are inevitably somewhat blurred. However critical perspectives are those which broadly tend to emphasize a normative position on issues of social injustice and express a commitment to challenge inequalities in social relations. Relational analyses tend to demonstrate the symbolic and material interdependence between white people and the 'other'. Contextual approaches are those which situate whiteness historically or in reticulation with intersecting sites of identity. Scholars within this latter approach thus see the importance to localize, 'provincialize' (Kapoor 1999) and 'historicize' (Shome 1999) whiteness, opposing the idea of developing any sort of grand narrative, as whiteness, like any other socio-historical construct, is constantly shifting. Whiteness is integrally intertwined with historical moments, location and social structures, and it is these times and places which are critical to understanding the power and multiplicities of its performances (Chen 2006).

Whilst not wanting to downplay the potential relevance of the former two approaches to discussions of whiteness, it is the concern of this book to explore the ways in which the particular *contexts* of expatriates' working and organizational lives are important in shaping resources available for identity negotiation. The specificities of the socio-historical conditions in which expatriates are situated help us to understand the diversities in white performances which exist from one context to the next. As McLaren (1998) has demonstrated, white culture is far from monolithic, and its borders must be understood as 'malleable and porous', and ever in a state of flux (p. 65). At the same time however, contemporary postcolonial contexts do share a long and continuing history of Western colonialism and neo-colonialism. This recognition is not to claim any fixity in white positionings, for, as Bhabha (1994) demonstrated through his concepts of colonial ambivalence, mimicry and hybridity, colonial power is necessarily unstable and open to challenge. However, these contexts all experienced variations of the violence by which 'the West' was manoeuvred into a position of ontological superiority over the non-West (Prasad 2006). Any investigation of race/ethnicity must therefore acknowledge the contingency of such histories as well as larger social conditions, whilst also recognizing the fluidity and dynamism of the lived experiences of those who are being studied (Davis et al. 2000: 536).

The purpose of this chapter is to show how the contexts of work and labour have long been organized to enable the makings of whiteness and superiority (Pugliese 2002). Whilst in no way denying the multiplicity and complexity of social processes contributing to the construction of racial categorization, it is clear from historical accounts of work that the organization of labour has offered a critical site through which whiteness – and consequent access to privilege – has been achieved.

Whiteness as a Resource in Historical Working Contexts

> The process of keeping blacks from competing with whites in the labour market
> is the foundation upon which American racism is built (Taylor 1995: 397).

The historical importance of work and labour in the construction of whiteness and white identities has been demonstrated particularly by scholars in the United States such as Du Bois (1977), Roediger (1991), Saxton (1990), Ignatiev (1995) Allen (1994, 1997) and Jacobson (1998). Their historical accounts attempt to show the ways in which the organization of work has relied on differentiation within the subject positions of workers. Roediger argues that 'workers, even during periods of firm ruling class hegemony, are historical actors who make (constrained) choices and create their own cultural forms' (1991: 9). These cultural forms were based on the negotiation of difference; and both work and political organization in nineteenth-century America were contexts which developed, and became wholly dependent upon, the manufacture of *dis*similarity between workers. In particular, this extended into the construction of a racialized and subordinate Other by both the white middle and working classes (Levine-Rasky 2002). In Allen's *The Invention of the White Race* (1997) we are shown how, prior to the American Revolution of 1775–1781, whites and blacks had associated together in the South, both at work as well as socially, and had united across racial lines in solidarity in their attacks against the plantation bourgeoisie. The solution to this mass labour unrest was the deliberate creation of a buffer social class of 'poor whites' which actually enjoyed little privilege in colonial society beyond that of their skin colour. However, it was this identification that protected them from the enslavement which was visited upon Blacks, and it was in this process of classification that the white 'race' was invented (Allen 1997).

After the American Revolution, many white people were still treated so poorly as to be described as 'white slavery'. Women and children working in textile factories had lives of particular hardship. However, the oppression of whites was increasingly held to be inappropriate in the new political context, and, as such, white workers were encouraged to abandon the 'slavery' metaphor in the interests of distancing themselves from the 'real' (black) slaves. Instead they were organized to form a more cohesive labour force through which white supremacy in the workplace could be maintained (Levine-Rasky 2002). This was a process which crucially relied on the development of an essentialized notion of difference, embodied by a racialized other. Pre-existing networks between white and black workers were severed and the language of work itself took on new nuances to distinguish white jobs from those held by blacks. Critically, Roediger argues, 'white urban workers connected their freedom with their work' (1994: 33). Thus the subjectivity of the raced and classed '*White worker*' was made: a subjectivity which positioned itself through a discourse of independence, freedom and dignity in work.

Roediger makes important connections between class, race and gender, seeing working class whiteness as a distinctively racialized and gendered phenomenon 'which expresses male longings' (1991: 11). Here Roediger's analysis nicely interweaves the *emotional* gains of whiteness with the merely instrumental, showing how whiteness brings 'pleasures' of status which function as an additional 'wage' or reward for white workers. These pleasures are complex however, based in part on a sense of envy for the 'other' and their way of life which is perceived as less stressful and more natural. Roediger argues that the new forms of work which emerged through capitalism thus brought with them various losses of humanity:

> The separation of work from the rest of life, the bridling of sexuality, the loss of contact with nature, the timing of labor by clocks rather than by sun and season, the injunction to save by postponing gratification – all these were monumental, and monumentally painful changes (1994: 64).

Roediger suggests that these changes in the ways in which work was done helped to intensify a growing sense of whiteness/belonging which brought together a very diverse white working class. 'All the old habits and styles of life so recently discarded by whites in the process of adopting capitalist values came to be fastened on Blacks' (1994: 64), and in order not to 'slip back', a sense of difference, development and superiority was created and sustained through legal, economic and cultural forms.

Other writers have pointed out that it was not just black people who were positioned as 'Other' in the changing work context of nineteenth century North America. The Irish, Hispanics and Jews were other migrant communities which became included in the emerging practices of racialization, becoming 'coloured' in the process. In the early years of their diaspora for example, Irish people were frequently referred to as 'niggers turned inside out' (Ignatiev 1995: 41). Italians and Jews became 'non-white' when the work they did during the Industrial Revolution was defined as menial and unskilled (Brodkin 1998). However the ambiguity of their colour meant that these migrant groups were gradually able to 'whiten' themselves through changes in America's labour practices. Whilst each ethnic group had its own journey to make in order to align itself with dominance and 'become white folk' (Brodkin 1998, Twine and Gallagher 2007), within these journeys, work was the key context through which this race making, and subsequent social mobility, was achieved. As Ignatiev concludes, the history of American labour shows that the definition of 'the white race' at every period included only groups that did 'white man's work' (1995: 112). 'White' was thus 'not a physical description', but 'one term of a social relation which could not exist without its opposite, "white man's work" was simply, work from which Afro-Americans were excluded' (1995: 112). Invented to justify the brutal but profitable regime of slave labour, race became the way that labour was organized and justified in the United States (Brodkin 1998) and white supremacy was maintained there (Twine and Gallagher 2007).

In the ways that they all reveal the unstable, shifting processes of inclusion and exclusion into whiteness, the historical accounts of race and labour offered by Brodkin, Ignatiev, Roediger and Allen help to challenge what it means to be white. Further, they also rearticulate and broaden the concept of racial identity itself, by confronting whiteness with questions such as 'when, why and with what results [have] so-called "white people" come to identify themselves as white?' (Roediger 1994: 75). Giroux (1997) argues that by historicizing discussions of whiteness and demonstrating the relational nature of all identities, these accounts have foregrounded the political significance and arbitrary nature of white racial identity 'as it has varied over time, place and class location' (Roediger 1994: 75). No longer the stable, self-evident or pure essence central to modernity's self-definition, 'whiteness' in the work of these historians is unmasked in its arbitrary attempts to categorize, position and contain the 'other' within racially ordered hierarchies.

Questions of where and when racialized whiteness emerged are also taken up by Bonnett (1998, 2000) in his historical discussions of European and Asian contexts. Bonnett also notes the vulnerability of whiteness in these different contexts, and the unstable nature of its constituent groups. As in America, who did what forms of work was a key determiner, and, in Britain, as late as the early twentieth century, working class membership into the white race was as yet insecure. There was a widespread conviction that the metropolitan working classes were 'a race apart' and still 'not quite' white. Whilst acknowledging the value of the racial histories provided in the American context, Bonnett (2000) reminds us that each context is different: the racial history of one society cannot be used as a template for others. Thus he argues that the story of 'how the working class became white' in Britain is very different to that of the United States. In nineteenth century Britain and Europe, the process of whiteness-making was bound up with colonialism and the creation of settler societies. Whiteness was idealized in the colonies as an 'extra-ordinary, almost superhuman identity', but it was solely 'an identity developed for and by the bourgeoisie' (1998: 318): the *middle class* men who were pursuing the colonial project. The Victorian working class, in contrast, were positioned as marginal to this construction. The understanding of the race order, just as those of class and gender, was framed through a scientifically based belief in hierarchy. As such, the inequalities of wealth and power between the working class and the bourgeoisie were legitimized and justified as reflecting a natural order of talent: the inevitable side-effect of the existence of economic growth and 'superior' and 'inferior' types of people.

However, from being marginal to whiteness in the nineteenth century, the working class came to adopt and adapt this as part of their identity in the twentieth century (Bonnet 1998). As the discourses of imperialism were disseminated within the nation, the populist nationalism which they furnished gradually brought the white working class British into the 'us' side of racial categorizations. The chasm of class identities produced through the Victorian period started to disappear, aided by the World Wars, and the marginalization of the working class from whiteness and Britishness became no longer tenable. 'In this new British social formation, racial and national identities once centred on the elite become available to the masses' (Bonnett 1998: 329). The global restructuring of capitalism brought by Victorian colonial activity overseas also restructured white identities at home therefore, where the meanings of whiteness shifted from being associated with *extraordinary* and heroic qualities of upper class masculinity to a politics of the *ordinary*: a lack of exceptionality, and the homely virtues of quietness, tidiness, cleanness and decency. Whilst emanating from different moments of capitalism, both discourses privilege whiteness and reflect an inherent racism which was, in particular, played out through *work*. That 'British jobs' should be occupied by 'British' (i.e. white) people was a discourse which started after the Second World War and which remains a site of contestation to the present day.

The Colonization of Work

European whiteness and nationality were not only constructed on home soil therefore. The contexts of colonialism and imperialism, heterogeneous as they were, were integral to the formation of these identities, and contributed to their plurality. However, in these diverse contexts, the non-white 'Other' was not solely in the imagination, but a real presence in the daily lives of the white migrants: the administrators, farmers and traders who were pursuing the colonial project. Their ongoing colonial 'encounter' has been argued as being one of the most decisive and meaningful historical processes that not only shaped the West's perception of the non-West, but also shaped the construction of a diversity of whitenesses (Prasad 1997, Said 1978, 1993).

Within the colonies themselves, early settler identities were constituted through a particular set of beliefs about whiteness which supported their presence overseas. The building of Empire was seen to demand particular sorts of masculinity, for these lands were seen to be places where 'adventures took place and men became heroes' (Green 1980: 37). However, these heroes were different from their chivalric forebears: constructed through the demands of mercantile and industrial capitalism *these* men needed to be rational, prudent and calculating (Dawson 1994). Typified by Robinson Crusoe, who 'on his island uses guns, compasses, scientific knowledge, diary and account-keeping, puritan spiritual techniques' (Dawson 1994: 59) to create order and value out of the wilderness in which he finds himself, as well as subduing the native inhabitants (Green 1980, Dawson 1994), these heroes saw they had a specific mission, and this understanding brought assumptions of entitlement by the white colonizers to the host country, its resources, and its peoples (Steyn 1999). In Africa, for example, Steyn argues that the colonial experience lent a particular intensity to the salience of 'whiteness', due to:

> The particular circumstances of being a small group of "whites", relatively isolated from the rest of the European tribe (both by distance and expense) but still in enough contact to retain a measure of identification with Europe's elite "whites" elsewhere, and most significantly, living in Africa among those who were marked in colonial discourse as the utter antithesis of "whiteness" (1999: 267).

Indeed, it was the very 'darkness' of Africa and its peoples which led to its construction as a continent of mystery and even treachery, and one which therefore needed to be 'controlled' by white people, with their direct line to order and 'civilization'. Early European settlers arrived already with an adversarial relationship to the continent and its peoples, who were cast as 'the nearest to animals of all the people being conquered by European expansion' (Steyn 1999: 268). Unquestioned were the natural abilities of the white settlers to make better use of the natural resources of Africa: its land was theirs to own and exploit, and the labour of the indigenous people was seen as part of this entitlement. It was through this constructed understanding of the direction of flow – from 'us' to 'them' – that whiteness was made. Based on myths of superiority and civilization, whites constructed themselves as the ones who 'provided order, government, leadership', and who took charge of the work to be done and assigned roles within this (Steyn 1999: 268).

This construction of whiteness was reflected throughout the expanding colonial Empire. As Miles and Phizacklea argue in their discussion of the making of 'Great' Britain:

The very existence of Empire was viewed as the outcome of struggle between superior and inferior "races", an outcome in which the labour of inferior "races" had been appropriated not only to ensure "their' advancement towards "civilization" but also, and especially, to "our" advancement to the position of Great Britain, workshop of the world (1984: 12–13).

Given that the Empire spread to cover nearly 85 per cent of the area of the earth (Loomba 1998, Prasad 2003), processes of race making were thus enacted on a global scale. Through these, workforces were produced and theorized as particular cultural artefacts, and subsequent material and organizational practices were based on these theorizations. These ranged from the more obviously violent practices of slave labour and forced migrations, to more subtle and covert practices of positioning people through the discourses and embodied performances of 'work'. A good example of this was the broader discourse of *control and surveillance* that pervaded many colonial societies and cultures. This transmitted itself into the sorts of work which colonial administrators undertook: for example, in nineteenth century India, colonial rule consolidated itself through a phenomenal increase in the search for 'scientific knowledge' of both the various populations as well as the land (Mohanty 1991). This was achieved through the introduction of a census, in which colonial administrators established a preliminary colonial taxonomy, the carrying out of which helped to position white people within a discourse of governance. The tasks which were associated here: of 'siting, surveying, mapping, naming and ultimately possessing' (Dirks 1992: 6) helped to define what whiteness was: equivalent to leadership, management and control, it employed intellectual as opposed to physical skills. Indeed it was felt that manual labour should be avoided by Europeans, thought as it was to be both physically dangerous and beneath their dignity (Duncan 2000). Morality tales emerged of early planters in Ceylon (Sri Lanka) who were forced to do physical labour themselves because they had no hired workers, and then lost their lives. These encompassed not only what Stoler refers to as the 'pioneering protestant ethic' (1991: 125) of European colonialism, in which ultimate success was seen to result from hard work and perseverance, but also warned of the dangers of acting out of one's race: 'Proper European work in the tropics was supervision, and the hardworking European was seen as the conscientious supervisor' (Duncan 2000: 42). In fact, many Europeans also worked as surveyors, engineers, government officials and planters, but this work was seen as distinct from manual labour, which was thought only to be appropriate for the indigenous peoples.

Important here too then was the need to position non-whites as manual labour as well as in service to the white population. A whole range of staff were seen as necessary to support the lifestyle and gendered identities of the white European population, as Alfred Weatherhead, a clerk in 1856 Hong Kong describes:

If you happen to be blessed with a stock of those lovely nuisances – children – you must have a distinct ahma for each olive branch. Should your tastes be "horsey" each animal must have his own proper coolie, besides stable boys, grass cutters, and so forth ... on the smallest scale you need indispensably a cook, to market for you and generally to control the victualling department. Generally, he transacts the mechanical portion of his duties by deputy-employing a scrubby juvenile assistant at a mere nominal pay. Next you must engage that indispensable factotum, known as "boy", by no means necessarily a youth ... His pigeon is to run errands – convey chits – attend on you at dinners and parties, make all bargains and give orders to trades people, and act generally as your interpreter and representative ... chair coolies – during the greater part of the year it is impossible to stir abroad in the day time, for fear of sun stroke, except in a sedan chair, and even in the cool of the evening, while the ladies take their after dinner promenade, dignity requires that their chairs should follow them. Consequently every member of the household must have a separate chair, each requiring two coolies ... (Wai Kwan 1991: 54, quoted in Wu 1999: 150).

Whilst these sorts of binaristic assumptions made by whites about the doing of work are revealed in a range of colonial texts and across a range of historical colonial contexts, it is also important to acknowledge the differences by which different 'races' were characterized. Tamil labour in India for example was described as 'docile, indisposed for exertion, but with great powers of endurance, influenced in their conduct by fear or by love of gain, rather than by motives of gratitude or a sense of duty' (Proceedings of the Planters' Association 1869–70: 56 quoted in Duncan 2000). In colonial Hong Kong, the local Chinese population was seen as anything but docile however, but rather as a 'thieving, piratical population' (Wu 1999: 149) made up of 'fearful criminals and thugs' (ibid: 151), which somehow had to be tamed to meet the needs of the colony's capitalist expansion. An Official Report to Her Majesty's Government explained:

He must be sanguinely visionary who expects that Hong Kong will ever contain a numerous and respectable Chinese population. There is in fact a continual shifting of a Bedouin sort of population, whose migratory, predatory, gambling, and dissolute habits, utterly unfit them for continuous industry, and render them not only useless but highly injurious subjects in the attempt to form a colony (Martin 1847: 407).

Cultural texts such as these had an important part to play in disseminating the ideological discourses necessary to position colonial administrators and workers. Mohanty (1991) notes how Kipling's fiction created children who embodied values and qualities that were essential for their roles as white colonial rulers if they were to survive and manage a racially tense social and political world. In *The Jungle Book*, Mowgli, like Kim before him, reveals the capacity not only to inhabit the jungle but to chart and track it as well. Kipling's characters learn to observe carefully, but also to observe without being observed, to contain the threat of any real encounter – in short to rule colonial India without seeming to do so.

One of the marks of this specifically colonialist desire is that white men are seen in a purely abstract and functionalist relationship to their world, wherein the object being analysed is reduced to something that can be manipulated. 'It is there only to be deciphered, read, and interpreted, without any significant cost ... The white man learns only so much from the world as is necessary to rule or subjugate it' (1991: 331). As Mohanty goes on to argue, 'This reduction is one of the essential elements of the racialization of culture, the inherent logic of the color line, then as much as now' (1991: 330).

By the next century, the ambivalences and contradictions within British colonial ideology start to reveal themselves more clearly. On the one hand, many of the autobiographical accounts by ex-colonials wives such as those in Callan and Ardener's (1984) *The Incorporated Wife* in which they look back on their lives in the 1950s and 1960s, show little change in positioning: Kirkwood (1984) unironically describes the lives and work of white farmers in Rhodesia:

> While the physical work was carried out by black labourers the farm owner normally had to plan and supervise, arrange for the marketing of the crop and negotiate the complicated financing of the farming operation (p. 153).

Gartrell (1984) reveals the importance of 'the enactment of whiteness' in her discussion of how remarkably few Europeans were required to run the colonial economy of Uganda: 724 colonial administrators ran a colony roughly the size of England and Wales, with an African population of about five million. In this situation

> the style of the ruling officials was itself a tool of domination. The impressive dignity and awesomeness of the District Commissioner was the "front line" of rule. More broadly, maintenance of a mystique of European superiority was believed to be essential to the maintenance of domination (p. 168).

On the other hand, however, Myers' (2002) discussion of Eric Dutton's *Kenya Mountain* (1929) reveals some of the broader ambiguities in the imperial project which were appearing. The idea of this as some sort of adventure, suitable for a hero, was being transformed into one of a 'game grown professional' (Belloc 1929), as colonial states expanded in size and reach, albeit struggling against poor economic performances. 'Rather than men torn from pages of ripping yarns, what the Empire needed most by then were good clerks and accountants, yet what it seemed to have were what Dutton called "faddling and lackadaisical administrators"' (Myers 2002: 24). There was a growing gap between the hegemonic ideal of adventurous manliness and the reality of mundane office work that dominated the colonial service. After the First World War, this became even more pronounced: broader discourses on masculinity were still dominated by militaristic and athletic ideals, and yet what the colonial service actually offered after the processes of exploration and pacification were over were 'roles as clerks and shop assistants' (Nash 1996:

443 in Myers 2002: 27). Added to this loss of glamour was the growing sense that the practical tasks of building the colonial order in, as Dutton (1929) put it 'brick and mortar', were not doing very well. In these uneasy circumstances, compliance with the structure of working relationships was seen as important affirmation of the economic, as well as the spiritual and familial bonds, between colonizer and colonized (Spurr 1993). Indeed the famous colonizer Stanley saw that it was the introduction of *paid work* which actually fulfilled the colonial mission through the 'transformation of the native's spiritual state' (Spurr 1993: 33): 'It created hope ... in every man, that he possessed something that was saleable ... that the force of those masses of muscle had become marketable and valuable' (1885, 1: 171).

One of the key principles by which colonial administration was achieved was by dividing the works amongst indigenous populations and classifying them as suitable for different sorts of people. Prasad (1997) quotes Lord Thomas Macauley who in 1785 stressed:

> We must do our best to form a class who may be interpreters between us and the millions we govern: a class of persons, Indian in blood and colour, but English in taste, in opinions and morals, and in intellect. To that class, we may leave it to define the vernacular dialects of the country, to enrich those dialects with terms of science borrowed from the western nomenclature, and to render them by degrees fit vehicles for conveying knowledge to the great mass of population (MaCauley 1972: 249).

By classifying the indigenous people in terms of the different jobs they might do, they were simultaneously racialized. Not only did work help to confirm the meanings of whiteness, but it was also a means of establishing who, amongst the native population, was more or less white. Spurr (1993) notes how Lugard divided the natives of British Tropical Africa into three classes: primitive tribes, advanced communities and Europeanized Africans. The latter were typically educated in England and returned to Africa to practice one of the professions, such as law or journalism. They imitated European dress and customs and were perceived as having little in common with the indigenous tribes. Lugard commented that each 'must be treated – and seems to desire to be treated – as though he were of a different race' (1929: 350). Lugard recognized the strategic value of the internal authority exercised by native rulers, and, by dividing them and promising them 'white man's work', he felt their authority could be turned to the advantage of colonial power. In this way, certain natives were prepared for positions in the colonial Civil Service, in the process becoming an integral part of the administration machine, and, into the bargain, revealing the fluidity of whiteness. Whiteness, it would appear, could be earned by the *doing* of particular forms of (European capitalist) work. Similarly, so could masculinity. As Dr Van Dort put it, 'the genius of labour ... stamps the physiognomy with an expression of manliness and intelligence which is never seen in the raw, uncivilized, newly landed cooly' (Proceedings of the Planters' Association, Kandy 1869–70: 55, quoted in Duncan 2000). These forms of work were thus part of the technology of the broader colonial project: civilization, and empire, were achieved by means of paper and psyche as much as by force (Richards 1994).

Not only did the *tasks* of work form an integral part of the racialization process, but so did the *spaces* and *places* of work – who did what work where. In colonial India, the definition of 'race' – and gender – was tied up with climate, and in particular the hot climate of the low country was seen as unsuitable for the health of white people: especially white women. Indeed the ability to cope with the work *and* the heat was a further testament to the superiority of whiteness, as T. Roger Smith explained in his 1867 talk to the Royal Institute of British Architects: 'The sun's heat is so powerful that nothing but English pluck prevents the attempt [to work] to being altogether given up...' (quoted in Metcalf (1989)). Beliefs such as this led to the development of hill stations and the gradual migration of the Anglo-Indians away from the larger cities (Kenny 1995). By the 1880s, the government planned a permanent move to the cooler hill country, and consequently 'every district collector was building a summer office on higher ground' (Kenny 1995: 700). Defending the move of the imperial, provincial and district offices into the hills for often more than half the year – and thus away from the indigenous population which they supposedly 'governed' – was the appeal to the greater efficiency of administrators there. This spatial separation of the doing of government helped to emphasize the separation of both race and nation: the viceroy Lord Lytton described the British attraction to the area as it was seen to be 'a paradise ... the afternoon was rainy and the road muddy, but such *English* rain and such delicious *English* mud' (Price 1909 quoted in Kenny 1995: 702).

The landscape then, as well as the climate, was a critical resource in the racialization process. Work such as tea and coffee growing, which involved taming and cultivating 'the tropics', were seen as living performances of the qualities of heroism, manliness and adventure which were elsewhere informing the construction of Victorian British masculinities (Duncan 2000). An advertisement for a plantation overseer in a London newspaper of 1885 read: 'we now ask for young fellows of the right sort – even public schoolmen, university men – anyone with pluck and energy who comes determined to fight his way against all odds' (quoted in Duncan 2000: 41). But it was not only the climate and natural landscape which was drawn upon to construct Englishness and whiteness: the physical character of the built environment was also critical in the construction and symbolization of white British rule and power. Simla (or Ootacamund) was amongst those developments of towns specifically 'created in order to carry out "European" work' (Kenny 1995: 711).

Historical sources such as these are invaluable in revealing the ways in which meanings of whiteness and social difference are constructed in the social imagination across the globe. This is certainly *not* however to claim that the old ways live on, and that past constructions of race are in any necessary way connected to those in the present. Rather, what they do underscore is an understanding of 'race' which sees the meanings of raced categories as contingent upon the different contexts of time and space. They emphasize the importance of recognizing the diversity within and between different (historical and spatial) contexts, but also, *inter alia*, how important the conditions and contexts of *work* and *organization* were to these processes of systematic social differentiation and power distribution.

These observations to some degree question the distinctions that have been made by some cultural studies scholars that a cultural approach is in some way to be distanced from 'a previous generation of scholars who have for the most part focused on the economic and politically exploitative dimensions of colonialism' (Chun 2000: 431). Chun goes on to argue that

> This is, of course, not to downplay the obvious effect of domination and destruction that has characterized colonial rule and that capitalized on the creation and maintenance of difference in social, racial and other terms but *instead* to highlight the role of both explicit practices and underlying mentalities in legitimizing and normalizing the colonial project (ibid: 431–432, my italics).

I question the use of the word *instead*. The economic cannot be neatly divided from the social, political and cultural contexts in which this is situated. Difference is legitimated and normalized through work: both through *explicit practices* – such as the allocation of who does what work, how, who can go where, who can talk to whom, and when, and how; as well as through the discursive *underlying mentalities* which frame the 'doing' of work. Work is both economic *and* symbolic and discursive – in colonial times it was an integral part of the 'routine colonialism' in which race was made, specifically concerned with 'the construction of the colonial subject in discourse, and the exercise of colonial power through discourse' (Bhabha 1994: 67).

However I do not wish to leave this discussion as a uni-linear reading of the construction of race in historical working contexts, as a monolithic exercise of power by whites over non-whites. The attempts to produce abstract workers: docile, useful, disciplined, rationalized, normalized and controlled (Foucault 1979) were very often *not* successful, and the relationships between white colonials and the people they attempted to colonize, as well as the meanings of whiteness, were complicated and fractured by acts of worker contestation and resistance. Whilst these were sometimes overt acts of rebellion, more often they were more covert forms of everyday resistance (Duncan 2002). On the colonial plantations for example, workers employed a range of 'weapons of the weak' (Scott 1985) to resist the demands and disciplines placed upon them. These included activities such as deliberate calculated errors and incompetence, exit strategies such as feigning sickness, 'forgetting something', hiding and even desertion, and forms of retribution such as damaging crops and equipment and hiding produce (Adas 1986, Duncan 2002).

In addition, although I have emphasized the economically and socially exploitative agendas of many white people, particularly through imperial and colonial governance, I also want to recognize the importance of a sensitivity to, and acknowledgement of, the nuanced differentiation of (colonial) discourses and relations. The hegemonic discourses of colonialism were competing with other discourses, beliefs and representations in 'home' contexts as well as 'away', and not all of these submitted to the dominant ideologies of whiteness and/or gender, nationality and class.

Space, Place and Work

The acknowledgement of context underpins recent studies of whiteness which take a spatial approach to explore the intersections of space, place and identity. These develop the approach to whiteness taken by labour historians by taking a 'contingent' approach. Emerging from writers located in invader-settler colonies, such as the US, Canada, South Africa, Australia and New Zealand, this approach constructs contemporary forms of whiteness as very specific and locationally contingent experiences, which are inextricably linked to other dimensions of social identity such as gender, class, religion, region, ethnicity, age and sexuality. For example, in Frankenberg's (1993) much cited empirical study of 30 white Californian women, connections are made between the women's narratives of their (classed) experiences of childhood, relationships, sexuality and domestic lives to establish that space and place, as well as time, are critical elements in the making of their racialized identities and everyday lives. Many had been brought up in highly specific, racially segregated environments, and their stories of their own personal experiences open a window onto the interplay of broader social and political landscapes with individual lives, and how our choices are contingent on these.

Frankenberg's work makes two important contributions to our understandings of whiteness which we can carry forward into our focus on work and organizational contexts. First is the acknowledgement of the role of individual *agency* in the ways in which she demonstrates how actively the women negotiate the 'repertoires' or discourses on race in the construction and negotiation of their identities:

> the subject constantly acts out, reformulates, challenges, and potentially relocates these constructs/discourses that assign her or him a place from which to speak. With these developments, the question of "who I am" has been "deterritorialized" so to speak, has been removed by the question of how to locate oneself (Michel 1995: 91).

Second is her underscoring of the argument already discussed at length in this chapter: that whiteness varies over time and space and as such can in no way been seen as an immutable, transhistorical essence. Rather it is a 'complexly constructed product of local, regional, national and global relations, both past and present, and the interplay of these with a range of other racial and cultural categories, such as class and gender' (1993: 236).

This 'co-constructional' approach has been taken up and developed in whiteness research across other invader-settler contexts. For example, Steyn's (2001) study of South Africa draws on its particular history of colonialism by both the British and the Afrikaans, and the subsequent entrenchment of hierarchies of race in all aspects of pre-Apartheid life, to explain the very specific constructions of contemporary whiteness there. She identifies two major factors which have contributed to the particularities of South African whiteness – firstly, the presence of a small group of people whose self-image and expectations were shaped by the dominant 'master narratives' of European whiteness, yet who were in an environment where they were vastly outnumbered by the indigenous population which they subjugated but never decimated. The second factor was that whiteness was shared, albeit reluctantly, by two different groups of Europeans: 'each of which has always considered the other group an unworthy custodian of the entitlement' (2001: 26). The British, with their history of Empire and their sense of superiority regarded the more rural and often illiterate Afrikaners as racially distinct, and 'not quite white'. In turn, Afrikaners regarded the British as imperialists who subjugated them alongside the indigenous black people. 'The texture of the Afrikaners' whiteness, then, was coarsened by discourses of indignation and rebellion toward the more confident whiteness of overlordship assumed by the English' (2001: 26).

Steyn's (2001) analysis also draws attention to the importance of *work* in the co-constructions of what was 'white' and what was 'not'. In the early years of colonialism, the British dominated the administration of the colony, and the exploitation of natural resources such as gold and diamonds. The Afrikaners took to the land, in the process displacing indigenous African people and replacing their livelihoods with paid labour based on unfair and unfree conditions. For both groups however,

> Nothing could better justify the colonizer's privileged position than his industry, and nothing could better justify the colonized's destitution than his indolence. The mythical portrait of the colonized therefore includes an unbelievable laziness, and that of colonizer, a virtuous taste for action. At the same time the colonizer suggests that employing the colonized is not very profitable, thereby authorizing his unreasonable wages (Memmi 1990: 145).

Until the achievement of black majority rule in 1994, it was clear that race was the defining factor in any South African's life. For whites, the privileges which accompanied their colour were taken for granted – for them it was unquestioned that 'White people lived in nice houses, went to good schools, did the work that mattered, had culture, and decided political issues. Other South Africans worked in our houses, on the roads, on the farms' (Steyn 2001: x). Race and class were conflated as 'workers': those who did the cleaning, gardening, childcare and farming, were always black, whilst for whites their colour was the sign that they were not to be destined for such 'menial' tasks (Steyn 2001: 52). Since majority rule, the diversities between whites have become more marked, on one level at least. Steyn's (2001) analysis reveals the divergent discourses by which contemporary whites in South Africa may now position themselves post-collapse of the singular, dominant 'master narrative' of whiteness. She not only shows that there are now 'many shades of whitenesses' available, but also points beyond essentialist, binaristic models of racialization to those which allow both whiteness and blackness to convey multiple meanings, subject to context and situation (Nayak 2005). Whilst there are those who still assume and live by the old patterns of power and privilege ('still colonial after all these years'), others see themselves as victims in a reversed order, whilst still others accept the change and are trying to find new ways of being white. There are also those who never internalized the racial hegemony embedded in the old order, and even others who are moving away from their whiteness in different ways. The key point underscored here is that white identities in the contemporary South African context need to be understood as multiple, through which the meanings of race are dynamic and subject to renegotiation. At the same time however it is still clear that in terms of work, whites remain privileged: it is not often you see a white street cleaner on the streets of Cape Town.

Steyn's (2001) discussion also draws attention to the importance of *nationality* as a differentiating aspect of whiteness. In South Africa, to be of British or Afrikaner ancestry is to mean very different white identities. Jackson (1998) also argued that it is important to contrast different meanings of the concept of whiteness within and between different national contexts – which may be as much the result of different intellectual traditions as a reflection of different empirical realities. This view is underscored by Elder's (2007) discussion of the construction of Australian national identity, in which the place of work is once again revealed to be important. In stark contrast to the 'clean hands' subjectivity of the colonial British, the manual labouring working man has long been valorized in (white) Australian culture as the 'quintessential Australian'. It is the labourer rather than the bureaucrat who is constructed to be emblematic of Australian whiteness: even Australian politicians still position themselves as 'working men'. 'The trope of the working man centralized what were regarded as unique and positive characteristics of being Australian' (Elder 2007: 43): hard work chiefly by someone not afraid of getting his hands dirty. Whilst early constructions were thus highly gendered, with little acknowledgement of women, more recent versions have morphed into men *and* women. However the sense of monolithic pride in 'being white' is undercut by Aveling's (2004) study of white Australian women, for whom whiteness was bound up with issues of guilt, fear and alienation. For some of these women it was *through* their work as lawyers, doctors, therapists or psychologists that they had become more aware of the meanings of whiteness in Australia, the differences between their (privileged) lives and those of Aboriginal people, as well as how much there was to learn from them.

In spite of this, there is a seemingly strong consensus amongst white Australians about their national identity when contrasted with the lack of collective identity between British whites. It is often argued that whilst strong national identities exist for the Scottish, Northern Irish and Welsh, there is no such coherence for the English and certainly not for the British which remains a highly contested identity (Langlands 1999, Cohen 2000, Byrne 2006). The slogan 'British Jobs for British workers' made by Prime Minister Gordon Brown during the recession of 2009 was greeted by a storm of controversy as members of white and ethnic communities debated what such a statement meant in practice. Further, the multiplicity in national identity is reinforced by a multiplicity within white identities – with the English still occasionally represented as 'more white' than the Irish for example (Garner 2006).

This chapter has taken a deconstructive approach to emphasize the multiple, fluid, contingent and sometimes contested nature of white identities. 'Whiteness' has been shown, both historically and spatially, to be in many ways an achieved location, within a hierarchy of 'more' or 'less' white. It is far from a self-sufficient category but is dependent upon other marginalized positions (Dixon and Jones III 2008). White identities involve mobilizing two *simultaneous* sets of borders therefore: those separating 'white' from a non-white Other, and the more fluid divisions between the nominally 'white' groups themselves (Garner 2007). However the achievement of whiteness should in no way be regarded as monolithic or stable: for whiteness has also been shown to be an ongoing process, constantly made and remade through its participation in these other unequal social relations.

Work and labour settings have also been shown to be key in the process of assigning subject positions *vis-à-vis* other whites and other non-whites; thus reinforcing the ways in which whiteness is mediated by both *class* and *gender*, *colonialism* in the past and a more or less enduring sense of *nationality* today. Whilst they might still enjoy the 'wages of whiteness' (Du Bois 1977), huge variations exist and many white workers are on a considerably lower wage than (fewer) other whites. This chapter asserts therefore the necessity to see identity formation as anchored in *material* conditions as much as *ideological* and *cultural* ones. Whiteness is a position of structural advantage, associated with 'privileges' of all kinds, including higher wages, reduced chances of poverty, better access to health, education and the legal system. As such, white social identities cannot therefore be fully understood outside the contexts of the modes of production and the labour force imperatives that shape them (Garner 2007). Further, albeit uneven, whiteness can also be a 'standpoint', subject position or location from which to look at oneself, others and society (Frankenberg 1993). It carries with it a set of ways of being in the world, a set of cultural practices which, although they may not be named as 'white' because they are looked upon by white people as just 'normal', are white nonetheless. In order to uncover and reveal these processes and practices at both the material and the discursive, we need therefore careful comparative and historicizing study, so that we may build up our knowledge of similarities, differences, and internal nuances within and between different contexts. In the next chapter I turn to consider more fully how this can be done.

Chapter 3
Researching White Identities

Whilst the *study* of whiteness has burgeoned in recent years, the *methodological tools* by which to conduct this research have not been at the forefront of debate. Yet the ways in which we understand and conceptualize whiteness both inform, and are informed by, the methods we choose to explore our research questions. Historically, some 'race' research has been criticized for sidelining issues around methodology, epistemology and politics (Twine 2000), and perhaps rather 'comfortably address[ing] the methods, settings and subjects/objects of research – the *hows, whens and whos*' (Alexander 2006: 398). In other words, the links between the methods employed and broader ontological and epistemological assumptions and/or questions framing the research are not always fully interrogated. How we understand notions of 'truth' and 'objectivity', for example, will affect our understanding of the relationship between ourselves as researchers and the research process, not only in terms of collecting data, but also in terms of the ways in which we analyse, produce and present our findings. However, some of the recent work on expatriates *is* becoming more self-reflexive and self-critical, recognizing not only the positionality of the researcher in the research process, but indeed making this a central feature of the discussion. Methodological issues are thus becoming tackled more openly, and the aim of this chapter is to provide an overview of the key approaches and debates.

Ethnography

Ethnography is the most popular method used for much of the recent work on expatriates, although it is perhaps a 'rather amorphous and ill-defined set of practices undergirded by multiple and contested epistemological foundations and assumptions' (Alexander 2006: 399). At its broadest, ethnography is seen to encompass all forms of qualitative methods, but it is usually assumed to involve a period of intensive fieldwork involving participant observation. Its aim is 'the study of people in their own "natural" setting', with a focus on capturing and re-presenting the subjects' own understanding of their world' (ibid: 400). This usually involves an extended period of time 'in the field', with an emphasis on gaining insight into the range of meanings, categorizations and theorizations by which people position themselves (Brewer 2000) as well as 'giving voice' to these (Wacquant 2003, Alexander 2006). In terms of its applicability to 'race' research however, ethnography has historically been subject to much critical scrutiny and challenge as regards its subjects of study, the nature of the research process and the relationships within this, as well as the status of the knowledge produced. This has drawn attention to issues of power which arise through the positioning of the researcher in the research process, and in particular to a seemingly integral process of 'Othering' by (the predominantly white) ethnographers in their undertaking of research on ethnic minorities. Some of this research has been criticized for being 'part of a process of neo-colonial control' (Sharma et al. 1996 in Alexander 2006: 401), and such charges have perhaps meant that ethnography has remained rather marginal and controversial in race research more broadly.

However more recently a new generation of ethnographers have sought to re-imagine the use of ethnography in race research through a central recognition of the issues of power involved in the research process. Some of the research with privileged migrants can be seen to fall within this 'wave' of whiteness research (Twine and Gallagher 2007) in its endeavour to recognize

> the negotiation and construction of "difference" in "the field" and in writing, the acknowledgement and partial amelioration of power hierarchies in the research process and the engagement with the broader local and global political contexts and realities of "race" (Alexander 2006: 402).

The new ethnographies are thus attempting to make explicit links between micro-level processes and relations – 'the mundane, the marginal, the everyday' (Burawoy et al. 2000: xii) – and broader structures of power including race, gender, class and nationality. In spite of its roots as a method intended only for the study of the small scale and the local, ethnography is thus increasingly being seen as a means by which to access and analyse the larger scale: macro level processes such as globalization and migration. Looking at the everyday lives of transnational migrants for example offers a valuable way of gaining insight into the ways in which globalization is lived and experienced (Burawoy et al. 2000), as well as how this is differentiated by features such as race, gender and class. Such an approach allows 'the pawns of larger structural forces to emerge as real human beings who shape their own future' (Bourgois 2000: 208). These insights are gained through the range and diversity of methods which can be incorporated within ethnography, whilst combining these with a thoughtful awareness of the researcher's own positioning within the research process and in the 'knowledge' produced. Thus research with *expatriate* 'pawns' (Bourgeois 2000: 208) often involves a very particular complexity of positionality issues which may be different to the norm of ethnographic research on more disempowered migrants. Whilst it may be true to say that expatriates are relatively powerless in the global scheme of things, they are still powerful compared to many other people, and many of them (particularly the white middle class males), are in highly prestigious and influential careers. For the researcher the enquiry may involve 'studying up', whereby the research subject occupies a more powerful position than the researcher (Fechter 2007, Hunter 2009). For white researchers, although the process of turning the 'white eye' back on itself will not involve being marginalized due to processes of racial 'Othering', the research relationship may still be far from unproblematic or egalitarian. The divisions which occur *between* whites, across *inter alia* gender, ethnicity, class, age, political persuasion and sexuality, inflect the research process just as they do in life (Gallagher 2000) and researching people who may be very different from oneself socially, politically and economically may necessitate some considerable negotiation.

Acknowledging differences between the researcher and the researched caution against any assumption that 'racial matching' is a 'guarantee of authenticity' (Alexander 2004: 142) or a sort of 'hotline to the truth'. However, having said this, gaining a sense of distance and positing one's difference from the subjects of research is revealed to be one of the messy difficulties of doing ethnographic research with white expatriates by white researchers, which often involves spending considerable amounts of time together. Whilst it may be relatively easy for a white researcher studying, for example, a white far right youth gang, to position themselves against the subjects of their research, this has often been found to be more difficult with expatriate subjects. Clearly 'expatriates' are extremely heterogeneous, and they cannot be viewed as a 'group' with any sort of coherence. Whilst the researcher may feel politically at odds with *some* of their research participants, they may feel senses of allegiance and empathy with *others*. Walsh (2006) centralizes this messiness in her discussion of her friendship with Jane, an expatriate woman in Dubai. Knowles (2006) describes an opposing experience with an expatriate diving instructor in Hong Kong whose political and social opinions were very different to her own. These experiences show how we need to challenge any sense of 'emotional, psychological and political neutrality' in the researching of race, and acknowledge that what we are involved in may carry with it a difficult emotional balancing act which Back (2002: 57) terms 'ethical ambivalence'. Having ethical ambivalence is not always easy: as Back (2002) and Knowles (2006) describe, 'being white' can be seen by some other whites as an entry visa to a privileged club, membership of which assumes a complicity about 'them' which may involve listening to unfettered racist allegations. However this sort of experience can also be seen as a 'necessary and productive tension' (Alexander 2004: 143), which leads us to think very carefully about how we position ourselves in both the 'collecting of data' and the 'writing up' stages. The complex strains and feelings involved *can* make for methodological thoughtfulness and creativity.

Important here therefore is the understanding of ethnography as a *dual* process of both *fieldwork* and *writing* (Alexander 2004, Clifford and Marcus 1986). Drawing on Clifford and Marcus (1986) Alexander (2004) describes ethnography as encompassing both the *politics* of doing fieldwork research as well as the *poetics* of writing, narrating and picturing. This is a conceptualization which pushes to the forefront the role of the researcher in the production and presentation of knowledge. Conventionally, whilst methods of collecting data are usually discussed in the writing up of research – albeit in sometimes rather perfunctory ways – the *analytical/interpretive* methods by which findings are then examined and presented are all too often insufficiently considered. In contrast, this approach, rather than pursuing any attempt to see researchers as objective, understands that the ways in which they situate themselves, negotiate their research subjects, manage the research process and interpret the data is a *personally* productive and creative process. Clearly, 'writing up' is not some kind of 'automatic transcription' (Back 2004: 204), but a highly subjective process. We will return to this point later in the chapter.

Recent debates on the uses of ethnographic approaches in race research thus argue for an explicit recognition of the position and partiality of the researcher (Alexander 2004). This is something which has certainly been taken on board in some of ethnographic work with white expatriates which has been undertaken in the last few years. For example, Walsh (2006) studied British expatriates in Dubai by spending 18 months there, living alongside them in the 'expat' community. Here she was both one of them and yet not one of them: an experience which enabled her on one level to 'belong': becoming thoroughly incorporated into the daily lives of the expatriates there and having access to unchecked and unmediated talk; yet at the same time experiencing exclusion from certain classes of the white community. Importantly, she adopts a self-reflexive approach by centrally acknowledging herself in the research process, and analysing some of the difficulties that resulted from her total immersion there – 'being there, doing it, and becoming part of what you're writing about' (Walsh 2005: 283). She has an open discussion of how her embodiment influenced her experiences 'in the field' and in the ethnographic process, which involved negotiating relationships with her respondents and having to make decisions regarding trust and boundaries. Gender, class and age were important factors in her experiences as a researcher, both positively and negatively. Thus whilst she was able to be invited into the heart of some feminized spaces, events and routines, and was invited out socially by the younger expatriates, she found she needed to manage the ways in which some (older) men were flattered by her interest in them, and how she was sometimes excluded or patronized by older women. Being a white researcher does not grant you unfettered access to *all* things white, and the ways in which expatriates particularly have been found primarily to 'hang around with those of similar backgrounds in terms of occupation or even class' (Walsh 2005: 289) may make it difficult to access groups of people who are unlike yourself. At the same time, however, Walsh (2005) also acknowledges the pleasurable side of doing research and the potential for identifying with, or even making rewarding friendships with, your 'research subjects'. 'Boundaries' can be complex in ethnographic research.

Fechter's (2007) study of expatriates in Indonesia also incorporates participant observation, interviews and informal conversations, combined with questionnaires, newspaper material, expatriate publications and the Internet. The research was based in Jakarta: a sprawling city which requires considerable travel to get from one place to another. This meant that in order to meet her research participants Fechter (2007) had to make appointments or attend events so that she could spend time with them. Her participant observation was thus tied to community and social activities, whilst informal discussions were often conducted on the hoof, travelling from one place to another. She also conducted interviews in homes, restaurants or at the workplace. The interview material is supplemented by fieldnotes in her discussion and analysis. Fechter (2007) also draws on Internet sites such as an expatriate forum entitled 'Living in Indonesia'. These sites abound in many locations of expatriate migration, and provide an interesting insight into local topics of discussion as well as the discourses by which people position themselves. While acknowledging the care which needs to be taken in terms of interpreting Internet sources, Fechter (2007) argues that these can provide key complementary data to material gained in other ways. More crucially, she suggests that they may provide valuable insight into the making of race and racism. Whilst it has been argued that such forums not merely represent but encourage the production of racialized discourses, and therefore offer distorted perspectives (Zickmund 1997), Fechter found that the postings on these sites were 'intensified and magnified expressions of sentiments and beliefs encountered during fieldwork' (2007: 15) which people were perhaps reluctant to express face to face. These particularly concerned expatriates' opinions of Indonesians, and racist and sexist attitudes in general. Aware of the fact that the medium of the Internet may influence the discourses conducted through it, Fechter (2007) nevertheless found a useful point of access to issues of race making was to trace connections between views aired on the website and the everyday lives of expatriates.

Fechter's (2007) close attention to, and exploration of, the detail of Indonesian expatriate lives reveals both how whitenesses are made as well as the ways these understandings and performances are sometimes contested within this diverse community. Through her explorations of the differently gendered and classed spaces of their lives as well as their talk, both spoken and unspoken aspects of whiteness and racisms are revealed. As well uncovering differences between her participants, Fechter (2007) is also aware of the differences between herself and her (more wealthy) research participants, exacerbated by her status as a (low income) student. In terms of power and status, Fechter acknowledges that she was in the main 'studying up'. As was discussed in relation to Walsh's experience, this position in a research context may make it difficult to access certain expatriate/white spaces which are not amenable to being researched by a (perhaps underfunded/less well paid) academic researcher. Amongst these I would suggest are (sometimes) the spaces of work and organization – particularly large corporations which may be wary of opening themselves up to sociological research on issues which are not of clear and direct economic benefit to them. Consequently perhaps, Fechter's work, like Walsh's, does not concentrate on working life, but on the daily domestic and social lives of expatriates in Indonesia, and the boundaries that are constructed within these.

Biographies and Narratives of Everyday Life

The increased awareness of our own positionality within the research process has also led to a growing interest in ways of widening research to include the voices of others. Issues of multivocality, centring on how to deal with participants' own representations of their worlds (Gubrium and Holstein 1995), have led to a growing creativity in research methods in terms of both data collection and analysis. 'Where the older ethnography cast its subjects as mere components of their social worlds, new ethnography treats them as active interpreters who construct their realities through talk and interaction, stories and narrative' (Gubrium and Holstein 1995: 46). In particular, biographical research takes personal texts as a central focus. These can include autobiographies, autoethnographies, biographies, diaries, letters, oral histories, life stories, personal narratives or experience stories: and thus it is a method which underscores the active, creative involvement of people in the construction of their everyday lives. It is particularly useful in revealing how 'participants work at characterizing their lives in relation to the interpretive horizons of social settings, using available interpretive resources' (Gubrium and Holstein 1995: 47). Biographical work can thus reflect *locally* promoted ways of interpreting experience and identity, so that what is constructed is distinctively crafted, assembled from the meaningful categories and vocabularies of particular contextual settings. This means also that this method is very specifically interested in the *language* which people use. As Gubrium and Holstein (1995) argue, if we treat talk and interaction as the means through which lives and identities are constructed, we need to look carefully at what participants 'do with words' to structure and give social form to their thoughts and experiences. Empirical research can thus centre on *how* participants articulate the stories they tell about themselves and others. Narratives in particular are thus to be seen as 'artful and situational constructions', offering 'a complex sense of biographical patterning' (Gubrium and Holstein 1995: 47–8). They also require, therefore, distinctive methods to analyse and interpret the language features and rhetorical devices used in order to explore the ways in which people understand, organize and represent their experiences and life stories (Gubrium and Holstein 1995).

Biographical methods have been found to be particularly useful for studying both migration and race, and are thus valuable for exploring expatriate lives. First, they have been found to be especially useful in the ways in which they place the 'act' of migration within the migrant's entire biography. This gives access to broader aspects of the migrant's life, their 'home' and 'work' contexts, as well as the complex and perhaps messy decision making and upheaval involved in the move itself (Boyle et al. 1998): the whole 'leaving of the old and negotiating the new' which I turn to explore in the next chapter. In particular, methods which encourage participants to talk at length and tell stories about their lives can provide invaluable access to the detail of expatriate lives. Second, such 'narratives of everyday life' also help to direct our attention to what narrators '*accomplish* as they tell their stories, and how that accomplishment is culturally shaped' (Gubrium and Holstein

1995: 2). In other words, discursive acts such as these help the narrator to establish their *identity*: who one is, and what one is like. As Wetherall and Potter (1992) put it, 'identity in talk is a construction, an achievement and an accomplishment' (p. 78). In their focus on the stories of lives, and the language and performance in the telling of these, auto/biographical and narrative methods are thus invaluable in enabling us to conceptualize migration and race in terms of identity (Boyle et al. 1998) and to see that migration is an 'expression of people's sense of being at any one point in time' (Gutting 1996: 482). Third, collecting narratives can allow for plurivocality: to include in the research a range of alternative voices to the dominant mainstream male/Eurocentric subject (McDowell 1992). Building up a deliberately socially diverse picture can give access to the interplay between the 'logic of individual action' with 'the effects of structural constraints within which life courses evolve' (Vandsemb 1995: 414 in Boyle et al. 1998): that is, the ways in which aspects such as race, gender and age affect people's opportunities and resources. Indeed, biographical approaches are particularly useful as a point of access to researching race. Through the ways people position themselves in the telling of their lives and talk about the contexts in which these are set, we can explore the ways in which raced subjectivities have been/are constructed. Although the individual subject is placed at the centre of the frame of analysis, through their personal accounts we are also given access to, and insight into, the broader social and political contexts of their lives, and the processes by which their race has been animated and given meaning. In the way in which connections are made between individual experience and larger historical and social scenes, biographical methods are thus capable of capturing the *micro* and the *macro* in the same frame (Knowles 2003, Harper et al. 2005).

With biographical interviews, researchers engaged in the specific exploration of race and ethnicity will have the opportunity to build in ways of inviting participants to reflect on the ways in which race, past and present, inflects their lives. However in other biographical material such as autobiographies, letters, diaries and so on, it is less likely that the subject of race is tackled head on. For example, in Chambers' (2005) autobiographical reflections on his career as a development worker in a variety of contexts, although an interesting and self-reflexive discussion of the circumstances of his career is offered, there is a silence on the issue of his whiteness. Rather he attributes his career fortunes to other aspects of his personal biography such as his education, his patrons and colleagues, being taught how to write well, being relieved of lecturing duties in academic appointments and so on. These are attributed to 'comparative advantages and luck' rather than acknowledged as the privileges of middle class male *whiteness*. Silences such as these require these sorts of texts to be subjected to close scrutiny to piece together the mechanisms by which lives are raced.

Auto/biographies and the telling of narratives are thus creative acts both in terms of what the author is doing *and* in terms of the activities of those excavating them. They should therefore be understood as *compositional* rather than *representational*, and, further, as compositional at variety of levels. In terms of their use in research, there is at the very least, a *double moment* of interpretation, as the narrative activity which involves 'reflection, theorization and the translation of living into text' (Knowles 2003: 55) is undertaken *first* by the narrator in their talk or text, and *second* by the researcher in their analysis. However in neither case can these interpretations be seen as completely free or unbound: for the author, the doing of auto/biography is governed by convention and as such personal biographies are often composed within a prescribed format. They are 'a particular way of accounting for the self, a particular kind of narrative, and a particular mode of self-understanding' (Freeman 1993: 28 quoted in Knowles 2003: 55). Individuals tend to *give* meaning and structure to their lives by (usually) placing events into a linear order, seeing their present lives and identities in terms of past experiences and future plans. In this creative act of interpretation, 'the self is constantly written and rewritten, constituted and reconstituted' (Knowles 2003: 55) and relationships between past and present are constantly (re)established. Further, in the ways in which memory is operated to select (and reject) past and present lives and experiences, multiple, fluid and sometimes contradictory identities may be (re)created.

This process of selection/rejection is then repeated by the researcher analysing the text. Further complexities, however are nicely emphasized by Gordon's (2008) discussion of her research with the 'Shell Ladies': the wives of engineers, developers and administrators employed by the oil conglomerate Shell. Drawing upon a selection of autobiographical narratives published as part of an historical memoir by the corporation, she notes how

> the stories are a *public* expression of their private thoughts and experiences and as such we need to be aware of the context in which they were created, what kind of data these texts yield, what they leave out and perhaps conceal, and how the contributions were selected for publication. Storytelling is a creative *social* practice (Gordon 2008: 23, my italics).

The Shell Ladies' stories combine to produce *both* individual biographies and a collective one. By bringing their personal memories together, the women create a sense of shared understandings and meanings. Connerton (1989) suggests that this kind of recollection can then become a political act in the way that it is then absorbed into the collective consciousness of the whole group, becoming a community or social memory. The selection, rejection and subsequent publication of such accounts can transform and mobilize both understandings of personal identities and what it means to belong to the group, as well as the understandings of these by other readers. In her analysis of the Shell narratives, Gordon (2008) also interweaves her own autobiography as a 'Shell daughter'. In doing so, yet another layer of selection, interpretation and meaning is added.

The aim of the Shell Ladies project was to give voice to the wives of Shell expatriates and gain public acknowledgement of *their* role in the life of the corporation. Gordon (2008) uses their autobiographical narratives as a rich source for tracing the associations and connections between the people and the sites of Shell, gaining access to the *multiplicity* of different contexts and expatriate lives and identities. Other researchers attempt to get closer to the 'situatedness' of expatriate life by focusing very closely on the autobiographical narrative and life of just *one* research subject (Harper et al. 2005, Walsh 2006). In our close examination of the life of Jack, a veteran Second World War soldier, we drew on his own telling of his life story to us, as well as his published autobiography *Banzai You Bastards!* to explore in detail the complex configurations of ethnic and racial boundaries which had shaped his life (Harper et al. 2005). Focusing on one subject in this way can thus give sufficient space and depth to explore the ways in which lives and identities are constructed through a range of narrative texts.

A further technique is to draw on *our* own experiences: using ourselves as the subjects of research. A*uto-ethnographies* are reflective personal accounts which attempt to make connections between personal biographies and history by focusing on the relationships and institutions that have shaped our own lives and identities. This may be done by interrogating some of our most emotionally stressful moments, particularly those that remain unresolved. This approach thus does away with a sense of linear progress where the past is 'dead and done with', but approaches lives through key moments or 'stepping stones' (Eyben 2008). It can also challenge the 'structures that keep the voiceless silent' (Eyben 2008: 151), returning to give voice back. For example, Eyben's (2008) auto-ethnography covers the years she spent as an aid/development worker and wife in a variety of expatriate contexts, and her personal, critical approach allows her to acknowledge the almost complete silencing of issues of race and racism which marked her earlier life. It is in many respects a reflective and retrospective account of whiteness, exploring how whiteness was made and performed across the diverse spaces and times of expatriate life. Eyben (2008) honestly admits to situations in which she remained silent in the face of racist comments and jokes. She is now however able to reflect back from the present to this past self, a self who failed to question the presence, behaviour and purpose of expatriates. Her highly personal account provides a rich resource and a methodology by which to explore the making of whiteness in expatriate lives.

Interviews and the Psycho-Social

The increased awareness of our own positionality in the research process has also been used quite deliberately within interviews which draw on psycho-social approaches for analysis. Psycho-social methodologies of interpretation hold that the interviewer's talk and responses are of equal interest to those of the interviewee (Wetherall and Potter 1992). *Both* are constructing narratives which draw on a varied range of rhetorical devices, an understanding which challenges the idea that interviewers should be or can be neutral and uninvolved. This acceptance opens the window for a more active and interventionist form of interviewing, perhaps involving the interviewer as a more 'animated conversationalist' or even as more argumentative, offering counter examples and questioning assumptions (Wetherall and Potter 1992: 99). This may be especially appropriate for approaching the study of whiteness where issues of empowerment/exploitation are different from research which involves more vulnerable groups. In psycho-social research, the focus of interest is in the emotions that such an encounter may create for interviewer and interviewee, as well as the operation and effects of power relations. The ways in which power relations are produced and negotiated by both parties recognizes the co-constituted nature of the research process, as well as the ways in which such relations may constantly shift and change throughout the interaction. The research space will involve the collision of a multiplicity of histories, experiences and contexts, which will be both produced and changed through the research process (Gunaratnam 2003). This is demonstrated nicely in Knowles' (2006) encounter with an expatriate diving instructor who we both met during one of our research trips to Hong Kong. On the one hand his racism and bigotry instigated feelings of anger, even repulsion. On the other Knowles came to recognize that these feelings were also the result of the mirror Diver was holding up to whiteness, thus forcing an acknowledgement of characteristics that she may in fact share with him. The ongoing ebb and flow of their research interaction was an emotional encounter which forced new insights. We can all learn from this: the researcher needs to be alert to the connective power of the emotions in play, and the ways in which these may bring together ideas, people and discourses in fruitful ways. This may also mean an acknowledgement of the silences, for emotions are often 'as much about what we don't say, and how we avoid saying it, than about what we do say and how' (Hunter 2009). This can be particular apposite for issues of social difference such as gender and race, which are often euphemized in everyday talk.

Discourse/Narrative Analysis

The discussion so far has revealed that how people *talk* about themselves is central to the examination of the ways in which racial and ethnic categories are produced and have meaning in individual lives (Gunaratnam 2003). The broad range of material which captures talk such as biographical texts and interviews clearly offers a rich and varied means by which to explore the links between the macro and the micro, both in terms of the relations between social and subjective process of 'race-making', and the relations between theoretical conceptualizations and lived experiences of race. However, in order to conduct this sort of analysis we need methodological tools: and tools which connect with our broader epistemological understandings of identity and race, and the relationships between these. In this book I have stressed complexity and diversity in the experience of race, its historical and spatial contingency, and the multiplicity of both performances and contexts. In tune with this epistemological trajectory, poststructural approaches can be seen to offer a valuable methodology both in terms of their theoretical assumptions on the nature of order and their practical applicability for the analysis of empirical material.

Poststructuralism recognizes experience as mediated by the continual negotiation of personal, interactional and social dynamics. As such our personal experiences of, for example, race, are only ever partial, as they are continually ongoing, constructed in and through the diverse contexts of our lives. These fragmented and sometimes even contradictory experiences challenge essentialist or fixed understandings of the relationships between our identities and social categories such as race and gender. Further, poststructuralists see that the ways people *talk* about themselves, positioning themselves in and through social discourses, frame the ways in which they both understand these experiences and themselves, as well as the ways they represent themselves to others. However people are far from consistent, and in the diverse, sometimes playful, and sometimes contradictory ways in which people locate themselves, hegemonic social discourses can be troubled. As Wuthnow (2002) explains: 'While hegemonic representations may categorize and define, there is always resistance to these definitions, and it is the subjective agency embodied in this resistance which constitutes the possibility for oppositional discourses' (p. 194).

Poststructuralism has a commitment to represent *all* voices and knowledges – the oppositional as well as the hegemonic – including minority voices whose knowledge may normally be subjugated. This approach recognizes therefore the dynamic construction of the meanings of 'race' and ethnicity through these multiple engagements with social discourse as well as through the subjective investments of individuals (Gunaratnam 2003, see also Brah 1996 and Hall 1996). It is interested in the multiple ways 'social discourses are enmeshed in lived experience and institutional and social power relations that have emotional, material and embodied consequences for individuals and for groups' (Gunaratnam 2003: 7). In this way discourses and lived experiences are constantly *co-constituted*: they intermingle and inhabit one another. Seeing situations and experience as co-constitutional means that the researcher's presence in the research process cannot be ignored, and attention in research must therefore be given to recognizing the ways in which both the research participants and the researchers are socially situated and contribute to the construction of the 'knowledge' produced.

In their concern to rupture the essentializing tendencies of modernist knowledges, poststructuralist epistemologies have some clear connections with those versions of postcolonialism which seek to avoid conceptual fixings of 'race' in their analysis. These also aim to challenge and reconceive the ways in which the 'West/Rest' have been positioned in global relations and in contemporary identities. As Ahmed states:

> postcolonialism is about rethinking how colonialism operated in different times in ways that permeate all aspects of social life, in the colonized and colonizing nations. It is hence about the complexity of the relationship between the past and the present, between the histories of European colonization and contemporary

forms of globalization. That complexity cannot be reduced by either a notion that the present has broken from the past ... or that the present is simply continuous with the past ... To this extent post-coloniality allows us to investigate how colonial encounters are both determining and not yet fully determining, of social and material existence (2000: 11).

This rethinking concords with poststructuralist approaches, as both seek to challenge any notion of fixed meanings and binaristic terms of opposition such as colonial/postcolonial, white/non-white. Derrida's (1978) deconstructionist analysis is useful here in its demonstration of how one term in any pair of oppositions inhabits and interpenetrates the other, producing a supplementarity or *double movement*, between the two. Using tools which work across poststructuralism/ postcolonialism thus means that understandings of 'race' are not produced in terms of unitary, hermetically sealed, homogenous categories of difference (Gunaratnam 2003), but rather the aim is to overturn these by showing how race interpenetrates *all* contemporary social differences. Categories of gender, sexuality, class, age or disability are *also* categories that carry racialized meanings, and, as such, the aim is to challenge knowledge based on discrete categorization, coherence and stability, moving instead towards more contextual, contingent and ambivalent forms of knowing. Poststructuralism aims to break down binaristic thinking, 'by uncovering and working through the tense entanglements, interdependencies and junctions between categories and social relations' (Gunaratnam 2003: 22). Employing this sort of reflexive analytical 'doubleness' thus entails interrupting binary systems of knowledge production and addressing the plurality and multiplicity of racialized identities and differences.

This aim is also reflected in Wetherall and Potter's (1992) *Mapping the Language of Racism*. Their task is to unearth analytically how a range of heterogeneous practices, arguments and representations constitute a 'taken for granted' racism for many white people in New Zealand. Here *language* is seen as a material which can be explored and charted, and thus Wetherall and Potter (1992) do not see deconstructionist approaches to language as *in opposition to* those accounts which claim to be 'materialist', and grounded in 'real' experience. Rather, looking at language is seen to be critical in seeing how experience is brought into being and has specific (material) effects in particular social contexts. Consequently, they focus primarily on *discourse*: on the meanings, conversations, narratives, and anecdotes of a group of white New Zealanders, as well as a range of other government and media texts. These are used as a means to look at 'the ways in which a society gives voice to racism and how forms of discourse institute, solidify, change, create and reproduce social formations' (1992: 3).

Wetherall and Potter's methodology involves a very practical engagement with text and talk. In line with the approach of this book, rather than seeing this as in any way representational or reflective of 'reality', they see that, in the ways in which these draw on and use ideological discourses, they are *constitutive of* subjectivity, identity, social groups and social categories such as race. For example, racist ideological discourses facilitate the assignment of minority groups to exploitative roles in a division of labour through certain formulations of capacities, talents, roles and rights. 'Ideology becomes in these accounts, not a set of ideas which simply legitimate disadvantage, but part of the mechanisms which institute disadvantage' (p. 60). Ideology is thus a form of 'practical action, instantiated in policy statements, in the statements of political spin doctors, in memos, in speeches, in documents, in newspapers, in conversations, accounts, explanations, versions, anecdotes and stories' (p. 61). By their nature, these are far from coherent, but fragmented and contradictory, with these variations being crucial to their operation.

Whilst Wetherall and Potter (1992) draw on a Foucauldian understanding of discourses as historically evolved, making up an important part of the common sense of a culture as well as providing the structure for the operation of its institutions, they also place much more emphasis on its function as a social practice, the context of its use and on the act of discursive instantiation. From this perspective, the sense of texts and talk is not seen as derived from their *abstract* meaning or organization, but from their *situated* use in actual settings and speech contexts. For this reason they move to use the term 'interpretive repertoires', by which they mean 'broadly discernible clusters of terms, descriptions and figures of speech often assembled around metaphors or vivid images' (p. 90). These provide a way of understanding the *content* of discourse and how that content is organized and used, and a way of approaching language and speech from a sociological perspective rather than a linguistic one: one that is concerned with 'language use, what is achieved by that use and the nature of the interpretive resources that allow that achievement' (p. 91). Rather than offering a consistent model of the world, however, discourse analysis of a social group or community usually reveals fragmentation and sometimes even contradiction: 'a kaleidoscope of common sense' (Billig 1992).

Clearly, to explore interviews and biographical/narrative analyses in depth requires that these are transcribed in their entirety. The language is then available to the researcher to explore for *discursive themes* (or 'interpretive repetoires' (Wetherall and Potter 1992)). This methodology provides a way of disassembling 'race' into the smaller concepts that give it meaning, a process which makes it much easier to deal with analytically, as well as offering a way to grasp its complexity in lived experience (Knowles 1999). It also offers a way in, when 'race' or 'whiteness' is not featured directly. As we have seen, in these cases 'we have to work much harder to understand its impact on, and significance in, lives' (Knowles 1999: 123). By exploring how race operates with and through themes in the making of identities in individual and local accounts, the researcher can make connections to broader discourses of race, the social and political context as well as the dynamics of the research interaction itself. This analytical approach thus offers a way of weaving the discursive, the material and the interactional together, as well as acknowledging the heterogeneity of raced experiences.

As well as exploring texts for key discursive themes, they can also be approached for the ways in which other rhetorical devices are used to construct meaning. These include *rhetorical constructions*, or the range of discursive features through which people draw upon to construct their versions of reality, including devices such as categorization and particularization, constructions involving consensus and corroboration (a sense of 'we' versus 'them'), the use of combinations of vivid and systematically vague formulations when referring to Others, the mobilization of narrative techniques, and basic rhetorical forms such as lists and contrasts. Second, once again *absences and silence* are of interest: what is left out? From a poststructuralist perspective, it is revealing to explore the ways in which arguments by white people are often fashioned against an absent Other, or silence alternative views of the Other. At the same time, silences *about* whiteness as a racialized identity have been seen as critical to the construction of power relations, serving the purpose of producing a de-racialized identity, and enabling those categorized as white to ignore, deny, avoid or forget their racialized subjective and social positioning (Simpson 1996). Further, at the intersubjective level of the relationship between researcher and researched, these silences may be connected with emotions caused by the interview itself. As Hunter (2009) has shown, feelings about difference are often 'caught up with discursively constructed Manichean positionings as either victim or oppressor' that may play out in the interview process. A third approach is to give *conflicts and tensions* a central place, directing attention to the way a particular version or argument is designed, often in a highly inexplicit and contradictory manner, to undermine one or more competing alternatives. A fourth technique is to search for *patterns of variation and consistency* which signal the different ways of constructing events, processes or groups which may be deployed, and the patterns of discourses that participants draw upon. Again these may be contradictory, such that people may shift between claims, being simultaneously racist and non-racist within the same interview. The analytic goal here is not to classify people however, but rather to reveal the discursive practices through which race categories are constructed and privilege is legitimated.

It is clear from this discussion that discourse analysis is an active process on the part of the researcher which involves developing, exploring and justifying interpretations and readings of texts. Documents and transcripts are searched for patterns of meanings in order that the argumentative and rhetorical practices through which key discourses are mobilized can be identified. A final stage of interpretation then lies in the hermeneutic act of drawing conclusions from this identification process: of making connections between the patterns of discourse and the contexts within which they are derived. This discussion needs to explore the social consequences and effects of these accounts and narratives in order to evaluate the extent to which they can be seen to be an expression of power or a resistance to dominant hegemonic ideologies. This final stage is essential if we are to argue that certain forms of discourse are implicated in the sustenance and maintenance of particular social patterns.

Visual Methods

People do not construct their selves and lives through talk and text alone however: they also do this in the *embodied* performances and contexts of their lives (Halford and Leonard 2006). If ethnographic and biographical methods aim to capture this broader construction of subjectivities and identities in full, then the inclusion of visual methods can offer a valuable and meaningful tool. Photographs are able to capture particular aspects of individuals and situations, whilst also inviting the viewer to speculate on the wider social and political ramifications (Harper et al. 2005). This is certainly not to claim that visual images are any less constructed than narratives: just as life stories are framed by powerful literary and discursive conventions which are then mediated through the researcher's interpretive repertoire, so photographs are formulated through, more or less explicitly, a *collaborative* relationship between the photographer and the photographed. In this way visual methods can be used as an additional means of *bringing in* the research subject's voice, rather than a method of objectification. The meaning of the photograph is then 'constructed by the maker and the viewer, both of whom carry their social positions and interests to the photographic act' (Harper 1998: 34–5).

The contrived nature of photographs makes them a particularly suitable method for investigating race, itself also a contrived social category (Knowles 2006). Knowles (2006) argues however that this arbitrariness creates two problems for the visual researcher of race: first, in the selection and arrangement of objects at which the lens is aimed, and second, in the theoretical analysis in which the image is then rendered. The first problematic refers to the staging of race in the staging of the photographic image, wherein all the complexities and subtleties involved in the investigation may be conflated into a 'series of short-cuts' (Knowles 2006: 513) which can be stereotypical. Visual methods by definition focus on visible differences: and historically the focus on race has been *by* white photographers looking *at* Others. Photography has thus contributed to the ways in which bodies, lives and spaces are theorized and categorized – as raced and othered by whites. However of course photography is not *inevitably* a racist practice: it can be used to challenge, reformulate objects of the gaze, re-position, and *re-theorize* (Knowles 2006). However when used to focus on *white* bodies the meanings of the image for white people traditionally start to disappear: are we looking at 'race' or just 'people'? Images of extreme right wing activists are clearly about race, but are photographs of the mundane activities of white people's everyday lives? Gradually, work is starting to appear claiming that they are. For example, in our discussion of Jack, Harper, Knowles and I (2005) combine biographical, autobiographical and visual methods to tell the story behind *why* an old man in his 80s remained in Hong Kong as an expatriate, when most men of his age had long returned 'home'. The images were co-constituted by Jack and Harper to reflect his daily life in Hong Kong, and the spaces and places which were meaningful to him. Whilst his white body and the symbols of white Britishness which frame parts of his life appear to clash with the Chinese landscape around him, he is clearly tied to that landscape and its history. The images point to the complexity and ambiguity of white British relationships to empire and race.

Photography has a valuable supplementary role to play in ethnographic research therefore, to reveal what words alone do not say. Both text and image are polysemic, inviting the reader/viewer into the making of meaning, and helping to reconfigure the theoretical frameworks we have to understand the world. They can also provide a way of connecting micro-lives to macro-processes and events. For white researchers of whiteness, taking photographs, just as scrutinizing interview texts, involves the personal challenge of attempting to deconstruct the normative positions by which we see the world. As Knowles (2006) argues, trying to see the mundane and unspectacular moments of 'normal' (white) lives as *raced* brings issues of culpability, complicity and difference to the fore. Research with white people is not and should not be always about their larger acts of overt racism, for the privileges of whiteness are deployed in multiple and subtle ways (Byrne 2006). In research with expatriates, their privileges are rarely discussed under a neat sub-heading: like whiteness, these usually remain 'unmarked, un-remarked on, unrecognized, and denied' (Knowles 2006: 517). Visual methods can help to expose such privileges however, taking us 'beyond words' and allowing our gaze to dwell upon the multiple and subtle performances of whiteness.

Doing Ethnographic Research with White British Expatriates in Hong Kong

In this chapter I have discussed a range of methodologies and methods by which whiteness has been studied, and which provide the level of micro-detail needed in order to pursue the study of whiteness in expatriate contexts. Ethnographic and biographical methods open a window onto the 'mundane routines' and 'banal' habits of everyday life, and create an opportunity to see afresh the formation of nationality and raced identities (Billig 1995). They are also methodologies which are self – conscious about the theoretical assumptions which underpin them, and the sort of knowledge which they produce. In particular I have made a claim for the value and importance of poststructural and postcolonial epistemologies and analytical strategies to make sense of the production of race and identity in context.

Bringing these approaches together: ethnographic, biographical and visual methods with poststructural and postcolonial analytical methodologies, was something I attempted to do in my own research in Hong Kong with white British expatriates (Leonard 2008, 2010), which I will be drawing on in later chapters. The aim of this research was to explore the postcolonial interplay between whiteness, nationality and gender with the construction of work identities. Hong Kong was selected as it is both a major global city and centre for work and lifestyle migration, as well as having a relatively recent history of colonialism and British administrative rule. Colonized by the United Kingdom in 1841, it remained under British sovereignty until 1997. White British people have had a long history of working in the Region, although the meanings of white Britishness have changed significantly over this time. During the period of colonialism and British sovereignty in the Region, British expatriates remained a dominant and privileged clique, enjoying superior conditions of service and a very comfortable lifestyle (Holdsworth 2002). These included long leaves 'home' or to 'exotic locations', school fees for their children in UK public schools, luxury accommodation, domestic help and large salaries. Indeed, the cultural stereotype of the expatriate which survived well into the 1990s was that of the 'blimpish senior civil servant or a well-heeled director of one of the British *hongs*' (Holdsworth 2002: xi).[1] These were inevitably a self-selected elite of white middle class professional men, accompanied by their 'trailing spouses', for whom there was an established lifestyle and set of gendered and racialized identities ready and waiting. However, since the handover of the Region back to China by the British in 1997, the social and political landscape of Hong Kong has changed rapidly, bringing an unsettling of old understandings of the privileges and entitlements on which white British identities and power relations have been based. The administrative workings of empire and territory are receding, being replaced by Chinese policies and practices. In spite of this, whilst employment opportunities for British expatriates have declined significantly, and many have left the Region, many expatriate packages *still* offer substantial material privileges and symbolic power to British people, meaning that the discursive legacy of racialized difference still actively mediates their experience of living in the Region.

An ethnographic and biographical approach was taken in my research there in order to explore the life stories and experiences of expatriate workers in a range of organizational contexts. Interviews were semi-structured to allow respondents to reflect on their lives in Hong Kong, the circumstances in which they had come and the choices which they had made, whilst encouraging them to reflect on issues of nationality, race, gender and class. These took place in a range of settings: primarily in places of work, but also at home, in clubs, café's and bars. Over the ten year period, interviews have been conducted with British women and men from various working backgrounds, including multi-national corporations such as banks, legal services and the construction industry, as well as clubs, schools and universities, and charities. Some are on highly paid short-term contracts whilst others have lived in Hong Kong for many years, working for the same organization since they were young. Some are no longer on expatriate conditions, some never have been. In all cases, interviewees were found through a snowball method, following initial approaches through multi-national organizations, the Chambers of Commerce, clubs, schools and universities and personal contacts. Interviews were supplemented by periods of observation as well as visual methods.

As discussed above, my analysis of the interviews started from the premise that these stories of lives were texts of identity, produced in context, in which 'participants work at characterizing their lives in relation to the interpretive horizons

---

1   *Hong* is the Cantonese term for a large multi-national corporation.

of social settings, using available interpretive resources' (Gubrium and Holstein 1995: 46–47, Halford and Leonard 2006). Rather than providing a straightforward window onto subjects and their lives therefore, the language used in interviews is seen to give rich insight both into the ways people represent themselves, the cultures of which they are a part (Cameron 2001, Lemke 1995) and how these may shift and change over space and time (Leonard 2008, 2010). Of key interest here is the extent to which race/ethnicity/nationality emerge as important. My interest on the contexts of work and organization means that I have also explored the language to reveal the ways in which individuals are made subject through *organizational* and other work-related discourses, and the ways in which they may try to position themselves against these: as Hardy et al. (2000) argue, 'most contexts – including organizations – consist of multiple and fragmented discourses that provide actors with choices concerning the discourses on which they draw' (p. 1232).

In my research, a poststructuralist approach is taken to allow the focus on these multiplicities of identifications: the inter-discursive and shifting ways in which individuals position themselves, and are positioned, through language and discourse (Baxter 2003, Jones 1993, Leonard 2003). The particular mosaic of discursive resources used to craft working identities reveal the choices made, the constraints of the context within which participants are situated, as well as the complexity and unevenness of whiteness and nationality in identity-making. A key discourse I identified however, and which has resonance across the global contexts of expatriate life which I discussed in Chapter 2, is that of '*the (British) expatriate*'. Early (white/male) versions of this discourse – of hierarchy, leadership, firm decision making, hard work, moral responsibility and an understanding that a certain class of white men do 'pretty well everything at the senior level' (Holdsworth 2002: 35) – could still be traced in the talk of some of Hong Kong's long term expatriates. However, as Britain's international relations have changed, so too has the discourse mutated. The contours of British expatriate identities are shifting, as traditional subject positions of whiteness, nationality and gender are being constantly reconfigured. In Hong Kong, just as the architectural landscape is a vibrant mix of old and new symbols, with British/imperial style dwarfed by postmodern global high-rise, so too is the terrain on which identities are constructed and performed. Organizations and work provide a particularly interesting site of change here, because the 'doing of work' has always been critical to expatriate/Hong Kong life, and not least for the construction of British white masculine identities.

This predominantly masculine discourse is complemented by a specifically feminine version: *the expatriate woman*. This is also a complex, diverse and changing discourse, with the retreating legacies of femininities from the colonial past competing with new subject positions. Trollope's (1983) descriptions of colonial women reveal the limited subject positions of earlier times: spinster in search of a husband; supportive wife, there to aid her husband 'in the lonely difficult and responsible business of setting up and maintaining colonial rule' (p. 30); or missionary. In the contemporary context, subjectivities for women are far less clear-cut. In Hong Kong, some white British expatriate women *do* find themselves locked into the position of the traditional expatriate wife, whose role it is to smooth the transition from one domestic space to another. However, as we shall see in subsequent chapters, the increasing arrival of working women help to broaden and update the discourse, and reveal the retreat of traditional versions of white British femininities and masculinities since the handover in 1997. Expatriate identities in Hong Kong are now open to question, and this new flexibility is reflected in other literature exploring identities under globalization (Hannerz 1992).

In Hong Kong, other discourses interplay with these discourses of whiteness and Britishness. A third discourse is the Hong Kong Chinese discourse of '*gweilo*' or *British cultural incompetence*. Again, this discourse has a long history in the Region: throughout the periods of both colonialism and territorial rule, the British have, in their turn, been constructed by the Chinese as 'Other': the term 'gweilo' or 'fan gweilo', literally meaning 'foreign devils', is used by the Chinese to construct a subject position for white people, which is tainted with some abuse and mockery of their cultural clumsiness (Holdsworth 2002). Ironically, many white people living and working in Hong Kong re-appropriate the term to position themselves. Their use of the term (rather less pejoratively) also refers to their 'non-Chineseness', and their difference, although its meanings are multiple and highly contingent. A fourth discourse is that of '*the HongKonger*': the local. Although in the main it is Hong Kong Chinese people who position themselves in this way, it was also noticeable that this discourse was adopted in the talk of some of the white, long-term residents of Hong Kong, struggling to position themselves away from the 'gweilo'. I will return to discuss these discourses more fully in later chapters.

In the rest of this book, I now turn to the task of exploring the making of whiteness in expatriate contexts, and the relationships that exist with other aspects of identity such as gender, class and nationality. This will involve looking at both the discursive and performative aspects of work: the organizational discourses at play in people's talk, organizational policies and workplace design as well as the material and embodied aspects of working practices, relations and routines. We need to see how whiteness is made in these contexts and its centrality in organizational life. To do this, I will draw on and review a range of the empirical evidence which exists on expatriates and work, including my own research in Hong Kong. However, whilst it is the argument of this book that work and organizational contexts are very important in the production of white identities and white advantage, it is also understood that they are not sealed off from other aspects of life. There is no clear and easy distinction or separation between the *public and private* contexts of our lives and they interplay and overlay in often quite indistinguishable ways. The interaction between these sites offer expatriates new contexts and cultures in which identities and relations are to be (re)negotiated, and so I will now turn to look at this in more detail. I start by looking at the decision to migrate itself, and the ways in which processes of leaving and arrival can themselves be racialized.

Chapter 4
Becoming a White Expatriate

This chapter turns to explore the mechanisms of expatriate migration: the processes by which homes are left and new lives are made. I have already made the point that the constitution of 'expatriates' as a 'social group' is far from homogeneous, and the exploration of the ways in which old lives and identities are left and new ones are then negotiated makes this particularly clear. In this chapter, I show how key differences exist according to *gender*, *location*, *time* and *occupation*; and that these reveal the wide-ranging heterogeneity of white expatriate lives and performances of whiteness. Thus whilst for some, expatriation is the result of internal movement within the same multinational organization, for others there might have been a more deliberate decision to travel, join another workplace or even change career. For all however, moving from one location to another offers opportunities – and sometimes the necessity – to reconfigure identities. Aspects of these, such as race, gender, nationality, as well as personal links with place, may have to be managed in new and different ways in the new contexts. Much of the existing research on this has focused primarily on cultural and domestic contexts, and this chapter builds on this to look particularly at the ways in which *work* and *organizations* frame departures and the early negotiations which occur in the new places of migration. Crucially, it will explore how organizations are *implicit* in the construction of new identities and lives, and how whiteness and nationality, together with gender, may be mobilized by both organization and employee as a key resource in the displacement process.

In the last few chapters, I have discussed the *situated* nature of identity, and the ways in which identity is negotiated in context, albeit in multi-faceted and sometimes fragmented ways. The importance of place in the construction of identities has been emphasized, as well as the ways in which we are also made subject through place and spatial contexts. The last chapter also demonstrated how personal biographies and life stories can reveal the ways in which people are connected to the places in which they conduct their lives – and how, when the places of our lives change, so do we. Whilst *working* identities may to some degree be constructed through discursive resources that stretch *across* places – certain organizational and professional resources and practices may be broadly similar across the global sites of their operation – they are always lived and performed *in* place, and through the particular histories, meanings and practices that accumulate there (Halford and Leonard 2006). Place thus offers a way into understanding human attachment and connection, and the meanings we attach to the routines of our everyday lives (Tuan 1977). But, if lives are made and lived in place, the *displacement* from the familiar and meaningful brought about by migration to new places is therefore potentially destabilizing; and perhaps even more so when this is a regular feature of one's life: 'You arrive in each new place all naked (as it were) and friendless and vulnerable, you gradually build up a little world around yourself, and then, bingo, you are suddenly sent off to the other side of the world to start all over again' (Keenan 2005: 10). Migration thus poses a special challenge to identity-making, and recent scholarly attention has revealed how migrants must renegotiate their identities after they have moved to places with different social and power structures (Chambers 1994, Rapport and Dawson 1998, Fortier 2000). Identities are constructed in place and in relation to others in that place: and when place and 'the other' changes, so do our senses of belonging and identity.

For white expatriates however the displacement of migration is a very different process than for the many other migrants in less privileged circumstances: the low waged labour migrant, the refugee and the exile; and from the start, their circumstances of arrival are a key way in which their privileged status is configured. Those expatriates working for large multi-national corporations, or those who are moving to join organizations within established sectors such as education and health, will often enjoy 'relocation packages' which may include familiarization talks and visits, help with (finding) accommodation and schools, and an existing expatriate community to 'show them the ropes'. However, whilst these privileges certainly help to mediate some of the stressful aspects of moving lives, it would be quite wrong to assume that *all* white professional and skilled expatriates move around the world 'with ease' (Scott 2006). Their migration still involves the process of fragmenting their personal ties with the places of their lives. Yet as we have seen, much of the early research on the so-called 'global elites' or transnational capitalist class has treated them as spatially 'disembedded', positing that place and spatial distance are now immaterial for contemporary social life (Featherstone et al. 2007). Despite the significant advances in understandings of transnational processes, and the importance of the local within these, discourses of 'ungrounded' and 'deterritorialized' trans-migrants still remain in many of the discussions of the highly skilled migrant, who is invariably made to appear to transcend the limits of space and the stickiness of place.

In contrast to this view, this chapter will continue the book's argument for the importance of the concept of 'place' in understanding the activities and identity makings of white skilled migrants. As Ley argues, 'the tyranny of distance and particularities of place continue to unsettle [even those] agents with a putatively global reach' (2004: 157). Many organizations know from bitter experience that encouraging employees to leave their places of home and resettle with their families in a new context is no simple matter (Selmer 2001). Increasingly, expatriate assignments are becoming unattractive to employees (Scullion 1994). The desire to 'see new places' can be now easily satisfied through cheap travel. There is a rise in dual career families and combining the loss of one career with deteriorating corporate policies on expatriate packages, as well as concerns over childrens' education, are all making employees increasingly wary of foreign assignments.

Indeed spouse/partner and family issues are the most important hurdles to accepting expatriate assignments (Hardill and MacDonald 1998). At the same time there is an increasing demand for expatriates, which has now outstripped the potential pool of male candidates, forcing organizations to consider women for expatriate positions (Mathur-Helm 2002). This chapter will begin by exploring who exactly are the ones to take the plunge and work abroad, showing the vast diversity in identities and biographies within this broad group. I will then proceed to explore the ways in which the initial processes of displacement – the leaving of the old and the arriving at the new – are organized and conceptualized by organizations as well as the individuals involved.

Situating Expatriate Skilled Migration in Context

In Chapter 2 we saw that migration by the middle classes of the West in search of upward mobility and a better lifestyle has a long history, bound up as it has been with Western imperialism and developing conceptualizations of 'citizenship' which saw that cosmopolitanism (engagement in travel and trade) was a fundamental right of the white middle classes (Tully 2008). The models of expatriates that dominated these times of imperial expansion until well into the 1960s were the connected yet somewhat limited ones of the colonial administrator, a 'blimpish civil servant' (Holdsworth 2002) whose role it was to administer western governance and ideology in lands far removed in both culture and distance, corporate expatriates working within the commercial sector for trade, oil and finance related organizations, and other employees such as Army officers. Today, however, there is far more diversity amongst contemporary expatriates, and, as Scott (2006) notes, five key structural shifts must be taken into account in any contemporary study of 'who they are'. First, *socially*, there has been a growth in the post-industrial middle class in terms of material wealth and skill levels, which means that the potential pool of skilled migrants is now wider and deeper than ever before. Second, *economically*, the power of transnational corporations and ruling elites has grown substantially meaning that world cities such as *inter alia* London, Paris and Singapore have become economically more dominant, requiring a constant supply of individuals with specialist high level skills to retain their position in the global urban hierarchy (Beaverstock et al. 2000, Sassen 1991). Third, *technologically*, world cities have become landscapes of hyper-connectivity, whereby the metropolitan middle classes are connected to international socio-economic and cultural networks. *Culturally*, the world has converged, as the global marketplace and its constituent transnational networks have permeated locations near and far. The international has become more culturally 'normal' characterized by three important changes: the globalization of the English language, the commodification of 'otherness', and the rise in (Western) uniformity or 'McDonaldization' (Ritzer 1993). Finally, *geopolitically*, within Europe at least, international mobility has been made more accessible for those outside of transnational corporations.

As Scott (2006) argues, these five forces open up the boundaries of skilled migration and demonstrate that migrants are drawn to expatriate life for a variety of reasons beyond the economic or as intricately linked to an 'elite' career path. It is thus 'no longer possible or appropriate to separate the cultural from the economic, or assume that skilled migration must have a direct link to *corporate* labour markets' (p. 1109). Rather we need to recognize the heterogeneity within the group, a fact which is reflected in the range of research interests contained within the contemporary interdisciplinary literature on 'skilled migrants'/'transnational elites'/'expatriates' and so on. What emerges from a review of this literature however is that four broad themes dominate the explanations of diversity: *gender*, *time*, *location*, and *occupation/organization*. I will discuss these more fully, as they provide a useful framework through which to flesh out the detail and 'human face' of 'who expatriates are' (Scott 2006, Nowicka 2006).

Gender

Routes into expatriate status are highly gendered, reflecting the predominantly patriarchal nature of 'transnationalism from above', which produces different sets of experiences for the men and women involved in global processes (Yeoh and Khoo 1998, Willis and Yeoh 2002). In spite of the fact that there is increasingly a requirement by multi-national companies for staff to be flexible and 'mobile', and that work abroad on an international assignment often forms an integral part of career development for potential senior managers in the contemporary global labour market (Derr and Oddou 1993, Hardill and McDonald 1998), today's skilled expatriate workers are still mostly male, just as they were in the colonial era. They are either young men with high potential, or promising middle managers, usually middle aged and married with children, who need to broaden their experience prior to taking up their senior management positions at home (Henry and Massey 1995, Beaverstock 1994, Hartl 2004). The dominant narratives in the expatriate literature tend to focus on 'white, company men' therefore (Beaverstock 1996); particularly those who are privileged in their access to, and control of, the uneven power geometry of mobility such as those pursuing careers in finance, science, management and technology (Massey 1994, Kofman and Raghuram 2006). 'Elite males' are almost universally seen to be the driving forces of innovation and financial acumen (Beaverstock and Boardwell 2000, Castells 1996) and international circulation often represents a vitally important 'career move' in their climbs to the upper echelons of corporate life. Meanwhile, for their 'trailing' spouses and partners, the experience usually offers a devaluing of their productive functions and a relegation to the domestic sphere.

The issue of women's availability for expatriate postings is complex, subtle and linked to stereotypical assumptions about women in (international) management and discriminatory practices in organizations (Adler 1994). Success in managerial and professional careers depends on 'commitment': that is, being highly flexible, working long hours and 'putting the job first', all of which are stereotypically 'masculine' notions. In some organizational contexts, women are seen as lacking in these characteristics and therefore lacking in the ability to be organizationally mobile (Fielden and Davidson 1996, Mathur-Helm 2002). As Hartl (2004) argues, it seems that the paucity of women expatriates is more a reflection of a *domestic* glass ceiling than anything to do with women's effectiveness on international assignments or their willingness to relocate (Solomon 1998). The term '*glass border*' would therefore seem appropriate to depict this phenomenon of gender (together with other distinguishing characteristics such as race and class) hindering individuals from being selected for expatriate positions (Linehan 2000)

As a result, women face difficulties in being sent on overseas assignments (Adler 1994). There are even fewer British than American women in multinationals (Kofman 2000) and it would appear that many women are not even given the chance to opt for overseas relocations: these decisions being made in advance within male networks (Forster and Johnsen 1996). When women are sent abroad, they are generally unaccompanied by their families (for example, only 25 per cent of American female expatriates were joined by their partners and families) unlike the 80 per cent of American men who are accompanied (Reynolds and Bennett 1991). Women's careers may be adversely affected in two ways therefore: by foreign assignments being denied to them in the first place, and secondly by the interruption/disruption to their careers caused by a partner's posting abroad.

Much of the literature on women expatriates focuses on their roles as 'trailing spouses': as the wives and mothers who accompany their husbands overseas, whose role it is to oversee the seamlessness of their partner's performance at work, uninterrupted as it must be by domestic concerns. Indeed, as Kofman and Raghuran (2006) note, it is largely through narratives of *reproductive labour* that women enter theories of globalization (Sassen 2000). Kofman (2000) suggests that in fact there is an *invisibility* of female migrants in studies of skilled migration – and the choice of research agendas has played a major part in this. Because the emphasis has generally been on transnational corporations which, in their higher ranks especially, remain resolutely male-dominated, the presence of migrants in other sectors such as welfare (education, health and social services) which are strongly feminized has been ignored. In addition, feminist research has also tended to obscure the role of skilled migrants in its emphasis on the unskilled. As a result it is virtually impossible to find much discussion of women or gender relations in studies of skilled international migration, except for a few statistics on the gender breakdown of employment and, as we have discussed, studies of women's domestic roles, lives and experiences as trailing spouses.

However more recently there is a growing recognition that women themselves are increasingly securing posts overseas in a variety of contexts. Kofman (2000) argues that it is necessary therefore to broaden the analytical framework and sectors of study in transnational skilled migration research to incorporate gender issues more fully. She argues that the dominant yet narrow focus on the highest echelons of inter-company transfers reflects a kind of neo-liberal agenda, in the extent that researchers have opted to study only what they see as the wealth generators: 'ICT migrants are seen as the jet-setters: they demonstrate the reality of globalization and a borderless world' (Kofman 2000: 52–53). In contrast, other sectors, such as welfare, represent a past world, and are definitely not a 'sexy' topic. The narrow focus assumes the normality of an exclusively male world unconstrained by any wider social relations, a perspective that has until recently characterized migration studies (Kofman 2000).

In fact, when the welfare sectors are *specifically* explored with regards to migration patterns it is clear that there is an increasing amount of female activity. An examination of changing immigration regulations and the ways in which migrants are differentially selected by countries highlights the importance of the welfare sectors as employers of migrant women in recent migration streams (Kofman and Raghuran 2006). It appears that many of the skilled women migrants are being enticed to migrate precisely in order to provide welfare, and a significant proportion of the migrants from Ireland and Australia for example are in fact such women (Kofman and Raghuran 2005). For example, studies from sending countries such as Australia (Hugo 1994) confirm an increasing trend of female professional immigration, particularly by single women. However there still remains little research on welfare migration – particularly *from* the West. Although some significant research on nurse migration is appearing, it focuses on the main on the West as *receivers* rather than *senders* (e.g. Royal College of Nursing 2002).

Kofman (2000) makes the point that whilst migration studies are willing to consider the relevance of households and networks for women, the male migrant is maintained as the '*heroic individual*' either making his decision alone or in a work-related context:

> It is as if social and cultural dimensions applied only to female migrants but that the economic domain exhausted men's experiences. It is therefore time that we seriously applied the full gamut of contemporary migration theory to the movement of *both* skilled women and men (Kofman 2000: 54, my italics).

However some recent work is starting to remedy this position (Yeoh and Khoo 1998, Mathur-Helm 2002, Moore 2007, Kofman and Raghuram 2006, Fechter 2008). Evidence is appearing to show that in the last few years the number of Euro-American female professionals working abroad is starting to rise – mainly due to the fact that women are participating in domestic labour markets in much higher numbers than in the past, thus leading to a greater representation in overseas paid employment. Women now form over 15 per cent of total international transferees (Hartl 2004). In the main they are young unattached professionals without partners and children (Barnes 2006): what Fechter (2008) terms 'expat girls'. They have a university degree, and have sought an international assignment after gaining some initial work experience at home. They tend to be employed in the fields of international education, cultural exchange and development, but can also be found in accounting, marketing and management consulting as well as the media, pharmaceutical and computer software. 'Although she does not choose the location of her workplace at random, the fact that she lives abroad is more important to her than the particular country where she is stationed for a while' (Fechter 2008: 193). In addition, whilst the older generation of expatriates typically moved as part of intra-company transfers, as part of a career within one institution, expat girls are employed on the basis of fixed term contracts or project work. In addition the number of *partnered* women being offered job transfers is also escalating, who, as the primary migrant, bring with them *their* 'trailing spouse'. The fact that these are still seen as a challenge to the 'norm' however is encapsulated in derogatory terms such as '*pantoflarz*' (Polish for 'under a women's high heel') (Linderman and Hess 2002).

However it must be acknowledged that many expatriate women are still the 'trailing spouses' themselves. They usually find it difficult to obtain a job in the new context, and for this reason, as well as the growth of women's careers and the number of dual career households, there now appears to be some reluctance on the part of some couples to accept international assignments (Scullion 1994, Hardill and MacDonald 1998). International migration disrupts the second 'follower' career in dual career households, and so it is often easier to encourage couples to move abroad whilst children are young (Kofman 2000) when one member of the partnership might be at home during this period anyway. In most globe-trotting families, this homemaker is the woman, and it is she who becomes the social reproducer while men engage in 'globalist capitalist games' (Kofman and Raghuram 2006: 287).

Time

Expatriate assignments vary considerably in their time scale. The United Nations' technical definition of 'international migration' includes only those persons residing in a country other than that of origin for more than a year: that is, longer term residents in the country of immigration but not necessarily settlers. From this perspective, an arbitrary, but workable, threshold between business travel and 'migration' is presented, and a large number of studies make a distinction between what can be called 'labour tourism' (business/regular commuting/extended visits); the 'nomadic worker' (temporary sojourns and flexible contracts); and more permanent relocation (the expatriate or skilled migrant). In recent years there has been a rise in the latter, but for shorter time periods of between two to four years rather than for a career lifetime (Findlay et al. 1996, Doyle and Nathan 2001 and Hardill and MacDonald 1998). Today the likelihood of longer term migration by skilled professionals is much diminished: as Hardill (1998) puts it, the time when 'our man' was permanently ensconced abroad is gone (Salt 1988: 389), replaced by shorter term placements as well as international commuters and virtual working (Hardill 2002).

There are a host of other differences between the lives of the older generations of expatriates who tended to expatriate for long time periods and those of today. Colonial officials, postcolonial technical officers, missionaries and the business people associated with primary products and early industries tended to stay in one country for their careers, even if they moved workplace and domicile within that country (Callan and Ardener 1984). Despite barriers of race, caste and residential location, they were therefore probably more immersed in the place in which they lived than many expatriates today, as knowledge about the country's political systems and ethnography was fundamental to their work and essential for administrative purposes. Today's more transient workers and their partners lack this imperative. Many of the expatriates who are now prepared to work in a range of countries are in their 20s and 30s, and spend only a few years in a particular place before returning home for good.

Forster (1996, 2000) argues therefore that the idea of the 'international manager': the globe-trotting nomad who moves from region to region at regular intervals, never putting down roots, distanced from family and friends or moving their children from school to school and adapting to new cultures every few years, is largely a myth. There are few, he claims, that are psychologically capable of doing this. Instead, a period of short migration is viewed strategically at different stages of a professional career. A temporal dynamic exists in the international career path whereby the value of migration varies according to seniority: at a junior level, moving overseas is part of a process of 'learning the ropes'; in the middle of a career, migration can be a 'defining moment' in determining professional status; and towards the end of a career, migration can augment one's elite status and is likely to involve a highly sought-after international posting (Scott 2006).

For some nationalities, particularly Australians and New Zealanders, a period of living and working abroad (principally in Europe) has come to be viewed as *a rite of passage* and an almost central part of reaching adulthood (Conradson and Latham 2005a, Scott 2006). As well as the young backpackers 'doing Europe', many Antipodean young qualified professionals in their late 20s come to Britain (and especially London) to work in hospitals, education, local government and engineering. Similarly, Scott (2006) has shown how a period in Paris is popular for middle class British professionals in their 20s and 30s. They may have left secure and well paid professional jobs to occupy new ones which may sit outside conventional career structures and offer few prospects of advancement. However, this sort of flexible employment does offer the opportunity to intersperse periods of working with periods of travel in Europe. Whilst there may be little ambition to remain in the long term, a period of travel and the experience of 'being an expatriate' are used almost *de rigeur* as part of a project of middle class self-fashioning: a 'prosaic process of sustained self-experimentation, exploration and development afforded by the liminality of travel' (Conradson and Latham 2005a: 290). For the British in particular, this 'educational migration' also has a raced and classed element – this is a strategy by which the young, white middle class 'Brits' gain credentials in an increasingly competitive world of employment. As such, this sort of 'lifestyle migration' is also temporally bounded, and at some point these migrants, like their more career oriented colleagues, know that they will have to return home to 'real life'.

Location

Location is also critical to the expatriate experience. As we have seen, members of the transnational elite are often represented as being able to locate in any part of the world due to the trans-local nature of elite space within capitalist flows. However we have also seen that gender, as well as other factors such as nationality, are important distinguishing variables within transient migrant flows. Not only are people posted to certain places based on their perceived abilities to 'fit in' to a particular location, but the recognition that these employee flows can also be intertwined with flows of kin means that the movement across international boundaries is rarely as straightforward as it is sometimes portrayed (Willis and Yeoh 2002). Partners and families may refuse to go to one place, preferring another; cities will often be chosen over rural locations. Family and/or friends who have already relocated may offer a strong pull factor to a particular destination. Many women express a preference for travelling to Western countries rather than those in, for example, the Middle East, due to a belief that 'women are not represented there' (Mathur-Helm 2002: 24).

Not all expatriates live in cosmopolitan, global cities however: expatriate professionals are found today in a wide variety of global locations. The fact that intra-company transfers lie in the hands of the organization rather than the employee explains the diverse destinations of people moving abroad: they are more likely to be found in economically significant places than in the usual lifestyle-led destinations to which many other Western migrants move (Sriskandarajah and Drew 2006), such as southern Spain or Florida. These include the European Union and post-communist Europe (Salt 1993, Townsend 1997) the Middle East (Findlay and Gould 1989, Walsh 1996), the earlier 'heartlands' of expatriate life, such as the former colonies of South East Asia (Findlay et al. 1996), India and Africa, the Commonwealth countries such as Australia (Elder 2007) and South Africa (Steyn 2005). Recently the commercial and financial opportunities in the Gulf region and China in particular have attracted a large number of professionals, particularly in the business, finance and hospitality sectors, and, in Dubai, in education and health.

However it is still the major 'Global Cities' which act as the spaces within which much transnational business practice is carried out (Beaverstock 2002, 2005, Sassen 2002, Willis and Yeoh 2002, Scott 2006), characterized as they are by the concentration of corporate activities and clusters of producer services which are important for highly skilled international migrants. A number of writers have described the world's major cities as the strategic sites of the global economy (Sassen 1991, 2002, Hardill and MacDonald 1998), and Sassen

(1991, 2002) has described the ways in which the restructuring and production of financial services in particular has made these places key sites of authority and power. The availability of social and cultural facilities also renders cities particularly attractive to professionals as places in which to work and live (Beaverstock 1994, 2005, Scott 2006), and major cities such as New York and Paris are often seen as 'centres of the universe', offering better opportunities in both business and scientific fields (Sriskandarajah and Drew 2006) and enabling careers to progress at a faster pace. The concentrations of skilled migrants thus create 'communities of transnationals' within such cities. In turn, transnational corporations depending on world cities for their global reach, capitalize on this diverse pool of skilled labour. Skilled international migration as a process therefore contributes to the production of the global city (Findlay et al. 1996).

More recently certain destinations have emerged as popular 'hotspots' for skilled workers, one such example being Dubai. Increasingly, such hotspots do not only attract corporate employees, but people who decide to migrate 'on spec', applying for positions through locally-based recruitment services, website listings or even applying once they have arrived, rather than being seconded through a company which they already work for (Walsh 2008). These local employment contracts mean that increasing numbers of expatriates do not receive the privileges traditionally associated with working overseas, such as higher salaries and accommodation allowances, but the tax benefits, increased promotion prospects, attractive winter climate and economically privileged lifestyle continue to attract new workers (Walsh 2008). Fechter (2008) found a similar situation in her study of the 'expat girls' in Jakarta, who had actively sought employment abroad, their mobility driven by their own sense of career rather than a corporate agenda.

History defines a country's relation with its expatriate groups in infinitely complex ways, and expatriate identities will be negotiated in that context. In ex-colonial countries, nationals of the former imperial power may form the dominant expatriate group, and still have a relationship with the indigenous population which is coloured by the past. In certain countries, indigenous women may have little autonomy and be actively discriminated against, and recent events in the news show how women expatriates can be included in this gendered marginalization, whatever their race and nationality.[1] The host country's culture may exert both legal and more subtle influences on foreign communities: some countries do not permit entry to unmarried couples, for example, whether in heterosexual or same sex partnerships. In many countries, the local culture requires women to make greater modifications in their dress and behaviour than is expected of men

---

1   In April 2009 a British woman, Marnie Pierce, was convicted of adultery in Dubai and lost custody of her two sons to her Egyptian husband. She denied all charges, claiming that her husband was violent and she had to flee to a refuge. At the time of writing she has been released and is fighting to see her sons again. See http://www.telegraph.co.uk/news/worldnews/middleeast/dubai/5229965/British-mother-jailed-for-adultery-in-Dubai-released.html (accessed 5 May 2009).

(Coles and Fechter 2008), and in others legislation may govern the consumption of alcohol. These differences in culture often exacerbate the tendency to maintain an 'expatriate bubble', in which the (often neo-colonial) lifestyles and cultural values of the home country are maintained.

Occupation

Just as expatriate life varies considerably by location, so it also does according to occupation and organizational context. Indeed, much of the work in migration studies in the 1990s which attempted to evaluate the characteristics of professional, managerial and entrepreneurial migrants working in global contexts focused on occupational and organizational issues, constructing explanatory frameworks such as the 'migration channels' approach. This approach explored the role of the internal labour markets of different multinational corporations, international recruitment agencies and international skill transfers by small- and intermediate-sized firms (Findlay and Garrick 1990, Findlay 1990) in the production of skilled migration, as well as the links between companies' personnel strategies and transnational production (Cormode 1994). Other areas of interest in this area were the nature of career paths and internal labour markets (Salt 1988), as well as business cultures and definitions of 'international expertise'. These meant that most skilled migrants were predominantly classified as what Sriskandarajah and Drew (2006) term 'gold collar workers', that is, highly valuable employees who should enjoy substantial benefits. Within this group, Salt (1997) has distinguished 12 different categories: corporate transferees, health, education and welfare professionals, military, consultants, entertainers, business people, academics, researchers and students, and spouses and children of these categories. However, the differing conditions applicable to each category mean that we need to be careful about how we analyse this heterogeneous group: not all have the same weight of gold in their collar! We have seen for example how both organizations' migration channels and occupational categories are gender sensitive, and that 'women and men circulate differently in an unevenly globalized economy' (Kofman and Raghuram 2005: 150). Men dominate the movements within transnational corporations, information and communication technology, science, banking and finance. Many of the moves in these sectors occur as inter-company transfers and may be arranged through male networking (Forster and Johnsen 1996). Women on the other hand often circulate as skilled labour within the reproductive sectors such as education, health and social work, which may be still heavily regulated by states and corporate bodies (Kofman and Raghuram 2005)

In general, the 'occupational' literature focuses on 'the range of institutional mechanisms controlling and promoting the new patterns of skill transfer which have emerged' (Findlay and Gould 1989: 5) rather than the individual experience of being part of the international circuit. At this level, the *processes* of the transition: of leaving the familiarity of home and one's work there, and arriving in a new and very different context are ignored. However, it is through looking at these transition processes in detail that the making of whiteness, nationality and gender can come further to the fore. It is in the *how* of these processes: the ways in which the move is managed at both the organizational and the personal level that social differences are made and refined.

Organizations, Migration and the Making of White Expatriates

The overseas deployment of skilled workers is in many ways a prime example of 'transnationalism from above': especially if this is the result of a 'top-down' company-based strategy which moves employees around the globe according to global need. By relocating, these migrants, at least in part, are subscribing to the 'objectives relative to the goals of the transnational and local companies which employ them' (Findlay et al. 1996: 50) and at this level can be seen to be the agents of globalizing processes. However, in the mechanisms by which transnational organizations 'organize' the move, migrants are also made subject. Through their policies and discursive practices, organizations play a critical part in turning the circumstances of departure and arrival into an identity making process in which race and gender are integral.

From the first, discourses which are fundamental to whiteness are often reinforced through an organization's *acculturation activities*. The new context of migration is often shaped by an advice framework instituted by the employer, and, as Hindman (2008) argues, new, about-to-be-expatriated migrants may be positioned from the start from seeing the indigenous population as 'Other', and, indeed, a people to be feared. This discourse of *fear* may be particularly revealed in the ways the advice may linger on the *dangers* that need to be reckoned with. The acculturation frequently provides families with cautionary tales about what *not* to do, advice about health and safety concerns, and things to avoid. For example, in the Middle East, women are told where not to travel alone. In South Africa, expatriate houses are constantly protected with barbed wire and alarms, and hotwired to armed patrols. In Nepal, full time security guards come as a standard part of the American expatriate's package (Hindman 2008). The discourse of fear is further reinforced in the ways that wives and mothers are typically positioned with the subjectivity of *protecting the family*. It is women who are usually expected to obscure the differences that relocation present to the family: 'if it is male labour that brings the couple abroad, it is the woman's job to erase that move' (Hindman 2008: 42). In other words, it is made clear in the talks given to women particularly before they head abroad that the job of the spouse is to create a space where the worker can be as effective and efficient as when working in the main office (Hindman 2008). Indeed, expatriate *success* is a technically defined ability to maintain the same productivity in the office at home or abroad, and, as such, this is deeply embedded within employers' concern with workers' families (Hindman 2008). As a result, predeparture 'training' for the whole family is a key component of how companies and governments seek to ensure their workers are productive and successful. In this way, whiteness is constructed as the ability to be consistently productive across place, time and culture.

As well as the discourses of 'fear' and 'protecting the family', pre-departure training may deliver a third gendered and raced discourse which positions the new expatriate woman in particular: the discourse of *consumption*. Hindman's (2008) research on employees bound for Nepal reveals how a critical part of the organization's advice is instruction on *how* to consume abroad. In their talk of where to obtain 'a basket of wants': goods families are assumed to need in their new posting; women are taught far more than merely what to pack or buy. They are also taught what 'type' of place they are moving to, as well as the sort of place it is *not:* not white, not Euro-American, not full of western-style products. Further, these training sessions often deliver conflicting discourses: on the one hand issuing warnings of danger, the need for security and taking adequate supplies, yet on the other, waxing lyrical about the *exotic* beauty of the country and the peaceful spiritual nature of the people. Both discourses however, fall within the broader discourse of *White/Other* by which 'race' is defined.

A further way in which race is made by organizations is through the '*compensation package*'. Compensation focuses on the family unit, offering salary supplements and hardship allowances determined by the number of 'dependants' that the employee supports. Particular destinations are positioned as '*hardship postings*'. The very words 'compensation' and 'hardship' frame the move in terms of loss, of trying to make a bad situation good. Often these compensation packages reinforce particular aspects of gendered behaviour within the family and create for women new roles, roles which are often perceived as the traditional ones of homemaker and protector. Such ideas on 'how to live as expatriates' thus not only come through explicit rules for conduct, but more powerfully as *implicit* structures, created by the very forms of acculturation, compensation and posting. Hindman (2008) argues that this means that, before long, expatriates find they are performing a set of behaviours and beliefs without really knowing how they came to have them. As Bourdieu contends 'what they do has more meaning than they know' (Bourdieu 1992: 79 in Hindman 2008: 57).

Perhaps helping to influence the ideologies on which these organizational discourses and policies are based is the Human Resource Management (HRM) literature on expatriate working. It is interesting to note how this can frame expatriate assignments in *heroic* terms (e.g. Torbiorn 1982, Osland 2000); reinforcing the idea that going to live abroad, coping with fear, hardship and the 'strangeness' of Others is only for the heroic. Indeed Torbiorn (1982) argues that expatriates *should* have a spontaneous desire to work abroad, and an element of idealism or a 'sense of mission'. The missionary subjectivity of superior and heroic whiteness is further encoded through talk of making *sacrifices*. For example Osland (2000) argues that the sense of mission is necessary because: 'Otherwise they are not likely to make the necessary sacrifices or be committed to achieving a real understanding or acceptance of the conditions in the other country' (p. 229).

Personal Factors

Skilled migrants should not only be seen as the (passive) subjects of powerful organizational forces however. People migrate for all sorts of reasons: not only economic (Yeoh and Khoo 1998), but also due to personal motives, political change or environmental problems (Li et al. 1995, Hardill 2002). The decision to migrate and processes of migration also need to be considered at the micro-level of the individual therefore, as part of 'transnationalism from below', to unravel the interplay of the individual with larger global/organizational structures forces.

Hardill (2002) notes that migration is often conceived of as the outcome of a conscious rational decision, but it can also be considered as the result of a haphazard, non-rational and non-economic decision. However, many expatriates say one of the key factors in accepting an expatriate assignment is whether the 'time is right' (Moore 2002). Professional as well as personal factors come together here, as employees weigh how the assignment will fit into the development of their career as well as their domestic/personal life. Parents, for example, assess the impact on their children's education, with high school generally considered as an inopportune time for relocations. For dual career couples, the partner's tenure, job satisfaction, desire for a career change and level can affect whether an international relocation is welcome at a given time. Spouses who were previously unwilling to relocate may change their mind if they become ready to make a career change themselves or after children are born. In some cases, the relocation provides the spouse with the opportunity to take time off for education, to care for the children full-time or to freelance (Moore 2002). However, these factors feed into an inevitable transformation of gender relations within a partnership, as one becomes the lead migrant and breadwinner and the other an accompanying spouse (Coles and Fechter 2008).

Once again gender and gender relations emerge as key here therefore. As Hardill (1998, 2002) and Walsh (2008) reveal, right from the start, the initial decision-making on whether to embark on a first posting or a longer term professional life abroad is already taken within gendered contexts. There is often considerable bargaining and compromising involved in relocation decisions among couples but, as I discussed above, the result of these negotiations is that usually the husband's job is prioritized (Coles and Fechter 2008). However having said this, studies also reveal that most women partners have a critical role to play in the move and exercise a degree of choice over it. Even though the man may initiate the move, the woman's affirmation is vital to the whole exercise (Yeoh and Khoo 1998, Coles and Fechter 2008):

> The move is definitely a "we" decision. My husband would have rejected the position in Singapore even though it is a good career opportunity for him, if I had said "no" (Jane, 37-year-old Canadian) (quoted in Yeoh and Khoo 1998: 420).

Typically much of the analysis and discussion on displacement positions men and women differently: as binary opposites in terms of what 'leaving' means to them. Men are usually positioned as '*winners*': 'leaving' for them is described as an unemotional experience, 'understood simply as the call of the outer world of work to which they belong'. In contrast, women are positioned as '*losers*': for them it means 'the loss of their more social networks centred on the home and the community' (Yeoh and Khoo 1998: 420). Gendered notions of what it is to be 'the good wife', who lends support to the husband's career, are seen to compete with their 'real' desires of staying at home:

> For me it was a difficult decision, for him [husband] it was easy ... because for him it's a job, whereas for us women ... it's leaving behind my friends and family and starting from scratch again ... so that's a little unsettling (Rebecca, 35 yrs, British) (Yeoh and Khoo 1998: 420).

More recently however evidence is appearing to counter this (traditionally) gendered discourse by recognizing that it is not *only* women who experience emotional upheavals and misgivings over departure. Men *too* worry about missing friends and family, or putting children in boarding school. These concerns may be exacerbated further if *they* are the trailing spouse: as we have seen it must be acknowledged whilst men are usually the primary breadwinner amongst skilled migrants, this is not *always* the case:

> the most painful part about being a trailing spouse is that I miss my children. Sometimes late at night or when Patricia's away on an assignment, I find myself crying, yearning for them so badly. I play music and yell. I miss them telling me about their day at school; I miss the way they annoy me. Guilt is the biggest thing. I am plagued by it (Patrick, in Cohen 1996).

It is instructive therefore to look closely at the *language* people use to talk about making the decision to leave, their reasons for going and the experience of leaving itself. We saw in the last chapter how key moments, or 'stepping stones', are often remembered as times of identity change. Leaving lives and homes can be conceptualized as one such watershed. This is supported in Osland's research (2000) on expatriate decision making, where he found that 80 per cent (all men) of his sample were 'extremely excited' about the possibility of going abroad, describing it as 'a rare opportunity' and 'flight into the romantic unknown' (p. 228). Some remembered what they described as 'the call' 'with the same total recall and enthusiasm usually given to marriage proposals' (2000: 228).

The discourse of heroism and adventure used by these expatriate men reiterates the discourses found in both the pre-departure training and the Human Resource Management literature. The *personal* discourse and subject position of *the hero's adventure* (Osland 2000, Leonard 2010) can thus be seen to interplay with the *organizational* discourses of fear and othering which we noted earlier. At both levels, it is understood that if foreign lands are dangerous places, then migrating to them must necessarily be a heroic endeavour. Osland's (2000) (admittedly gender-blind) analysis of men's expatriate stories shows how their narratives can be likened to Joseph Campbell's (1968) 'hero's journey myth'. This has a plot common to mythical stories which consists of three parts: first, separation from the world, second, initiation involving the penetration to some source of power, and third, a life enhancing return. As Osland argues, mythical heroes

> either seek to find their destiny outside their known world or inadvertently stumble into another world. In either case there is what mystics call an awakening of the self. Magical friends guide the heroes past the dangerous guardians of a different world. Next the heroes undergo a series of trials that ends with a decisive victory and brings them to the realization of higher consciousness or a hidden power within themselves. After this transformation, the heroes return home from their journey with the power to share the prizes they acquired on this adventure (Osland 2000: 228).

As we shall see in the next chapter, 'hero talk' is often used by expatriate men to narrate the ways in which they consider and then eventually decide to go abroad (Osland 2000, see also Amit 2002). They too may talk about the way they embarked on a fascinating, adventurous, but initially lonely, overseas assignment, leaving behind the social support of the domestic office of the organization, and an established life. The new location is 'shrouded with ambiguity, due to unknown language and customs' (Osland 2000: 228). Osland argues that one of the major differences with an *international* relocation concerns the nature of this cross-cultural experience, and it is in the coping with this that the 'heroic' qualities of the expatriate are represented:

> Usually one's normal defence mechanisms and mental maps must be reorganized to cope with a different culture. Before that process is complete, the expatriate, like the mythical hero, will endure a high degree of uncertainty, anxiety and unavoidable adventure. Not everyone is willing to withstand the discomfort (2000: 229).

We saw in Chapter 2 how whiteness has traditionally been made through hero talk such as this, part of a broader hegemonic discourse which historically framed a range of key subjectivities for white men. These are well documented in the colonial literature (Dawson 1994, Rutherford 1997) and I have shown how these were particularly influential in the construction of *British* imperial masculinities (Bonnett 2000), where going off to the colonies became a way to redefine oneself through class, gender and race as well as, for some, to achieve social mobility. The colonial 'explorer' was seen to embody the characteristics of what Bonnett calls 'hyper-whiteness' (2000: 33): a hero-like figure of tremendous energy and sense of adventure. In Amit's (2002) research with British and Canadian expatriates she found the quest for 'a little adventure' was commonplace. In my own research in Hong Kong, I have also found that 'hero talk' continues to be used by male respondents. For example, Rob, a senior police officer who has worked for the Hong Kong Police for over 30 years, told me of the way he came to the Region almost by accident, as a result of his quest for 'adventure'. A small town, working class boy from an unfashionable seaside town in the north of England, the theme of *adventure* is drawn upon in the construction of his early memories:

> I looked at the section for all the job applications and all that and there was nothing that interested me in the UK and so I looked at the foreign section and there was this supplement concerning the Hong Kong Police Force.... I had had thoughts of joining the military-initially the Royal Air Force as a pilot to fly and then in the Royal Navy as an observer ... but failed [to get in] ... so then I came across the Overseas Section! The parents came down at half term and questioned my plans and I told them of my wish to go to Hong Kong to train as a police officer in this really lovely restaurant. My father dropped his spoon and my mother nearly fainted, they could not believe it! I had been abroad but only in Europe and had never been out to the Far East so it was a bit of a culture shock initially I must admit ... I never thought of being a Police Officer before, especially in a foreign colony anyway as it was then ...

Fechter's (2008) notes that her 'expat girls' *also* drew on the discourse of adventure, revealing perhaps a narrowing or blurring of the gender gap here. For example Lucy from Michigan says:

> Everything in my home state is predictable. You know where you are going. You know what you can find in the stores. You know that if they don't have it in one place they will have it another. I think therefore it's the adventure of discovering a new place (Fechter 2008: 203).

Migration is also attractive in terms of social mobility and a discourse of *class* has been noted amongst the talk of some British migrants, especially those from less affluent areas of the UK (Sriskandarajah and Drew 2006). As one respondent put it:

> I left because of class. I had this funny accent and I grew up on a tenement and I knew as God made little apples that I was going nowhere in Glasgow (male, New York City, US) (Sriskandarajah and Drew 2006: 42).

In contrast, a dominant discourse among female expatriate employees is less to do with personal mobility and more about a notion of '*doing good*' for others (Fechter 2008). For many women, a key motivation to work abroad is to make 'a positive impact on their host society' (Fechter 2008: 199). As we have seen, women are usually to be found in welfare occupations: education, health, aid and development, and these views are perhaps unsurprising. However similar positionings are drawn upon by women in the corporate sector who see their expatriate status less in terms of adventure or making money but in terms of being able 'to make a difference'. In addition, they recognize a gendered difference in motivation:

> Most of the guys who are here, when you ask them why, they say, so I can make a ton of money and go back to Australia and retire. Well I'm not going to knock the money back-but it's not the biggest motivator. I do feel I am making a difference (Suzy, in Fechter 2008: 200).

As Fechter notes, the emphasis these women place on this charitable dimension is intriguing because it echoes one of the main occupational roles of more traditional/colonial versions of the expatriate woman. For both men and women therefore, it would seem that the discourses drawn upon to explain their reasons for becoming an expatriate have strong resonances with the race and gender making of former times.

Arrival at the New

Coming to terms with a new cultural environment and working context is not easy, and most accounts of expatriate arrivals reveal that they experience a sense of dislocation and 'culture shock' (Oberg 1960, Furnham and Bochner 1986, Pederson 1995, Yeoh and Willis 2005b, Walsh 2006, Forster 2000, Sriskandarajah and Drew 2006, Jervis 2008), although older expatriates find it easier to adjust more quickly (Selmer 2001). In general, many expatriates say this stage lasts about six months and is characterized by 'uncertainty, difficulty, strangeness, exhilaration, ups and downs, and intense, accelerated learning' (Osland 2000: 230). It is an emotional and often bodily reaction that discourages a sense of belonging to the new context (Walsh 2006) and a clinging to old identities and performances. According to the literature, the initial 'honeymoon stage', in which the new expatriate is filled with fascination, optimism, excitement and the sense of adventure (Pederson 1995) can then be followed by a range of other feelings such as being anxious, overwhelmed, suspicious and 'looked at' (Pederson 1995) and being conscious of one's race and nationality (Walsh 2006). It is perhaps to cope with the emotional and bodily aspects of displacement and isolation that many expatriates take refuge in work as well as the 'expatriate bubble' of the local 'expat' community, both of which offer prescribed models of appropriate behaviour in the new context.

This chapter has commenced the discussion of the role of organizations in framing the expatriate experience and the making of race and gendered identities. In the next chapter, I turn to develop this discussion in more detail by looking at the ways in which organizations 'organize' whiteness through the practices and routines of expatriates' daily working lives.

Chapter 5
Organizing Whiteness Through Organizational Practice

In the last chapter we saw how, from the start of the migration process, organizations can engage in the construction of boundaries, with the identities of both the corporation and its employees being shaped through metaphors, images, statements and practices about what it is to be 'us' rather than 'them' (Moore 2007). These devices position the new expatriate, framing both their knowledge and understanding of the new migratory context, as well as their new lifestyles, personal identities and relations with others (Foucault 1977). Organizations then continue to exercise a powerful control over the lives and identities of their employees, 'organizing' their careers and working lives, their relations with local colleagues as well as their work performances, through the discursive and material practices of worktasks and routines. This chapter now turns to explore these processes in more detail by looking at a variety of migratory organizational contexts. For manageability, this chapter will focus principally on the relationship between whiteness and masculinity, whilst Chapter 6 will look at the ways in which these experiences may differ for women. The two chapters work together to show how race intersects with gender to be a critical differentiator in expatriate lives. This chapter starts with a look at organizational contexts in which the more traditional meanings and performances of whiteness have been able to be largely maintained, despite broader challenges of multiculturalism and localization. We will then move onto explore other contexts, in which the privileges of whiteness are more openly questioned.

The Multinational Corporation

As we have seen, many expatriates work for multi-national corporations or MNCs. These can be defined as corporations with physical or conceptual bases of operation in two or more countries simultaneously, often of which at least one is in a 'global city'. The head office and its branches are linked to each other by lines of communication and trade (Moore 2005). Whilst globalization has led to a dramatic rise in the number of multinational corporations, whether this has led to any decline in the importance of nationality within those organizations is highly debateable. The conventional view is that, whilst MNCs are decentralized, with multiple divisions and functions being spread across the world, they still tend to be strongly influenced by *one* particular national culture, usually that of the 'home country', and the dominant mode of organizing reflects this. However, more recently, studies have demonstrated that whilst the culture of a corporation's head office can be a major influence on its branches, *at the same time* so are the influences from the host country (Mueller 1994, Moore 2005). This research concludes that what needs to be taken into account is the *interplay* between the home country, the host country as well as corporate cultures within branches (McSweeney 2002). The resulting 'third culture' is a synthesis of elements from both inside and outside the organization (Ghoshal and Nohria 1989) and branch offices can consequently be highly diverse. What is ever at play here are the power relations *between* the different cultures. It is not so much therefore that MNCs are '*nationalityless*' but that, by virtue of their involvement with the processes of globalization, they are engaged in complex and ever changing 'trialectics' (Soja 1996) between two local cultures and at least one transnationally operating global culture (Moore 2007).

The ways in which MNCs attempt to exert cultural influence over their employees is revealed in some of the emerging research on expatriates. This shows how, through established *organizational routines and practices*, subject positions are constructed both for expatriates and locals which draw on race and gender as well as notions of nationality. As we saw in the last chapter, these processes can commence from the start in the very early days of the migration process through both the terms and conditions that the expatriate is placed on, as well as the sorts of advice they are given. Hindman's (2008) research on American expatriates in Nepal shows how their first amorphous anxieties on arrival are given shape by the framework instituted by the employer: the need for 'secure housing', a guard, a driver, and consumption of American goods. These combine to create a sort of 'hypernationalism' as well as distinctive gender roles. My own research with white British expatriates working in MNCs in Hong Kong supports this finding, but found in addition that, as well as these forms of 'domestic control', the everyday routines of life *within* the organization further position expatriates in ways which make the meanings of race and nationality to be 'all about difference'.

For example, Properties Inc.[1] is a major player in the global construction industry. Although British, with a Head Office in the UK, it has a long history of operation in Hong Kong and has been a major presence in much of the development of the Region. As such, it plays a careful game with its symbols of identity: at times its Britishness is drawn upon to represent ongoing ties with pre-handover institutions, on other occasions its links with other countries are used to represent its globally engaged, flexible profile. At still other moments its '*Hong Kong-ness*' is emphasized, to represent its local importance and commitment. As Moore (2007) notes, for multinational corporations, identity may be less about the *maintenance* of boundaries than about the *flexible* selection of symbols which best express the desired identity under specific circumstances. However, in spite of this flexibility in identity making, Properties Inc. still remains predominantly white/British in

---

1   Not its real name.

its senior management: a division of labour which sustains the association of management with whiteness in global organizations (Meier 2006). This making of a raced division of labour is supported by a variety of organizational practices.

These are illustrated through a focus on Jim, one of their senior Construction Managers. Jim has been in Hong Kong since 1977, escaping a poorly paid position as a junior architect in the UK. From the first, he was positioned by the organization as an *expatriate* rather than a *local* manager, which meant that his whiteness and nationality worked to bring him privileged *terms and conditions* which have continued over the course of his career. These include a large salary, regular long leaves 'home', school fees for his children in top UK public schools, luxury accommodation, domestic help and club memberships. Jim admits that at first he could hardly believe his new life:

> ... it was fantastic and everybody is in the same boat as you, they have just arrived in Hong Kong, they've all got young kids, with parties every Friday, every Saturday night, it was fantastic. Great social life, great sports and then you had leave to go sailing, play badminton or squash, it was ridiculous. It was just like a holiday camp. You know, you didn't have a very serious job, everybody around you was just working part time really. It's a very great waste of talent and money. They were paying good salaries and people went just potty for six months: if you can't beat them you join them, and you can see people all round, sort of slacking off.

In Chapter 3, I discussed the predominance of the discourse of *the British expatriate* in the talk of the people I interviewed in Hong Kong. Colonial (white/male) versions of this emphasized hierarchy, leadership, firm decision making, hard work and moral responsibility, but here Jim exposes the inherent contradictions which also exist in the discourse. Competing with the supposed attributes of Puritanism and the 'Protestant Ethic' were the hedonistic privileges of the colonial lifestyle, provided by the advantaged terms on which expatriates were placed. As Hindman notes (2007), although these conditions of expatriate employment aim to facilitate their new life, in terms of helping them know *how* to cope with finding somewhere to live, or enjoying their leisure time, they also end up teaching them *what* to do. In this way, expatriates receive powerful messages about what being a 'white expatriate' means. However, for Jim, times changed, and now looking back, he reveals an uneasy awareness that his working life was not morally tenable. Yet whilst he now works hard and very long hours, he realizes that the organization *still* positions him within the discourse of the privileged British expatriate. His terms and conditions have not really changed over the years in spite of the changed political climate, a positioning which continues to differentiate between nationals of the home country of Head Office and local employees in a way which makes him feel uncomfortable:

> I am lucky, I have one of the old fashioned expat style packages, so I live in a nice big apartment and its quite different from the sort of place that my Chinese colleagues live in … I don't invite many of my Chinese colleagues to my home, as I don't like to rub anybody's nose in what I've got … really too much.

However, whilst material privilege in terms of generous compensation packages for white expatriate employees still exists within MNCs, this is a culture which is now starting to change dramatically. Hypercompetition in the global marketplace has required international business firms to focus on cost reduction and effectiveness, and many MNCs have changed their international assignment policies (Selmer 2001, Brewster and Scullion 1997). Increasingly, expatriates are receiving *no* special perks and compensations (Mervosh 1997). In addition, localization policies are progressively being introduced, partially due to changes in local laws but also as a form of cost reduction, meaning that expensive expatriates are a dying breed. Further, in Hong Kong, whilst localization policies have established the non-discriminatory employment of Chinese people at all levels, other changes in the pattern of skilled migration have added to the new power relations in race and ethnicity. These include the return of wealthy western educated Chinese from Canada, Australia and the United States, and the opening up of the border with mainland China. There are now fewer white British faces to be seen within organizations, such that whites and Chinese now work alongside each other at levels right up to the Board Room. As a consequence, expatriates such as Jim, are perhaps now more sensitive about their privileges:

> … localization is taking place, people would prefer to have a Chinese local person in a professional capacity in their office rather than an expatriate. Now with most companies here a Chinese speaking person is more valuable than a non-Chinese person. Skill for skill.

However, in spite of changes in the balance of staff, it is clear that in other ways the raced basis of organizational practice is more resilient. Although to a certain extent Jim has had to renegotiate his own sense of working identity in the new climate of diversity, it is clear that he is still comfortable that the discourse of the British expatriate continues to provide the dominant framework for *organizational practice*, both structurally and culturally. The *structure of the organization* into operational departments has remained largely unchanged over the years, each headed by a white British male with his own cultural stamp. The *culture* of the Construction Division is a tough, masculine and Western one of hierarchy and strong leadership which includes the 'naming and shaming' of poor performance in large meetings. This culture conflicts with Chinese values of 'giving face' and showing respect in public contexts. Whilst Jim reveals some clumsy attempts to be culturally sensitive, what is not resisted or contested is the priority of 'home' (Britain) in the culture of the meeting room or indeed the management of the organization itself:

> A Chinese person would try not to expose himself whereas the average British
> guy, we're used to it, I think it's a part of our culture, you tend to own up whether
> it's publicly or privately to anything that is going wrong. Chinese, I think, have
> more difficulty with that. And so you have to have regard for that when you're
> dealing with a mixed group of nationalities and make it easy for a Chinese
> person, you have to ask your questions in different ways, sometimes, to get
> them to open up.

Jim's talk reveals that personally he has not yet successfully positioned himself
outside of the older versions of the British expatriate discourse, based as it is on
understandings of 'otherness' and difference, and nor has the organization made
any real steps to adapt their practices to reflect the changing cultural makeup of
its staff. British 'ways of doing things' are still expressed as 'the norm', which
the Chinese are seen to have 'problems with'. This situation is supported in the
broader literature on expatriate managers, which has found that typically they
apply the same management style as they used in their home country and do not
adjust well to the norms and practices in the host country (Selmer 2001b). Black
and Porter (1991) also found that US managers continued to apply an American
style, which is quite difficult to that of local Chinese managers. In Jim's comments
on how his Chinese colleagues feel the need to negotiate carefully before the start
of a meeting, it is clear that it is they, rather than the expatriate, who are active
in taking on the burden of a great deal of 'identity work' behind closed doors. In
Jim's discussions of the everyday routines of his relationships with his colleagues,
whiteness and Britishness are revealed as embedded in the regular *doing of work*
in the organization:

> The way I find it happening, as people get more and more used to the personality
> that we British tend to have, they will come and before the meeting starts they
> will come and have a word with you. I've got a meeting this afternoon where we
> will be discussing some pretty punchy things, and already two of the members
> of that committee have been to see me or phoned me, to say "Jim, before the
> meeting starts I just want you to know ..." I think the assumption is that I will
> have regard for their face at that meeting.

Clearly, in spite of the fact that the organization's 'home' culture is clearly at
odds with Chinese ways of doing things, any need for change is not felt. Jim's
apparently 'liberal' talk reveals that in spite of his attempts to position himself as a
knowledgeable local, he is as yet unable to let go of his identity as a white British
man or to see over the parapet of Properties Inc.'s dominant culture of British
white masculinities. Nor do the everyday routines of organizational life require
him to do so. However the cultural reproductions of an MNC's Head Office are not
'mirror images': they have to be done *in place*. We can see here how the interplay
with the local culture, people and practices reveals the constant *negotiation* of
race, identity and power. The work performances of white/British masculinities

are clearly mediated and moderated by the activities of Chinese colleagues. Subtly this negotiation means that the white man *is* being asked to listen, and to change his behaviour in meetings. The organization of working practices and work identities in multi-national corporations is not and cannot be a 'one size fits all' approach therefore, but is constantly made *in place*: a continual and ongoing process within which spaces may exist for resistance and change.

Development and the Foreign Service

Jim's story supports an understanding of identity which is not only conscious and instrumental, but also habitual and unreflexive, achieved through the iteration and repetition of consistent organizational norms and performances (Bourdieu 1977, Butler 1990, Kothari 2006). Writing about administrative officers in colonial times, Kothari (2006) shows how Jim's attitudes reflect those long delineated in the rules and protocols of white/British administrative policies, hierarchies and systems. How these colonial forms of rule, cultures and practices have travelled over space and time to be subsequently reworked by white expatriates working in contemporary Development and Diplomatic Services in the post independence period has been the subject of some fascinating recent postcolonial analysis (e.g Kothari 2002, Kenny 2008). This shows how ideologies that were constructed and used to sustain forms of colonial rule and authority are still highly influential today.

As in the corporate sector, development organizations tend to be bureaucratic in structure, form and practice, just as were their colonial predecessors. Coles (2007), writing about her lifelong experiences as an expatriate for both the Foreign Office and the British Department for International Development, regards a love of '*Office Procedures*' as critical for shaping the identities, attitudes and behaviour of staff, both at home and overseas. For example, recent introductions of business management techniques such as 'government by objectives' which give employees highly structured work plans, listing activities to be undertaken and a statement of hoped-for results, mean that tasks need to be 'ticked off' within a tight time frame: typically between two and five years. Further, rather than evaluating the success of an initiative organically, the extreme emphasis on *written skills and paper* means that:

> Carefully worded minutes, concise, critical but ultimately constructive provided a paper trail against which progress could be measured and a record against which individual staff could be held accountable. ... A project memorandum (PM) complete with professional annexes ... was one of the main ways in which an overseas office ... showed its competence. Much effort went into its perfection, to make an elegant, crisply worded PM of precisely the correct length (Coles 2007: 129).

Within these organizational contexts, staff behaviour was expected to be 'neutral'. This is an interesting word, meaning in practice the avoidance of any show of emotionalism in the office. Disagreements are therefore couched largely in terms of procedures or professional judgements. Coles (2007) argues that this is a culture which is predominantly male-centred and consequently the discourse is masculine, with sports based metaphors such as 'levelling the playing field' and 'going for the goal' sprinkling the talk. This not only masculine, but also white and English culture plays itself out in diverse ways in both the long established regional offices, such as Bangkok, Nairobi, Harare, Southern Africa and the Caribbean, as well as the newer offices such as India, Bangladesh and Nepal. Here, each develops their own identity, 'an identity that partly, but only partly, reflected the characteristics and culture of the host country. Each was also strongly influenced by the management styles of both the first and current office heads and his or her senior advisors' (Coles 2007: 132).

Coles notes further that clearly discernible underlying values and assumptions are held by overseas staff. Historically, many of these had an academic background in a subject such as anthropology, and tended to transpose this approach to the 'Other' into their work. As such, their strong commitment to helping developing countries may be touched by 'lingering colonial values and a hint of missionary zeal' (p. 133), especially for the longer serving expatriates. For the younger staff, their idealism was tinged by the material recognition that their civil service conditions of service were higher and more secure than their NGO (Non-Governmental Organizations) colleagues. However, in spite of this, there tended to be little *real* concern with the culture of the country in question within field offices: briefing for postings were erratic and induction usually strictly task-related. Little information on the culture was given, and there was no encouragement to learn the local language. This 'continuing and partly conscious Britishness' (p. 133) was further encapsulated in the clothes and appearance of employees, who stuck rigidly to European dress. There was also a strict ethnic division of labour: local staff could only fill junior posts and their knowledge of the local context, their contacts and their continuity in terms of long term memory 'often went unappreciated' (p. 133). In this vein, any individual efforts made by staff to get to know local professionals or partners were not always acknowledged or valued by more senior staff.

A key way in which whiteness is performed in development and diplomatic contexts is in the *language* that is used in relation to the people that they are trying to 'help'. In particular, the ways in which the 'Other' is positioned gives an indication of the extent of the survival of colonial cultural footprints within an organization and its members (Kenny 2008). Kenny's research within a development organization reveals the dominance of two organizational discourses: '*Saving the Other*' and '*Knowing the Other*', albeit that both are marked by contradiction and ambiguity. Although these discourses were challenged and resisted by people over time, they remained central in both ways of speaking about the Other, and to the practice and outcomes of the organization's work.

First, it appeared at meetings, in documents, mission statements and in interviews with employees that the idea that the Other can be 'helped' and 'saved' was taken as a given. The white man was positioned *literally* as 'arriving bearing gifts'. As one interviewee put it:

> See how you can be useful to them ... I have an old apple mac laptop ... it's crap, it's 27 hertz ... give it to them and they will use it ... arrive bearing gifts ... (2008: 62).

Second, the idea that the Other can be 'known' was also widely held. Spending a long time in the field with a local driver was a key strategy to this end, as was having 'sensitivity' to their culture':

> Before I go into the field ... I need to know what's on their minds ... before I go to India, if they call Superman "Shaftiman", well then I can drop that into the training programme: "You don't have to be like Shaftiman" and get a laugh out of them ... culture is important (2008: 63).

A further methodology here involved *categorization* and *quantification* of the Other, recalling not only Robinson Crusoe's approach but also the activities of the colonial administrators which were discussed in Chapter 2. Through the use of questionnaires, field notes and comparison across countries and regions, the 'Other' is manoeuvred into an ontological position from which to assess, categorize and analyse (Kenny 2008). Fundamental to this methodology was the capturing of data in comparable, generalizable and quantative formats:

> It's all about linkages and triangulations between countries ... we want to look here [Ghana] does that correlate to there [Solomon Islands?] Oh yes it does! Just three indicators, three simple indicators with one question for each yeah? We can check those boxes then you in the Solomon Islands, Emily in Ghana ... we can really nail those bastards ... (2008: 63–64).

Constructing the Other as inferior with phrases such as 'Once the South gets itself sorted economically' clearly goes hand in hand with constructing the organization and its employees as superior. This is unreconstructed whiteness, but it would be too simplistic to say that all the employees of the organization subscribe to these discursive positionings. Alternative discourses emerge which constitute the Other as being outside the scope of the power of the organization to 'save' or 'know':

> I mean development generally comes from within ... if you look at South Korea, if you look at China or India or all those kinds of places, they have developed themselves, no-one else has done it for them ... and (a friend) was saying there is anecdotal evidence that Africa might have developed further if it wasn't for development workers ... (2008: 65).

Time spent in the field is critical to the construction of such ambivalence. However this can also result in the view that the local people *are* fundamentally different in terms of culture, race and language, and as such *unknowable:* inexplicable, irritating and opaque. Thus whilst the organization is clearly very powerful in terms of shaping the ideas and the identities of its employees, the co-existence of competing discourses points to a diversity of white positioning as well as the ambivalence of colonialist discourse as an instrument of power (Bhabha 1994). This ambivalence is supported by other discourses which were present but *silent*, such as views that the 'Other' is neither in need of being 'saved', nor could be. Further unarticulated was the fact that it is actually the 'Other' who is 'saving' the development workers and diplomats: providing them with jobs and a raison d'etre. These views were however sometimes expressed through jokes and asides, a form of 'easy white talk' (Simpson 1996) which reveals how neither the white man nor the 'Other' can be fixed fully or finally.

The Club

Life for white expatriates has long been made easier by the existence of 'The Club', which has played an integral role in structuring the social fabric of expatriate communities across the world since colonial times. In addition, clubs also play a critical part in oiling the wheels of working life: business meetings may be held here, and much networking is done between members. Club membership is a way of constructing the identities of organizations as well as employees, and this is especially the case in Hong Kong where clubs built around sport or occupation: the Hong Kong Cricket Club, the Royal Hong Kong Golf Club, the Foreign Correspondents Club and so on are spaces where business and social lives blur. As in other colonial spaces, clubs were originally set up by the British as oases of European culture, aiming 'to reproduce the comfort and familiarity of home for those living in an alien land' (Sinha 2001). They were for a long time symbols of racial exclusivity, dominated by white and usually British members. They were always self-governing institutions, with a tight role-defined administrative structure which reveals acutely the interplay of class and gender with race and nation in the relations produced by imperialism:

> The club formed part of an elaborate set of mechanisms that articulate the legitimate boundaries of an acceptable image of "whiteness". Through gendered, raced and class-specific assumptions, the concept of "clubbability" rendered whites "visible in a certain way" in the colonial domain (Sinha 2001: 504).

This particular mobilization of whiteness was articulated through the alleged 'unclubbability' of non-whites (Sinha 2001), and certainly Hong Kong clubs have remained dominated by white cultural norms. More recently, because of the political changes, they have opened their doors to local members and now some have more Chinese and Indian members than white. However, a quick look at the management structures of many of the most socially prestigious clubs confirms that white men still dominate here, maintaining their visibility not only as 'the people who know how to do clubs properly', but also as arbiters of Hong Kong life more generally. Managers make decisions as to what members should be doing and how, where and when they should be doing it, and, in the process, are able to sustain the values attached to symbols and daily routines of white middle class culture. Whiteness and British/middle class power relations are thus made and sustained through these key organizations, both through the daily operations of club management and the routines of everyday club life.

Harry has lived in Hong Kong since the early 1990s, having first come out as a junior hotel manager for an international hotel chain. An ex-private schoolboy, Harry has the typical self-confidence of his upper middle class, masculine background. As his biographical narrative reveals, the markers of his whiteness, combined with his gender, class and nationality, have been clearly beneficial to his life course. Not long after his arrival his contacts meant that he secured a job in one of the major clubs in Hong Kong. Now the manager of a very prestigious club in the New Territories, with a long history of white British rule, he is well aware of the power of his present position in Hong Kong society:

> you've got 30,000 members whose private lives you have an impact on. It's a bit like running their homes ... if you're anybody you have to be a member of [a] club. It's very much part of the culture in Hong Kong and consequently, clubs are taken seriously here.

Harry's early positioning as a green expatriate who knew nothing about Hong Kong and Chinese culture has been replaced by a work subjectivity shaped through a discourse of racial difference and white male superiority. The interplay of whiteness with nationality, class and gender reveals itself in a highly developed sense of difference, and it is clear that Harry has taken on the traditional subjectivity of the white British colonial-style boss with some alacrity. Imperialist attitudes to 'Others' are actively sustained and enacted through the assumptions on which his daily relations with Chinese employees are constructed:

> They're more reliable, you can rely on them to work. I've always felt that English people particularly in this industry, your washer uppers, your waiters and bar staff, are very transient, they do not have a service mentality, they don't really like what they're doing, they don't really want to serve. Whereas the Chinese tend to adapt to it quite easily. They seem to have a much better understanding, perhaps an innate understanding, so their training is much easier than UK staff. There isn't that service mentality in the UK that there is in Hong Kong. And Asia to a degree works like that.

Harry's talk reveals how the everyday club routines, reliant as they are on racialized notions of working class Chinese as docile, 'naturally' servile workers, are essential in constructing and maintaining both his own sense of his white British self, the way the club is organized, as well as the identities of club members:

> Ordinary workers are basically hard working, willing, keen to learn and very good when pointed in the right direction and being shown what to do. They have a positive working attitude. They will work, they don't drift around. That's the best you can say about them. If you've got properly trained staff with confidence in them, they will go off and do everything. So, basically you want good people who are going to stay. You don't want over ambitious or dynamic people, but people who are going to talk to the members and be nice and friendly with them.

In his careful talk about the multi-cultural make up of the club, Harry reveals that he is aware of the contemporary social and economic realities of Hong Kong's postcolonial state, but has an unstable relationship with these. On the one hand, he wants to make clear that it is (wealthy) Chinese members who now dominate the committee structures, and that his job is to make sure that the way in which the club is experienced is politically irreproachable, in terms of both race and gender. Whilst women have been part of the membership for many years, their participation in club life is now widening and they are no longer debarred from the facilities or committee membership. However, in the multi-faceted relations he has with his Chinese acquaintances, the contradictory and fragmented nature of his performances reveals the simultaneity of the colonial and the postcolonial, as well as the intersections of race, class and gender. Whilst he is prepared to respect the wealthier, middle class Chinese, underlying racist prejudices are confirmed in his talk about his Chinese subordinates, and he clearly needs to negotiate a position of difference and superiority over them. Further, the ways in which everyday relations and routines are operationalized in clubs have wider symbolic power. British cultural performances such as flower arranging, bridge clubs, festivals and social events still dominate activity, revealing how the club can provide a performative space in which some of the broader political and social changes of Hong Kong may be resisted, and where British expatriate identities based on traditional colonial understandings of whiteness, nationality, masculinity and middle class superiority are still acceptable.

Organizing Identities in the Public Sector

Organizations within the 'public' sector, in which broad church I include institutions of education, health care and the police, may also be heavily influenced by the countries of the West, especially if they were established in the colonial area and the nations continue to have postcolonial links. However the changing politics across the globe have brought changes to these organizations' structural hierarchies, with most now adopting localization policies. These mean that expatriates are now less likely to be found in senior management positions and more likely to be in functional specialisms. Typically, however, these organizations may still follow the Western bureaucratic and supposedly 'meritocratic' form by which they were set up, and this can produce complex and ambiguous positions for white expatriates working within them. They may need to negotiate their identities at the workplace with a little more care than white expatriates who work in the contexts discussed above. This is illustrated through the example of Rob, a senior officer for the Hong Kong Police.

The Police

The Hong Kong Police Force is a particularly strong example of a Western-style formal bureaucratic organizational structure, in terms of its methods of recruitment, selection, and career ladders. From its inception it was run by white middle class British men, ruling over a multi-racial staff of other Commonwealth expatriates, other Europeans such as the Portuguese, as well as Chinese and Asians. Although it has had a somewhat chequered history, and was for many years considered to be the 'poor relation' of the public sector, it now prides itself as a 'stable force' within the Region which has helped to manage the transition from colonial rule to postcolonial administration. Whilst many expatriates left with the handover, taking their generous pay offs and returning home, the life stories of those who stayed on to work within the new Chinese administration reveal how their white identities have been both sustained and challenged.

Rob is in his early 50s, and has worked for the force for over 30 years. His entry in the late 1970s was at managerial level, in spite of a lack of work experience and a rather humble background, revealing the middle class subjectivity that was automatically accorded to all *white* male recruits: an immediate readiness to lead. His talk reveals how the organization of the expatriate *career* crafted the racialized, classed and gendered subject position of leader:

> I joined at managerial level. Going out on the beat and checking your beat officers were okay. So I started off in what you would call Patrol Sub-Unit Commando, you had a sub-unit of so many officers and they did go out in force while you did your administrative work in the police station ... you are then trained to go into riot and emergency situations and use different weapons. You then go onto a regional attachment after your training course and most of your time is spent there unless anything happens and then you are on anti-crime patrols. So you are back again to beat recovery but in a very heavy handed slum type of police script where you are putting a large number of police officers into a possible crime area. ... [After the Emergency Unit] I went on a long leave then because of my conditions of service – two and a half to three months leave and I then came back and went

> into an admin job which most of my career has been ... The second tour I was on leave again and got back into basic patrol, uniform work and then got sent off to detective training school for CID and then went to the Complaints Office where I did a 2 year tour. I left there and no secrets now and I have trained at Special Branch for two and a half years and then onto Criminal Intelligence Bureau and then I moved into the one I am in now which is the Technology Crime Division. So basically I have covered a wide spectrum of the job ...

In the detail of Rob's language, we can see how the career of a white British officers in the final decades of British colonial rule was pre-scripted and automatic. Rob has been constructed by, and positions himself within, the strategies used by the Police Force to slot abstract white male bodies into the organization (Acker 1990). Here, whilst he shows himself to be power*ful* in terms of the seniority of his positions, he also appears, simultaneously, as somewhat power*less* to change the direction of a career which had already been mapped out for him. Thus whilst whiteness has brought entitlement, it also, perhaps, has meant a loss of individual identity and agency, and a self which has been gradually moulded through the daily routines of tasks and responsibilities. This is how a white officer was made, and what is interesting about this speech is Rob's silent and unquestioning understanding of what whiteness meant in Hong Kong: a lifestyle of responsibility regularly interrupted by perks such as long leaves and regular, termly bonuses. An entitlement that was his by virtue of his whiteness and nationality, any acknowledgment of this difference as a privilege is absent here, remaining unseen and unmarked by Rob.

However with the handover in 1997, the social and political climate has changed significantly since the early days of Rob's career. The Police Force has changed with it. Now the senior managers are all Chinese and the 'automatic' script which Rob's career was following has disappeared for white expatriates. For those who chose to stay on post handover, the ways in which their white identities are made and perceived by the organization is now a lot less clear cut and the crafting of Rob's identity needs much more careful negotiation on his part. Rob prefers to believe that his presence is still highly desired by the force:

Pauline: Was there a slight pressure that you should be leaving?

> No, I did not find that at all, in fact they wanted particularly, as the police force is in a strange situation here, it has always been looked on, despite certain parts of its history where corruption has been involved it, has always been the sort of stable force within the colony then or the territory. It has always been seen to employ the largest number of ex-pats as well, maybe a racist thing or, I don't know, but they would like to see the white face within the police force. It seemed to give stability to the force, so in fact staying here was encouraged as they try to keep as many officers as they could ...

However this surface rhetoric is undercut by a competing (but in the main somewhat silenced) discourse which reveals an organizational ambivalence (or even antipathy) to expatriate presence:

> but they did not personally bring this across and officers left and now people are retiring and some are not finishing contracts and things like that and numbers are slightly dwindling ...

Rob knows that in order to continue in his career he needs to embrace the localization policies the Force have instituted and the fact that now careers are supposedly constructed through merit on an equal playing field:

> Localization – yes, with the handover localization was brought into the police force – some time prior to the handover in fact. However, back until shortly we were still the largest expatriate employers ... most of the other Departments had localised long before we had, but then there was a general localization programme so come 1997 it wasn't a huge shock. ... of course promotion is still done on merit and through the promotion boards ... a dead man's shoes as one goes the next one goes up and it is done on merit and not necessarily on seniority... the only thing now is that unless you are a Chinese national or of Chinese origin you cannot become a commissioner or deputy commissioner – the top three posts you cannot hold.

On the other hand however he reveals that he still clings to idea of the endurance of an exclusive 'club' of whiteness within the organization which may bring benefits:

> [however] I am sure it does help if you do know the Chairman of the Board or something like that who is familiar with your work. The Chairman of this Board is a gentleman that I have known for a number of years [gives a Western sounding name] voted through the ranks and I have worked with him and know him ...

There is little evidence of a 'remaking' of a coherent 'new' identity of whiteness in Rob's narrative, and although alert to the need to demonstrate a willingness on his part to 'localize': primarily through the organization's expectation that expatriate officers should be fluent in Cantonese, he is embracing this very half-heartedly. Although he is keen to show how well he and his colleagues work closely together: they are a team, they support each other and he relies heavily on them; his reluctance to speak to them in their own language reveals an ambivalence towards change, based perhaps on the longstanding racial division of officers within the organization:

> **Pauline: So do you always understand what is going on?**
>
> Well they tell me. We are still a disciplined force so we are clear of our officer duties which are a clear picture, and of course you are supposed to know what

is going on in your section and as Chief Inspector I am in charge of four units within my section so I have four inspectors working for me and under them they have junior police officers working for them – so you rely heavily on the Inspectors to keep you addressed of what is going on...

I could [speak Cantonese] but I am lazy as I don't push it enough, and I also work with a lot of people who speak very good English. So that's a bit unfortunate, it's my own fault, I don't blame anybody else; it's just that I have not pushed it enough. We are supposed to have learnt it in the first two months when we came out here ... expats went to Cantonese schools and local officers went to do voluntary work so the two of them did not really mix initially...

Rob's story suggests how race is made through specific historical and political contexts, and the importance of organizational life in its construction and performances. He shows how his early (unmarked, yet) raced identity was displaced by the organizational one offered by the then colonially administered Hong Kong Police, in which whiteness and membership of the British Commonwealth were crucial markers of superiority and success. His migration transformed the meaning of these social markers, and he was able to draw on them to secure a successful and well rewarded professional identity, with a pre-established career path and privileged lifestyle. Since the handover, in some ways Rob's position appears to have faced little challenge. He is still able to mobilize the ideological and material privileges attached to whiteness embedded in the organizational structure and culture of the Police which were established by the British in colonial times. He can still be accused of viewing the world through an imperial lens. At the same time however, there is a sense of ambiguity: he *is* aware that the world is changing and with this so are the meanings of whiteness:

Pauline: Do you enjoy working here as much as you did or has it changed?

Maybe not, but that could be because I am getting older ... they are still paying the money and that is the main thing and it is a very good deal ... Hong Kong has been a very good deal for me and my family and I have got a lot out of it and I am very grateful to the Hong Kong Government. You would find that there used to be a lot of ex-pats who would complain about the service and the conditions of service but the Hong Kong Government is a very, very good employer and you would find it very hard to equalize and in fact it is something which my eldest son was thinking he would get a job like his Dad, but these jobs no long exist and Hong Kong was like the last jewel in the crown of the colonies and there are very few left now, such as places in the mid-Atlantic, which are very small colonies and by no means as vibrant as this place, but the jobs just don't exist and the terms of service which I am on are so very, very good and you get very good ex-pat terms of service so no way can you complain about that at all. The place has been good as I say for me and for my family ...

Higher Education

Higher educational institutions are now in a position of increasingly employing expatriates at all levels of the academic structure, as the badge of 'international' is critical to attracting both students and research funding. As academics establish research links and networks across national boundaries, the academic job market is increasingly becoming an international one, as new research teams develop, requiring experts from specialised fields to work together. For some an international posting may be a quick way to get promotion. This was the case for David, a young British academic who is a year into his first contract at Hong Kong's New University[2] having never lived abroad before. New University was established 25 years ago, and is now very keen to be seen to be competitive within the globalized markets of higher education, employing academics from all over the world. Western expatriates are sought to represent an engagement with that knowledge which holds cultural capital in Anglo-American contexts.

Being a more recent expat, David's terms and conditions are not as substantial as Jim's or Rob's, but he is still on an attractive package:

> To be very crude about it, they pay lots of money and that's a factor. I don't live in university accommodation because they now provide a system where you can take the goods in kind, where you can live on campus or they will pay your mortgage. So it's an extremely generous system.

David comments that whilst in many ways the organization is still 'very British' in terms of its culture, at the same time he finds there are key differences:

> It's a very formal place ... it's more British than Britain in many ways its run. All of the formalities of an old university like [names an established British university] are carried over and added to wholesale in a place like this. It's also very un-British in the sense that the president has power over the institution, far more than [names an established British university]. The Deans have a lot of power too, so I guess it's more like an American university. We are in a phase of transition, it was set up as a polytechnic, it got university status the same way as British universities did, and is now trying to transform itself into the next stage which is an American campus.

The management of the University is primarily Hong Kong Chinese and Chinese/ American: 'Every single vice president except one is Chinese. The Deans are all Chinese', and whilst he, like Jim and Rob, is still positioned as a white British expatriate, the different context of power means that David feels far more ambivalent about this subjectivity. At first he felt he had 'extremely happy working relationships' with his Chinese colleagues as he went about his everyday

---

2   Not its real name.

teaching commitments. However, a few months previously, he had been asked to take over a managerial post as Head of Department. The taking on of some degree of organizational power has brought about some stark differences in his working life, and he must now engage with the organizational culture and hierarchy more directly through the continual regularity of decision making and meetings. Differences between British/American organizational cultural ideas, routines and habits and Chinese ways of doing things are revealed through David's talk about his working life. From David's perspective, he now feels that he is more noticeably positioned by his colleagues within the discourse of British expatriate. On the one hand he bemoans that he feels locked into a stereotypical identity, particularly in these meetings. On the other hand however, his talk reveals how, in the ways in which he positions himself, he also constructs *for* himself an identity established on national stereotype and racial difference:

> ... you're not trusted, I don't mean they mistrust you, it's just that if anything goes wrong, they won't give you the benefit of the doubt. They tend to think you're English, you're alien, you don't understand anything about it ... there's a series of stereotypes about how Chinese and Westerners do things, one stereotype is that Chinese like to have consensus, there's never any open disagreement and therefore what you do, any one who's in a position of power, you go round checking before meetings that everyone's in agreement. The stereotype that they have of the UK is that it's kind of macho management, people come in and they fight things out with committees. When that happens with me chairing it's read as me being the Western stereotype, the fact that I don't understand how things are done, and why didn't I check beforehand? And when it happens under a Cantonese chair, then people don't even notice it's happening. So there's much less that I can get away with, so you just have to be much more careful ... Chinese bosses can be pretty tough. If anything goes wrong they immediately assume "does he know what is going on and how we do things"?

In his talk, David reveals not only the strength of his feeling that the discourse of British expatriate positions him unfavourably within the culture that exists at work, but also how, simultaneously, he draws on these very same discourses to position himself. He recognizes that the key problem is that he is unable to 'read' Chinese colleagues once he has risen above the level of only interacting with those who are subordinate to him such as students and secretarial staff:

> I honestly don't know what my colleagues think of me ... in the UK you have a better sense of how you are perceived. It was a shock to me in the four months as Acting Head when I suddenly found that people were openly hostile, because I felt I had a good personal relationship with people and I wasn't particularly doing anything different. Now I had hysterical responses, very emotional. In the UK it wouldn't have provoked the same responses; it wouldn't have been looking for "the problems". In the general office, the secretarial support, they are

very nice. People in low-level positions are nicer. Chinese bosses can be pretty tough. I guess in the beginning I knew what was going on but when I became Head I didn't have a clue what was going on!

For David, the problems connected with his raced identity began once he started to engage with people who held more powerful positions, and he was more isolated from the community of whiteness. Although he thought the organizational context and overt culture were familiar, the localized activities and responses of his colleagues are different to his expectations or his cultural knowledge. He finds himself unable to move beyond the subject positions he feels are on offer, and admits to 'a certain sense of frustration that I was being misjudged, that I wasn't this Western stereotypical character'. He has tried to be reflexive: 'I don't think that there was much that I did that was an expression of my western background, and I've been very observant, to look out for certain instances', but his perception of his Chinese colleagues as the problematic 'them', based on a cluster of stereotypical attributes *of difference* – such as inscrutability, toughness and a dislike of conflict, prevent him from learning and changing. For David, located much further down the organizational hierarchy than Jim, whiteness is performed through this confusion and the sense of bewilderment that anything he could have done might have caused offence. His inability to read the meanings of his own performances is augmented by his inability to read those of his colleagues, making it difficult to build connections with local colleagues or interact at work in ways *not* through the lens of race.

Work Makes Race and Ethnicity

The discussion has revealed how whiteness, combined with nationality, *continues* to be of ongoing relevance in organizational identity-making and organizational practice in global contexts. This finding is reinforced by other recent research which also to some degree contests the argument that identities constructed through racial, ethnic and national boundaries are *disappearing* through globalization (Smith 1995, Hirst and Thompson 1996). For example, Meier's (2006) research with white Germans in Singapore shows how they drew on updated discourses of the *white expatriate* which emphasized 'creativity, informality and independence', in the constructions of their identities. They were keen to contrast themselves sharply with the local Singaporeans, who were positioned as 'uncreative and dependent' (Meier 2006: 128). Meier found an ongoing and *omnipresent ethnic division of labour* in multinational corporations in Singapore, with all whites marked as 'foreign talent' who thus tended to position themselves as 'desired' and 'required' by Singaporean society as highly qualified personnel. In turn this leads to the practice of *dividing work tasks* by ethnicity: once again underscoring the ways in which work makes race. Beaverstock's (2002) research in Singapore similarly found that expatriates trusted locals to only do so much of the work, and that the final 'closing off' of deals required a white expatriate to oversee it. Whiteness here, therefore, is about having the final word:

> For my company [US bank] because the sales profession are expats, the big problem here is the locals may identify a deal, the proposal generally has been written or will be written by an expat. But you could do a hundred deals like that, you can write a hundred proposals, but it would take a special person to close the deals. And that's where you would come in. The identification of the decision makers within organizations ... in most markets ... is that the decision maker is of a level to have to be an expatriate. The decision making process on large deals ... need the involvement of an expat ... or someone coming in from head office ... parachuting in an expat specialist (Beaverstock 2002: 533).

Because whiteness is such a visible marker of difference, *clothes and appearance* tend to be less important as an indication of group formation in Singapore than they are at home. Meier (2006) notes that finance workers for example tend to be much more casually dressed than in other contexts such as London and New York where clothes are used to indicate professional memberships and affiliations. In Singapore, whiteness alone is enough to show the membership of a privileged elite.

However Moore (2007) reminds us that the construction of boundaries is *not* just about race, but can also be about *other* social divisions such as ethnicity. Her research on (white) German expatriates based in a multinational bank in London reveals how ethnicity is used strategically, and that this can lead to multiple identities being expressed both consecutively and simultaneously. She found that English employees would draw on their smatterings of German or links with Germany when necessary, whilst Germans would at times emphasize their cosmopolitanism or Europeanness rather than their home nationality. However, interestingly, as the bank went into a difficult period of restructuring, the staff retreated to more rigid boundary-based, ethnicized identities in order to cope with the stresses of the new climate. Problems were expressed almost *entirely* in ethnic terms, and specifically in terms of a boundary between English and German identities. New bosses who had transferred from the Head Office in Germany were described by the English as 'typical Germans, always keen on procedure' (Moore 2007: 57), and discussions about change were inevitably brought back to a German-English divide. Thus whilst a more flexible concept of identity had been used previously, the tough organizational changes brought about a more explicit discourse of bounded ethnic identities.

Moore (2007) suggests that this inflexibility is actually *not* inconsistent with the normal uses of identity in global environments. Contrary to arguments based on macro-level evidence, ethnographic research focusing on micro-level processes at the level of the individual and the organization is revealing how race, nationality and ethnicity *are* still important aspects of organizational and personal identities in globalizing working contexts. Also critical is gender, and it is to this which we now turn.

Chapter 6
Gender, Work and Expatriate Life

With women increasingly entering the international workforce, work is now a key context not only of expatriate men's lives but of women's as well. Traditionally, the focus of interest in ethnographic studies of gender and expatriate life has been on domestic contexts, studying women's relations with the home, the expatriate community and the partner's employment (e.g. Callan and Ardener 1984, Coles and Fechter 2008). Clearly however this focus now needs to be broadened to take account of the gendered changes occurring in skilled labour markets, and to include women's relations with work and workplaces as employees themselves. Although there may quite a contrast between the work experiences of the expatriate women who work: from the newer wave of, in all probability, younger women migrants travelling the world in the pursuit of their careers, to the 'trailing spouses', who may gain their employment as and where they can once they arrive, it is often *through* contemporary work contexts that meanings of gender and race in expatriate subjectivities are being challenged and transformed.

The last chapter explored the ways in which organizational practices can exert considerable power over migrant subjectivities, organizing and positioning expatriates in ways which sustain their senses of whiteness, nationality and difference. Women however can have their own particular gendered challenges to negotiate. For example, the stereotype of the white male manager still persists in many international contexts (Linehan 2000), such that expatriate women may find that they are positioned *against* type, in contexts where (professional/managerial) work is assumed to be done by a white man. However, emerging in the research on expatriates is new evidence which shows that work may provide a liminal space for women: a space which offers opportunities to contest and *renegotiate* gendered and even raced/national expectations. Many of the expatriate women's narratives I discuss here reveal a greater flexibility in their identities and relationships than the men I discussed in the last chapter, suggesting a motivation to challenge the discourses of gender and race which have traditionally dominated not only the contexts of work but also expatriate lives more generally.

Challenging Who Goes Where

In Chapter 4 I discussed what in some ways can be seen as a 'new generation' of skilled migrants: those who actively seek work abroad, driven by a personal sense of career and lifestyle rather than a corporate posting, and who do not necessarily expect or want 'compensation' in terms of a lucrative expatriate package. A growing proportion of this new generation are women, 'expat girls' who are travelling the world in search of new work experiences and lifestyles (Fechter 2008). These women are not overly bothered where they work: they just want international experience and to enjoy the work, social and tourist opportunities that expatriate life can offer. They are usually unattached, and are less likely than corporate employees to be active in the expatriate community or live in an expatriate compound, but will live in cheaper housing in expatriate zones within the local community. They have a sharpened sense of their own career, and choose their jobs strategically. They see often themselves as 'trailblazers', challenging the gendered discourses which have long shaped international work (Fechter 2008). However, whilst the expat girls can increasingly be found in the fields of accounting, marketing or management consultancy, they are still more likely to be clustered in the conventional 'female' occupational sectors in which women have always been active: education, health, culture and development. As Fechter (2008) points out therefore, this qualifies the extent to which expat girls can be seen to be totally breaking new ground; their gendered subject positions having not changed quite as substantially as at first might be supposed. Rather than completely dismantling the barriers of male enclaves (Adler and Izraeli 1994, Hartl 2003) and renegotiating the boundaries of gendered work, their occupations are not, in fact, perhaps so very different to the roles which unmarried women followed in colonial times, whose primary occupations were also the more 'care-oriented' ones of teacher, nurse, missionary or colonial administrator.

However, in spite of their continued predominance in the feminized spaces of working life, the 'expat girls' are helping to *broaden* the meanings of gender in expatriate contexts. Their growing numbers across all occupational sectors means that it is becoming far less unusual to find single white women working overseas, challenging the married male's dominance of work and work-related spaces, as well as the domesticated restrictions of feminine subject positions. Further, they themselves are usually very keen to position themselves *against* the dominant gendered subjectivities of expatriate life as exemplified through the lives of the expatriate wives (Fechter 2008). They see themselves as leading very different sorts of lives, having little desire to join in social activities such as coffee mornings, bridge, charity work and shopping trips. The key source of this sense of difference is their work, and the having of a career, and it is this which sets them apart from the other women, and even gives them an increased confidence and sense of superiority.

This sense of difference might be also somewhat misplaced however. We also saw in Chapter 4 that the expat girls tend to position their work subjectivities within a discourse of '*doing good*': as someone who is making a positive impact on the host society, rather than working for high renumeration or status, or living the sort of empty or self-indulgent life of luxury they imagine of the expatriate wives. In fact, as Fechter (2008) points out, many expatriate wives *also* tend to be heavily involved in 'doing good' activities through their charity and volunteer work. Yet this desire to contribute to other societies and cultures *is* seen to be a particularly 'girl thing', and as such the expat girls feel it sets them apart from their male colleagues:

> Most of the guys who are here, when you ask them why, they say, so I can make
> a ton of money and go back to Australia and retire. Well I'm not going to knock
> the money back, but it's not the biggest motivator. I do feel that I'm making a
> contribution (Suzy in Fechter 2008: 199).

For the expat girls, migration can bring a sense of freedom and flexibility. They
are often highly mobile: moving on when a project finishes or a more exciting one
beckons. Their low level of incorporation confers a degree of agency and control
over their lives which is represented in the way in which their talk is sprinkled with
references to 'having choices' within their working lives (Fechter 2008). However,
this was perhaps somewhat counterbalanced with an unspoken awareness that
choices in their *personal* lives were perhaps being implicated as a result of their
highly mobile, career-oriented lifestyles.

Challenging Who Does What, and How

The narratives of the expat girls reveal how they feel they are challenging the male
stronghold on expatriate work. This is further reinforced in their references to the
ways in which the 'doing of work' has also changed for them through migration.
Many find they are given more responsibility, resulting in a sort of 'ego-boost'
which enables them to be more efficacious or creative than they were at home
(Fechter 2008). For (young) women this might be particularly exciting, as Katrina
describes:

> It's because I am doing what I want to do ... [at home] there are people above
> me telling me what to do, and I will not necessarily agree. Whereas here, you are
> encouraged to take risks, try out new things, so nobody says anything if something
> goes wrong because there are so many disasters anyway! (Fechter 2008: 201).

The broader evidence reveals other women who also draw on the discourse of
'a sense of freedom' to describe the feeling of release that their migratory work
contexts have brought them, as compared to the gendered expectations and
constraints which exist in the work contexts of home. Whilst in the workplaces
of the West women can feel that they have to behave 'like men' at work, often by
adopting a 'male management' style in order to compete on equal terms (Halford
and Leonard 2001, Baxter 2008), some expatriate women suggest that migration to
new contexts has helped them to *change* their former (male) style and to develop
methods of working and relating to colleagues which are more individualistic.
Thus in contrast to Jim's rather macho style of management discussed in the last
chapter, this female director of a manufacturing company explains:

> I developed my own managerial style over time. First of all, when I started out in
> management, I tried to be more male. Looking back on myself in the early days, I

had to swear as good or as loud as the next guy. I had to be as aggressive as the next guy and I got on that way. It was when I went to Singapore and I became part of a totally different environment, where to swear would be so rude and insulting and they would be horrified by it. I looked inwards towards myself and ... changed my management style. First of all I dropped the habitual cursing: there is no benefit in women cursing and swearing. I became more structured ... (quoted in Linehan 2000: 96).

In my own research, Kim has felt that coming to work in Hong Kong has enabled her to step away from the limited range of gendered positions that had restricted her career at home. In her 50s, Kim is a very senior manager in one of the most prestigious hotels in Hong Kong. When I met her she had lived in the region for 15 years, coming out 'on spec' after redundancy from a university administration post of no real distinction. In Hong Kong, from the start, she was offered an exciting range of jobs which she felt she would never have been offered at home. She has held a wide variety of management and consultative positions in multinational organizations, working closely with Chinese and Asian businesses and colleagues. Her gender has certainly been no disadvantage in the landing of a succession of high level posts, supporting, perhaps, Selmer's (2001) research which found that expatriate women in Hong Kong were regarded by Chinese men as foreign first and women second. And not only have her gendered subjectivities become more ambivalent: so too have the ways in which she performs race and nationality. Her organizational experiences have been conducted in completely mixed racial environments, although most of the top management positions are held by Chinese. She presents a different and certainly more contemporary representation of white relations and identities to the men discussed in the previous chapter. Through her narrative, it is clear that she decries the attitudes and behaviour of traditional white British expatriates as '*very much an old guard inherited sort of situation*'.

Kim is keen to move on from the racially stereotypical behaviours of the colonial period and recognize that it is important to change behaviour and attitudes in the new context. She explains:

I don't think those kind of prejudices should remain any more ... And I think it's also about changing attitudes as well. I think there's a mutual respect in terms of we've both got work ethics. It's pretty similar I would say, people are prepared to work very hard here, they play hard, but they're prepared to work very hard because they know that's the path to success. So you can't afford to slack in Hong Kong ... I think a lot of it depends on attitude, and I think there has been a history in the past of a superior attitude, if you like, from the Brits which did not go down terribly well. I think that has changed as the Empire has faded, if you like, and the old guard has faded, but it hasn't been true for many years. Although there were some last vestiges, from long stayers, but no matter where you go in the world, you can't take that attitude and come and say "This is the way it's got to be done". Because you are essentially still a guest in that country. I'm a permanent resident, and I regard this as home, although Britain is still home as well, split personality, this is where my life is. But it does depend: if you are taking an open attitude I don't think there's a problem.

Kim has attempted to displace the 'old guard' colonialist identities, preferring the energizing relationships she has with local Hong Kong people. She has had to work hard, but Hong Kong has offered her great opportunities to develop and diversify her career:

> I don't know anywhere else in the world that it's this easy, because it a very fast integration process in Hong Kong. You are just absorbed as you arrive and you meet people very quickly and that openness of being willing to help gets you around very, very quickly indeed. So your initial contacts, you take every invitation that comes, because you want to establish yourself and then you narrow it down to people you really want to be with. But at least it spans right across the whole international spectrum.

This 'can-do' attitude is a finding which was also found by Willis and Yeoh's research with British women in China, many of whose feelings were encapsulated in the phrase 'Coming to China changed my life' (2008: 211). Willis and Yeoh (2008) note how time away from home can provide all skilled migrants opportunities for new experiences and challenges, but this may be particularly true for working women. Once again, migration is seen to open up a liminal space, where women may be freed from old ties and have the chance to adopt new subjectivities and values and stretch, or even jettison, the old. Indeed, for some women, the real excitement of migration may lie in the fact that it is no longer appropriate or necessary to draw on previously ascribed aspects of identity, as Kim explains:

> It's that kind of flexibility and taking the opportunity to move on and people are so positive about it. So it's a completely different ball game and a completely different mindset.

Challenging 'The Expatriate Woman'

Building or continuing careers in a posting overseas can also be difficult for many women however. Various factors often combine together to shape a context in which work and women are seen as almost mutually exclusive. Those following a partner overseas may find that, in expatriate contexts, their partner's employing organization has strong expectations that wives/partners do *not* work, seeing that they should be 'playing their part' in developing their husbands'/partners' careers (Coles and Fechter 2008). Added to this is the difficulty faced by women in actually finding a suitable job in a foreign context or negotiating complex bureaucracy in order to secure permission to work. Local laws governing immigration and work are often predicated on the gendered division of labour and as such will present hurdles for expatriate women hoping to enter the labour force. If they *do* manage to find employment, it is likely that they will experience downward mobility and deskilling (Kofman and Raghuram 2006), and most work is of a part time nature (Yeoh and Khoo 1998). Stereotypical perspectives of women's inferiority for leadership and discriminatory practices against women trying to attain higher managerial positions may also exist in the new context, and language barriers and lack of demand for their particular expertise may present further difficulties. Furthermore, if a couple move through a series of postings over several years, their itinerant lifestyle can make it even harder for women to establish or maintain any sense of career (Coles and Fechter 2008).

This lack of opportunity or support to work for expatriate women living in some circles means it can be very unusual for them to do so, and as such the gendered discourse of '*the expatriate woman*' outlined in Chapter 3 remains salient. This pushes women firmly back into the domestic and social contexts of the expatriate community to forge a life for themselves, and wives in particular are positioned as being:

> dedicated to supporting her husband and children during their stay abroad. She runs the household, manages their domestic staff, and occasionally entertains her husband's dinner partners. She is a member of a national expatriate women's association and attends their monthly coffee mornings. She is closely involved in the parents' group of the international school that her children attend and participates in charity work. She holds a professional qualification and worked for several years, but has given up her job in order to follow her husband to his posting, and to devote more time to family. She has found this transition not always easy, but a continuation of her career would have been difficult given the family's recent itinerant lifestyle (Fechter 2008: 193).

However those women who do manage to work can find that it offers a freedom from the gendered cloisters of expatriate life, where female subjectivities are so narrowly defined. So, whilst paid work may certainly not be looked for out of economic necessity, for, as we have seen, migration within the corporate context usually means upward social mobility in terms of housing and lifestyle at least, employment *does* represent a strategic means of coping socially and psychologically with the pressures of being in a new and often alien environment:

> Working keeps me occupied ... it makes me feel good about myself ... besides, it allows me to meet more people and get involved in the local way of life (Silka, 33 yrs, German) (Yeoh and Khoo 1998: 424).

Not only can work offer alternative femininities, but it can also provide a space from which to question and challenge the racialized discourses which abound within the expatriate community. In my own research, Penny has found that work has enabled her to resist what she sees as a key danger of white expatriate life: a sense of (misplaced) superiority. In her mid-50s, Penny is a proud working class woman, originally from the north of England. Although in Hong Kong she has had to construct her work identity through a mixture of poorly paid, semi-skilled jobs as well as voluntary work, it is clear that she has found the contexts of work to be essential in the construction of her migrant self. Not only has her involvement in work set her apart from other expatriate women, but it has provided coherence to the performances of her identity between the places of home and away. She centralizes the unpretentiousness of her home background in her talk, where she would have been expected to work and not to have any put-on 'airs and graces'. She sees that this biography has made it important for her *not* to use migration, whiteness, nationality or gender to 'indulge' herself with the privileges which expatriate life can bring. Indeed, Penny's talk of the 20 years she has spent in Hong Kong reveals a careful and deliberate positioning on the margins of the dominant expatriate community, such that she now describes herself with some pride as '*not your typical expat*':

> We never joined a club ... we never had a maid – I don't believe in that because
> I didn't want to spoil my children ... nor did I want to spoil myself.

Penny's making of gendered whiteness relies on *not* 'spoiling herself', contesting the subject positions of the 'typical expat wife' as well as the asymmetrical racialized relations which are structured through the use of domestic service (Pratt 1997; Walsh 2005). In contrast, she is proudly self-sufficient and has always worked: in a paid capacity as a secretary to the expatriate manager of a small organization, as well as voluntarily, working with underprivileged Chinese and Vietnamese refugee children. Having these jobs is clearly integral to her sense of self and the way in which she sees herself as different to the bulk of white expatriate women she meets:

> In the main, women come with partners, so you put your life on hold, you come
> in a supportive role ... I was glad to work – you meet more people and I like to
> contribute financially to the family purse. I've met a lot of women who never
> bothered, but I'm not that sort of person who can sit about, I feel an obligation
> to be part of something.

Her experiences of working along Chinese people in her voluntary work has also had the result of destabilizing her views of Britishness and opening her eyes to other ways of doing things, outside of both her home in Britain and the expatriate community. Unlike David, who we saw in the last chapter, Penny reveals a willingness to step outside her cultural safety net and learn other ways of doing things:

> My schooling told me that Britain was the greatest country in the world – but you come to the Far East and you realize that there are many ways of dealing with problems: Britain is not necessarily the best democracy. It is changing now and I worry, but they are bringing in more Chinese ideas, and these are more for the common good; these suit my psychology.

Kate has also found that work has provided her with a buffer against the narrowed performances of the white expatriate community and a space in which other identities can be articulated. She has lived and worked in Hong Kong for nearly 25 years, and reveals an articulate awareness of the ways in which the gendered discourses of British whiteness have contained her life. However, in the new postcolonial context, she feels that at last these are starting to be dismantled, and she is much happier now that there has been political change.

Arriving in Hong Kong in her mid-20s, an inner-city teacher 'travelling' the world, Kate met and married a well-positioned Government employee. Her identity at home had been constructed through the political discourses of socialism, feminism and anti-racism, all of which had been central to her work and career, and she thus found it hard to position herself solely within the discourse of the good 'expatriate wife'. In particular, the version which was expected of her had seemingly changed little from the historic discourses of British colonialism and imperialism which had long dominated Government circles:

> It's very tight, and as your husband rises up into power, you become more and more concerned about behaving yourself, because you don't want to rock the boat … for that reason I kept my maiden name for a long long time …

She was very aware of the subjective constraints on her, and felt under constant scrutiny:

> If you're in a society in which the oil of the machinery is still geared around the cocktail party and the dinner parties and the lunches … then there is a tendency for people to feel they have to watch their back …

However her work in a Chinese International School has enabled her to position herself simultaneously within the alternative discourses of cultural diversity and equality which the culture of the school prioritizes. Just as was the case in her previous job in London, her daily working life involves her in taking a stand against instances of racism and sexism, and this has spilled out into other aspects of her life:

A well-known Indian journalist wanted to interview me. So I met him [at a colonial club for British women]. We were sitting talking; when the worst kind of expatriate woman came over and told us we couldn't conduct business there. The journalist immediately got up to leave, hugely embarrassed. But he had forgotten his briefcase – so I went back to pick it up. I then accused this woman of being a racist. Three days later I received a letter terminating my membership of the club ...

As Kate attempted to negotiate a more radical identity in her career, based on alternative notions of gender and race, alongside her subjectivity of expatriate wife, her identities became fractured. However, it was in the context of the politically active, multicultural environment of work that she felt most comfortable, and as such she now spends a large proportion of her daily life there. Work has provided Kate with a transformative space in which she has been able to 'lose' those aspects of her whiteness and Britishness which her gendered role as the wife of a Government employee demanded that she perform. However, she feels that things have improved significantly since the handover. This has led to changes in the power of the traditional discourse of the British expatriate, as well as changes in the meanings of whiteness, and its relationship to work:

I am certainly more at ease living here now that I was prior to 1997. I didn't like personally being apparently a representative of colonialism, I didn't like that at all, and I found that quite a heavy burden. Now that I'm on an equal footing, it's really nobody else's business why I'm here; I'm here to work, not to have any kind of special favours.

Other women I talked to in Hong Kong shared Penny and Kate's concerns with the ways in which gender, race, nationality are framed within expatriate subjectivities. Tina's case further reinforces the importance of class in this intersection, in that she *must* work in order to support herself rather than this being a matter of identity or lifestyle. Now a British relocations manager for an American company based in Hong Kong, she has for many years been neither incorporated nor partnered, and as such has found making a living for herself a pretty hard graft. Tina came out 'on spec', a young, working class, divorced woman for whom migration was a way out of disappointing personal circumstances. Her early days were clearly very different to those of men such as Jim, Harry or Rob, or women such as the expat girls, buffered as they are by their different combinations of accommodation packages, secure jobs and contacts. The way in which Tina had to very consciously manage herself in order to find work reminds us that the subject positions of young white men and women in the expatriate context can be very different, and that opportunities are not always available for renegotiating gendered and raced expectations:

> I couldn't get a job. I was very naïve and gave off that appearance of being a bit green: I came in with long curly hair, permed, and I tried to look a little bit older. It was only after I got this job that you find out it's very different.

Now, however, after ten years of working at middle management level in various MNCs, Tina feels embedded in Hong Kong life. Yet her position within the organizations she has worked for has always remained vulnerable: not for her are the privileged expatriate conditions or easy lifestyle. She has been made redundant a couple of times, but has survived, and perhaps because of this her talk reveals her keenness to negotiate a position for herself *against* that of the privileged British/expatriate/wife. She attempts to disassociate herself from these, embarrassed by the blinkered behaviour of many expatriates in Hong Kong. She has a nuanced abhorrence of expatriate life and its diversities, and this escalates when she considers the gendered subject positions available:

> Ex pat wives! ... Husband's got his job, kids are in the school, it's the rainy season and she's left floundering in an apartment [so you get] "Oh, my tap's broken" or the prima donnas: "I want a maid here in fifteen minutes!"... some people think it is all for them ... [I think] you're in a foreign country, you bend to the way the country runs.

In addition to her resistance to the sorts of expatriate performativities which dominate the spaces of non-work, Tina also purports to detest the traditional (male) expatriate ways of behaving *in* work contexts. Top of her list here is the British Chamber of Commerce: 'the most stuffy, old fashioned, pompous people you have ever met!' However, nevertheless, like many expatriates, she spends a lot of her time involved in the networking activities organized by such institutions. Indeed, membership of the various 'Chambers of Commerce' and 'Business Councils' peopled by the expatriate communities of (in the main) Britain, America, Australia and New Zealand is a key part of daily business life for most expatriates, and it is here that much of the 'doing of whiteness' is done (see also Beaverstock 2002). Many corporate employees have their memberships paid for them by their organizations, who then expect them to attend functions regularly in order to interact with other expatriates as well as locals, building contacts and generating business. This sort of network formation is seen to be 'vital for the success of their expatriation, and transnational elite status' (Beaverstock 2002: 533), and as such is further undertaken through the pub and bar culture and sporting activities. Whilst these spaces and activities clearly have gender connotations, and can be quite problematic for women at home, many single women find they are able to use these to their advantage in expatriate contexts. Here they soon get used to the more 'upfront' style of expatriate life, where it may be more acceptable to go into a bar, start talking to strangers and give them a business card than it was at home (Willis and Yeoh 2008).

Tina needs to network as she is quite vulnerable in her employment status, having always been employed on 'local conditions'. Unlike her (male) American bosses who are on full expatriate terms, she knows that as an expatriate woman in the Hong Kong of today she is increasingly marginal in terms of employability: 'Today I wouldn't get a job – if you're not Chinese speaking, forget it'. Her response to this is to attempt to position herself as a local, away from the stereotypical short term corporate expat. She claims she is seen differently by her Chinese colleagues:

> Me … I'm an ex-pat in name only. When you see an expat, most people now look at it as people working for large multi-nationals being given packages and relocation and housing allowances. … I wouldn't class myself as an expat here … you get your levels. [The Chinese] look at me as a Hong Konger: I don't get treated as a British person ... I understand Cantonese, I don't speak it, but I understand it. I know the customs, so they treat me as a long-term expat … Now, my immediate boss, he's been in Asia for a long time, but he hasn't got a clue here in HK, so they will look at him as an American: (mimics) "I'm an American, it should be like it is at home in America … I'm an expat, you will jump".

Tina sees that she is attempting to challenge what it means to be a white expatriate in Hong Kong. She is keen to emphasize this is not always about privilege and racial homogeneity, and that the differences between expatriates need to be acknowledged. However, at the same time, Tina's talk about her behaviour at work reveals that her attempts to position herself against other white expatriates and incorporate more sensitivity to Chinese ways of doing things into her daily working life are uneven and incomplete. As was the case with both Jim and David, she still holds an underlying view that the doing of work 'properly' is about using white/Western working methods, and that Chinese people can be 'difficult' to work with:

> I'd go in and give [my Chinese boss] face, "yes, yes, yes, you're brilliant, yes, yes, yes", and then go and do what *I* wanted to … It's very different if you've got a Western management or Chinese management. Chinese management is all face, you can't stand up and say "Oh I think we should do it this way" … but I did and that's why I lost my other job …

However, she also has a sense of the difference *between* her Chinese colleagues, and finds it is far easier to work with 'Western Chinese', towards whom she has to make little compromise:

> The staff here tend to be very un-Chinese: you get a group that are very much more geared to Western people, so they tend to be more on that guideline, rather

than if I went into a very small company and they are very Chinesey, for want of a better word.

Although Tina is keen to position herself within a more local subjectivity, her talk reveals ambivalence and slippage therefore. Her position as a working woman enables her to challenge the traditional feminine subjectivities on offer to her, but, in contradiction, her continued attachment to Western (white) working practices and sense of her own rightness means that she is unable to sustain a coherent place for herself outside of the discourse of British expatriate. As much as she might think differently, the ways in which she works mean that she is, in some times and spaces at least, still 'doing whiteness' in traditional ways. New places can thus help to challenge old identities, but the extent to which expatriates *do* re-negotiate the raced and gendered aspects of their identities is highly complex and far from stable.

The Blurring of Work and Leisure

In expatriate life the 'separate' spheres of public and private often take on a new shape and meaning, and the spaces of 'work' and 'leisure' can become very blurred. Organizations may have greater expectations of their employees to socialize and entertain other colleagues when they are 'in town', and the popularity of confined expatriate spaces such as 'the Club' means that leisure and sporting pursuits may be well be undertaken with colleagues and clients. There is also an intensity to expatriate social life, in which discourses supporting the 24/7 culture of work – as something that should never go away or be forgotten – are constantly at play. For example, in Willis and Yeoh's research in Shanghai Jinni found:

> There's such opportunity to meet people at different functions. 'Cos in some ways our friends out here, you're not always working but you're always networking ... Whereas in the UK if you go out at night you don't talk about work or you don't do work, whereas here people are much more, kind of, their work's on their mind ... And there's a lot of the name card giving ... At night you could be out in a bar and you're giving out your name cards and taking a few in, so you tend to meet a lot of new people as well that way (Jinny, in Willis and Yeoh 2008: 218).

Willis and Yeoh (2008) note that the women expatriates talked about this in terms of something they would never dream of doing in the UK. This contrasts with the way the men presented these activities as a regular part of their working lives *regardless* of location. For working women especially therefore, the broader contexts of migrant work may offer new and exciting opportunities for identity making.

In many expatriate contexts specific organizations also exist for working/ executive women. These are specifically designed to foster and merge business and social contacts, not only between expatriate women but also with local women. Hong Kong has a woman-only club, for example: the Helena May, established by Lady May the wife of the Governor Sir Henry May in 1916. This acts as a meeting place for women and women's organizations, as well as promoting charitable events and causes. It hosts a range of female-oriented events such as lectures by women of status in the community and evenings focusing on fashion, flowers or food. However, whilst supposedly having a non-racialized 'face', these organizations can in practice be very 'white'. As Fechter (2008) also notes in her research in Jakarta, the events and lectures are usually white/Western in focus and any claim of 'cosmopolitanism' is pretty ambiguous. And it was from just such a club, moreover, that Kate's Indian journalist friend was asked to leave.

The Challenge of Not Working

The discussion so far has revealed that work may provide a context within which women can renegotiate the gendered and raced expectations by which they are positioned. Although I have shown that the making of such 'new identities' may be far from coherent, opportunities can be seen to exist for challenging normative performances. If a woman is partnered however, the same liminality may not exist within the contexts of her partner's organization. Men are usually seen to be the 'key migrant', and male partners' organizations can exert considerable influence over the 'trailing spouse', as the rich literature on 'The Incorporated Wife' has shown (Callan and Ardener 1984, Coles and Fechter 2008). The working woman might find herself multiply and simultaneously positioned by both 'new' and 'old' identities therefore; as a competent professional in the context of her own work, but as a domestic support mechanism by her partner's organization. We have seen how stereotypes can abound within expatriate organizations and communities, especially for the wives of the well-paid men who work for multinational corporations such as banks and finance. From the 'Jumeira Jane' in Dubai (Walsh 2008) to the 'tai tai' in Hong Kong (Leonard 2008), the image of the typical expatriate wife is of someone with plenty of time and money on her hands to devote to leisure pursuits such as shopping, the beauty parlour, expensive lunches and the occasional game of tennis. Because these stereotypes have endured over time, they appear to be more stable and as such can provide powerful discourse structures within the local expatriate society (Mills 2005). They are also iterative, ceaselessly repeated in the highly gendered 'how to' guides which abound in expatriate spaces and on the 'expat' websites. These feed expatriate women with advice on how to behave, how to look, where to shop and where to lunch: but rarely on how to get a job. Smaller or newly established expatriate communities may be particularly demanding of their members, in order to foster a sense of cohesion and of a (white) 'us'. Within powerful multinational contexts, conformity to group expectations and their boundaries are also seen to be particularly important, and it may take substantial amounts of courage for these wives to reject or challenge the dominant subjectivities on offer to them (Eyben 2008). Any sort of deviance, such as wanting to develop a career, or have a life away from the organization's bubble, may be seen as a threat to the accepted performances of gendered and classed whiteness by which the organization is understood to work and be successful.

For many expatriate women, work may be seen as just too difficult an option, and their 'new' identity may become one in which the traditional subject positions and performances of gender are reconfirmed. Embarking on a posting can mean therefore that gender becomes reconfigured and even magnified. What might initially have been small differences in income and career prospects between husbands and wives may become dramatically widened by the migration process and the giving up of paid employment by the woman. Yeoh and Khoo's (1998) study in Singapore found that 81 per cent of expatriate women had been engaged in paid work in their own countries, but only 44.8 per cent had then secured a footing in the local labour force. At first, some women may experience a honeymoon period in which the temporary escape from the hectic work routine of home is enjoyed:

> I had no problems giving up my job ... it [the move] was like a pleasant extended vacation, and I would have been silly to fret over it! I was looking forward to the time I would have to catch up on all the things I wanted to do (Mindy, 42 yrs American, quoted in Yeoh and Khoo 1998: 422).

> It has allowed me to think about myself, what I want to do with my life, what I like doing ... I've enrolled on a homeopathy course, and I do quite a bit of charity work ... I may do tennis but at the moment I've been too busy. I do a lot of shopping ... spend time at the club, I've joined a choir: or I'm at the hairdressers! ... I am content (Cathy, 45 yrs British, Leonard 2008: 52).

In contrast however, others feel lost and overwhelmed by the initial experience of having a large amount of time on their hands (Hardill and MacDonald 1998, Yeoh and Khoo 1998, Coles and Fechter 2008), and the research reveals how a discourse of *boredom and isolation* is common in narratives of early experiences. This period can be an unhappy and lonely one, and the adjustment to a life of not working is not easy: 'I felt very bored because I'd always been used to working and being independent' (quoted in Hardill and MacDonald 1998: 26). Indeed, with a spouse who was working very long hours, this respondent 'got to the stage when I was so bored I thought I would go mad' (ibid: 26). Forster (1996) notes an increased use of alcohol, drug and cigarette use amongst stay at home expatriate women. Similarly, one of Walsh's respondents graphically reveals the tedium of the early days for white women:

> You've got that typical thing when couples first arrive and they're staying in a hotel or hotel apartments until they find a villa. You wake up at the crack of dawn when your husband leaves for work and then time stretches out in front of you, empty, and you're still waiting twelve hours later for him to get back. If you've

got kids, you usually arrive in the summer before the start of term and it's awful. You might spend the entire day stuck in the hotel room because it's too hot to go out and you don't know anyone, and you don't have anywhere to go to, and you don't have anything to do. It's awful. The men are always straight into work so they're sorted ... (Walsh 2008: 75).

Inevitably, as the reality of the new life starts to hit home, women start to think of working:

I wondered what I could do with all the time on my hands, and I considered looking for a part time job (Mindy, in Yeoh and Khoo 1998: 422).

However, we have seen that finding work is not always easy. Inevitably, as an adaptive strategy, expatriate women often turn to the diverse groups which may exist within the local expatriate community: anything from bridge clubs, flower arranging classes, bowling leagues and volunteer agencies; to mitigate the displacement of life abroad. However Hindman (2008) notes that some of these local social organizations may merely result in contributing to the expatriate woman's anxieties and fears, confining her even more to the realms of expatriate life. With their prescriptions of what they should and should not do: 'don't go there, don't wear this, don't do that...': newly arrived expatriate women may be offered nuggets of advice which both reinforce traditional gendered identities and performances as well as their sense of racialized otherness.

As we have seen however, it must also be acknowledged that, with the gendered changes in international labour markets, it is increasingly not only the woman who is the trailing spouse. There is a growing band of 'trailing husbands' for whom the new life of migration may also be difficult. Like women, they must also face up to the 'culture shock' of life in the new country, and may also have to deal with a loss of status and work-based networks and identities. In some cases they, too, may need to meet the challenge of adapting to a new role as homemaker. Cohen (1996) argues that trailing husbands may have an even more difficult time adjusting than trailing wives, as there may be even less support for them in the new location: it is not so easy for them to join in with flower arranging or tennis. Indeed, Moore (2002) found that male spouses can experience a more difficult period of adjustment because they are often left out of the informal 'wives network' which can serve an important social support function, as well as a communication mechanism for information about the host country. Support groups and clubs organize activities for 'expatriate wives' but many have yet to recognize the need to cater for 'expatriate husbands':

Even in cases of apparent role reversal, the social infrastructure undergirding skilled migration-social norms, expectations and facilities – continue to entrench gender roles and identities along well worn paths (Yeoh and Khoo 1998: 421).

This chapter has examined further the ways in which the contexts of work can be critical to the makings of gendered and raced identities in expatriate life. Expatriate women's everyday lives are framed by particular and powerful discourses of gendered whiteness, which mean that the lives of many of today's expatriate women retain strong connections with femininities of the colonial period. In much of contemporary expatriate life there is a 'continuing dominance of the male order' and the appropriation of apparently male values or interests by women reveals the 'powerful and reinforced homology between what is socially valuable and what is male' (Moore 1986: 184–185 quoted in Mills 2005: 69). However for the postcolonial expatriate, work can offer a resource by which gendered versions of whiteness may be challenged: a liminal space from which to contest the limits of the subject positions which dominate the expatriate community. Whiteness/gender are ever in process therefore, being complicated and multiplied through the ways in which working women are attempting to re-position themselves and re-draw the boundaries around their lives. The ways in which these subjectivities of gender and race are further intersected by class, ethnicity and age broadens further the heterogeneity of the contemporary 'expatriate woman'. However, whilst women are contesting gendered expatriate subject positions with more or less coherence, the challenge to the privileges of whiteness remains as yet uneven. Race, together with class and gender, are not only identities achieved through *language*: through what these women say, but also through *practice*: through their work and social relations and performances. Whilst this chapter has revealed some instances of challenge to what these mean, in terms of material effects, the success of this challenge is still far from constant.

Chapter 7
Expatriate Places and Spaces

This chapter examines the ways in which expatriates' negotiations of their new migrant identities occur *in place*: through the particular places and spaces of their work organizations and the distinctive ways in which these connect with the broader landscapes in which they are set, both local and international. New identities at work are constructed not on the head of a pin, but within a *material* context – a spatial and physical architecture and landscape that is integrally entwined in the productions of the social actions, relations and identities of organizational members. History will have already played a part in defining the extent and manner of racial and gender segregation here (Holloway 2007), but the new expatriate will then bring their own biography to bear in their negotiation of this. Further, this material landscape is also an *imagined* context. History again, for example in terms of a past history of colonialism, together with personal history, will play a critical part in the ways in which the nation-state and new workplace are imagined, constructed and understood, and the diverse ways in which individual expatriates position themselves within this conceptual framework. Links will be also retained with the material and imagined landscapes of 'home': at both the organizational scale of the 'head office' as well as the local and national scales of urban/rural geographies. Thus whilst the contemporary fascination with processes of flow and mobility of labour in a globalized world often posits the 'end of place' and the arrival of non-place, I, along with others (Cresswell 2004, Savage et al. 2005, Conradson and Latham 2005b, Dyb and Halford 2009) would argue that this is certainly *not* the case and that, in contrast, migrant identities, space and place are highly contingent. This is especially the case in the new contexts of work where 'people are creating places at all scales and everywhere in a myriad of ways' (Cresswell 2004: 82).

This chapter thus develops the exploration of the *how* of whiteness by giving attention to the ways in which space and place are integral to the production and performance of white skilled migrant identities. As I noted at the end of the last chapter, whiteness is not only achieved through language – speech and talk – it is also performed in practice, embodied and lived in and through the places and spaces of lives. Part of learning to *be* white is to learn the specific places *of* whites, as well as how to perform within these in ways which produce and maintain power, distance and authority over other people in other places (Kothari 2006, Meier 2006, Frankenberg 1993). The social category of whiteness, as well as the individual, *also* makes material and imagined connections between spaces and places, such that, as we will see later in this chapter, an office in Hong Kong can be re-configured and re-imagined as an office in London; and it makes *virtual* connections with the white spaces of home by regular telephone and email contact.

In this way, whiteness is constituted *in* particular spaces and places, but also, through performance and activity, it contributes *to* the construction of those places and spaces as white: 'what begins as an undifferentiated space becomes place as we get to know it better and endow it with value' (Tuan 1977: 6). The inscription of meaning in places is therefore *intertwined* with the performances which take place there and the people who are making these. Place and space do not therefore merely provide a backdrop for the negotiation of raced and gendered identities, but are central resources in the construction of these, and in our work selves particularly (Halford and Leonard 2006). Further, and perhaps more critically, space is also implicated in the construction and structuring of our relations with others, and, as Gregory and Urry put it: 'Spatial structure is now seen not merely as an arena in which social life unfolds, but rather as a medium through which social relations are produced and reproduced' (1985: 3). Space is thus central to the production, organization and distribution of identity, race and also power (Foucault 1980, Shome 2003, Doel 2000).

Conceptualizing Place

This approach to conceptualizing place draws on contemporary geographical understandings which stress that the grounded locales of everyday life are produced by a range of social, economic and cultural processes from the very local to the global (Massey 1994, Cresswell 2004). As Massey (1994) argues:

> the identity of a place is formed out of social interrelations, and a proportion of those interrelations – larger or smaller, depending on the time and on the place – will stretch beyond that "place" itself. In that sense, if social space is conceived of as constructed out of the vast, intricate complexity of social processes and social reactions at all scales from the local to the global, then a "place" is best thought of as a particular part of, a particular moment in, the global network of those social relations and understandings (1994: 115).

The identity of a place then is also necessarily unfixed, and places are entangled with the different meanings and images which have occurred and are still occurring over time, as well as the way these might be conceptualized in the future. Places may undergo major shifts and restructurings, or they may be more subtly tinkered with and re-shaped in the course of everyday routines, practices and imaginations. However this particularity cannot be understood through a perspective focused solely on the local: the global world is always constituted in and through the local, and a place is made distinctive through the specificity and uniqueness of its interrelations with the outside world (Massey 1994). This specificity can be understood through an analysis first, of the particularity of the social interactions which intersect at that location, and of what people make of these in their interpretations and in their lives, and, second, of the fact that the meeting of those social relations at that location in itself produces new effects and new social processes. In other words, place is where encounters happen: and through these, important connections are made between the identity of place and constructions of personal subjectivities. As we are 'always multiple and contradictory subjects, inhabitants of a diversity of communities ... constructed by a variety of discourses, and precariously and temporarily sutured at the intersection of those positions' (Mouffe 1988: 44), we bring multiplicity to places and with this help in turn to produce the multiplicity of place (Massey 1994). If places are conceptualized in this way, taking account of the construction of subjects within them which, in turn, produce the place, then the identity of place is '*a double articulation*' (Massey 1994: 118) of both person and place. This is especially interesting perhaps when we think about the movements of migrants across borders: their 'displacement' can be seen as occurring between contexts which are already complex and dynamic constructions.

This mobile view of place also points to inevitable contradictions and conflicts which will occur 'on the ground' (ibid: 118) in terms of the different meanings attached to place. The multiplicity of place identities may not always happily co-exist. Edward Said (1978) shows this with his discussion of the Orient, in part a product of the European (imperialistic) imagination (Meier 2007):

> Just as none of us is outside or beyond geography, none of us is completely
> free from the struggle over geography. That struggle is complex and interesting
> because it is not only about soldiers and cannons but also about ideas, about
> forms, about images and imaginings (Said 1994: 7).

Similarly, Cresswell (2004) cites the example of the colonialist Vancouver, whose work it was to map the coast and name it as he travelled – making it a place of empire. 'Naming is one of the ways space can be given meaning and become place' (p. 9). Vancouver was confused by the weaving movements of natives in the sea around his boat: while the colonialists looked at the sea and saw blank space, the natives clearly saw a meaningful place. 'Two world views were in collision: and the poverty of white accounts of these canoe journeys reflect the colonialists' blindness to the sea' (Raban 1999: 103 in Cresswell 2005: 9). Clear-cut and confidently monolithic distinctions about places struggle to be retained therefore. And, in today's time of global migration flows, we are increasingly witnessing a 'third worldling' of the 'first' and vice versa (Shome 2003).

Struggles over meaning are as true of workplaces as any other place, and organizations, like seas, cities or local suburbs, should also be seen as places constituted by a divergent range of meanings, spatial scales and power relationships. The links between the local, the national and the international can sometimes be clearly seen in multi-national organizations, but this approach to place shows how it is analytically rich to see *all* organizations in this way. *All* organizations are made up of complex configurations of multiple, distinctive and differentiated *spaces*, each offering different potential for the negotiation of identities. Some of these spaces are appropriated by white expatriates for particular purposes, and layout, architecture and decor may be used to communicate and support messages about status and difference (Halford and Leonard 2006). Spaces are thus often physical representations of discursive constructions, and the ways in which the spaces of workplaces both constitute and are constituted by *racialized* (and gendered) discourses will be a consequence of the ongoing and complex interplay of these operating at a range of spatial and temporal scales. In other words, the racial and gender dynamics operating at broader levels in both contemporary and historical moments will play themselves out at the level of the particular work context and, in the negotiations that will result, workplaces are made and re-made. In keeping with the theoretical framework of this book therefore, 'place' is thus interesting as both the *cause* and *effect* of working life (Dyb and Halford 2009): at the *macro*-level of structure and discourse, and the ways it positions people, as well as the *micro*-level of the individuals negotiating it. At both levels however, it has to be constituted and reconstituted through reiterative social practice: made and remade on a daily basis (Cresswell 2004, Halford and Leonard 2006).

I now turn to explore these contingencies as they apply to processes of race and identity making more closely, and to look at the ways in which the places and spaces of organizational and working life both position expatriates and their colleagues as well provide a range of resources through which they may negotiate their racialized selves. To do this I will look at spatial practices, performances and imaginings within a range of (intertwined) spatial scales to show how race and power are produced in, articulated through and mapped onto place and space (Kothari 2006).

Global Spatial Practices

Expatriates make strategic use of the spaces of the globe in their work practices. They continue to use travel and migration as a resource in the building of their careers and work identities, despite improvements in information technology and high costs (Beaverstock and Boardwell 2000). Over the course of their careers, diplomats, for example, will work up from countries which are constructed as 'peripheral' to those which are seen as more 'centre stage'. Similarly, employees of multi-national corporations will change firms and workplaces across borders as an important way of accumulating the social, organizational and geographic capital necessary for a successful career. Some senior executives and scholars believe that international assignments are one of the most powerful experiences in shaping the perspectives and capabilities of effective global leaders (Stahl et al. 2002). Particular cities are seen as especially important 'escalators': routes to distinction and a marker of 'having made it' (Fielding 1991, Scott 2006). For example, Meier's research with German bankers reveals that they regard London as 'the navel of the world' (2007: 123) and for them working there was seen as evidence of personal achievement and advancement: 'the image of the globally important and successful centre of control, the City, is transferred to the own self'

(Meier 2007: 123). Paris is similarly viewed by some British expatriates (Scott 2006). Beaverstock's (2005) research with inter-company transferees in New York, another high prestige location, found it was seen as being towards the top of the escalator: 40 per cent had lived or worked in other financial centres such as Bangkok, Singapore, Geneva and Frankfurt, with either current or former employers before getting there. This transnational experience, involving both physical movement and virtual communication, was highly beneficial to their career path trajectory, both with respect to promotion within the firm and as regards the intellectual and social capital they accumulated through their business interactions. As one respondent commented:

> if you get someone from an overseas office you're getting someone who's already travelled and also knows the ways of the firm and it also brings someone who's got some contacts as well as experience. It helps push globalization (2005: 257).

Similarly, a global 'cosmopolitan' flexibility is important for development professionals, for whom technical skills gained across nations are valorized over embeddedness in one country:

> You don't get promoted in the [World] Bank if you have only worked in one or two countries, however long your association might have been. You need to gain experience of many different places otherwise they say, "oh he only knows Mozambique" (quoted in Kothari 2006: 248).

Indeed, development and foreign service professionals are often esteemed for their *resistance* to becoming familiar with one particular geographic area. Kothari argues that this is motivated by the imperatives of a globalizing discourse of development, whereby *issues* and *policies* rather than *places* become more important:

> The rolling out globally of neoliberal ideologies of privatization and trade liberalization and participation, map a unitary language and process that is interpreted through the practices and techniques of western trained advisors (Kothari 2006: 248).

However this view of totally 'ungrounded' and 'de-territorialized' transmigrants has recently been challenged by scholars who wish to reinsert notions of 'settlement' into the debate, and stress the duality of mobility *and* stasis (Featherstone et al. 2007). In the main, the organizational rationale for overseas postings is about the ability to transfer specific skills into the local workplace (Beaverstock 2005), and it may make little business sense to move employees from one region to another every year or so. Rather, the need may be for someone to develop 'local expertise' within a particular area. Multi-national and development organizations alike remap the globe into postcolonial spaces such as 'Asia-Pacific', 'The Middle East' or 'Africa', within which expatriates are expected to accumulate specialized and localized skills, such as nurturing and developing relationships with clients. This is particularly the case for expatriates working in professions such as law, construction and finance, for which frequent and local travel within a region may become a key part of their working life. Expatriates working for these sectors in Hong Kong for example, will usually also travel frequently to other global cities in the region such as Beijing, Singapore, Kuala Lumpar, Jakarta, Bangkok and Tokyo. This is seen to be important for local knowledge accumulation and career development, but also for global knowledge transfer, the engendering of an overall 'organizational spirit' and projecting the image of the organization into the global arena: an activity which is also seen to be good for attracting clients at home (Beaverstock 2002). These 'hyper-mobile' routes and journeys also help to 'localize global knowledge' and enable expatriates to learn the 'tricks of the trade' through network interaction with work colleagues, both local and experienced expatriate.

For younger expatriate professionals, such as those from South Africa, New Zealand and Australia, spending time in certain cities such as London plays a particular role in the transnational imagination, being attractive not only because of their labour markets but also because of wider social and cultural affordances. London for example offers the opportunity to gain important professional experience which can be difficult to access in, say, the Antipodes. However for others, rather than migrating to *improve* career opportunities, well paid, secure professional jobs are *left behind* for temporary ones, which may actually be a downwards move. For these privileged whites, confident of their ongoing and sustainable social capital, migration is seen to offer a break from the routines and stresses of work and a chance to enjoy new places. This is a time for tending careers rather than progressing them, and cities such as London can offer a vital context in which to locate this 'project of the self' (Rose 1999). As a legacy of their colonial ties, there are few language difficulties for white Africans, Australians or New Zealanders, and their qualifications are recognized. It is also a 'world city' offering a wealth of possibilities in a dynamic and multicultural social milieu whilst not being too 'experimental' (Conradson and Latham 2005b). Critically however, this is done *not* by mixing with the British, but through sustained friendship networks with other white Commonwealth members also living in the city. For these transmigrants, their friendship networks from home are picked up and then re-enacted and reproduced in London: in fact, migrating can be a way to *remain* socially embedded. Further, Conradson and Latham (2005b) argue that mobility and travel are key aspects of (white) New Zealander identity. Since settler times it has been seen as an important strategy for social advancement and security, embodying 'certain ideals of personal autonomy, resourcefulness, adventure and self-expansion' (Conradson and Latham 2005b: 299). For New Zealanders, gaining 'OE' (Overseas Experience) is a key part of the *doing* of whiteness.

In their different ways therefore, global and regional space are thus seen as key resources for the careers *and* personal biographies of expatriates, which depend on travel and the building of networks and connections across the globe. They are also important resources for organizational identities: whilst territories can no longer be claimed politically, they still can be claimed within the organizational imagination. And through the movement of expatriates across these imagined spaces of organizational reach, neo-colonial subjectivities of 'ownership' and control are constructed: '*I'm in charge of Europe and Africa*' one (white) expatriate recently informed me with some pride.

This (subjective) sense of ownership of space is by no means exclusive to the employees of multi-national corporations. In my research in Hong Kong, those working in public sector contexts also revealed the continuities of colonization through their relationship with the landscape. For example, in Chapter 5 we met Rob, an officer with the Hong Kong Police. In the ways in which he describes the neighbourhoods that he polices, his narrative reveals the ongoing interplay of the discourse of British (colonial) expatriate with that of *control and surveillance* which I discussed in Chapter 2. In his talk, Rob positions himself within that long historical involvement of whiteness in the carving up of foreign landscapes, and then maintaining the subsequent cartographies through the doing of spatial control:

> The Police Tactical Unit dealt with illegal immigration and you had a system of "touch base", as the British Colony sits on the arse – excuse my language – of China. Hong Kong has thrived from illegal immigrants coming from China after massive upheavals, but you always had a steady flow of illegal immigration from China, always. We used to have a Holding Centre whereby all the illegal immigrants caught the day previously were put into this Centre and we would then go along and put them in lorries and they were taken to the border at Man Kam To. ... Your duties were to patrol these vehicles so as not to let any immigrants escape. They used to come across the waters, on the trains and simply anyway they could come ... they would even come across the oyster beds – high tides, shark attacks and low tides coming across the mud flats and the oysters where they would cut their feet and be lacerated by the time they got across. They would still do it, however, as they saw Hong Kong as a haven paved with gold.

In a similar vein, Meier notes how, in Singapore, expatriate whiteness is about 'making geography and bringing order to a previously disordered area' (2006: 140). Through the demand for German supermarkets and Swiss butchers, for example, space is appropriated and reconfigured. '*Creating spatial order*' is still a critical part of whiteness, and in the ways in which expatriates use the city and exert influence over it, white spaces are formed, power is mobilized and colonialist subjectivities extended.

Constructing Expatriate Space

For many expatriates, when not travelling, much of their working lives are spent in 'global cities'. According to Sassen's (1991) definition, global cities have as many ties to and networks with other cities around the world as to their host countries, if not more so (Moore 2007). Within these cities, expatriates can also be seen to use space in a racialized and ethnicized way, as, just as in colonial times, their lives are often disembedded from the local and indigenous life of the city (Kothari 2006, Castells 2000, Meier 2006). Whilst global labour brings highly specific knowledge, skills and networks *into* the city, corporations and expatriates also *use* the city as a resource to reproduce their cosmopolitan interests and practices (Beaverstock 2002). Castells has argued that the activities of global elites carve up the city into business, residential and leisure oriented spaces, wherein dominant functions are clustered into 'carefully segregated spaces' (2000: 446). These 'design spatial forms aimed at unifying the symbolic environment of the elite around the world' (2000: 446). Similarly, Hannerz has noted that it is the transnational relationships of people that 'play major parts in the making of contemporary world cities' (1996: 129) and he suggests that, as many of these elites are from elsewhere, because they have 'hyper-mobile international careers and cosmopolitan cultural distinctiveness' (Beaverstock 2002: 526), they 'stand a better chance than others to extend their habitats from the world cities into their other locations' (Hannerz 1996: 139). However, this has not always been recognized theoretically. The 'world city hypothesis' (Friedman 1986, Sassen 1988, 1991, 1994) emphasizes the rise of the *low-waged* immigrant sector as being crucial in the making of global cities, yet the role of *professional* migrants is downplayed (Beaverstock and Boardwell 2000). Yet it is *these* transnational migrants who have a high degree of 'sociospatial agency' (Smith 1999), and who, together with the intensified activities of international companies, also bring about the establishment of particular transnational social spaces within cities (Pries 2001). Transnational elites thus not only bring flows into and through the city,

> but the territorialization of their cosmopolitan practices and discourses are deeply embedded in specific transnational space, which are at intersecting points of particular corporate, capital, technological, information and cultural lines of flow, and connections (Beaverstock 2002: 560).

Despite the fluidity and transience of many transnational elites therefore, their presence affects the global city in the generation of a multiplicity of 'contact zones'. Yeoh and Willis (2005b) argue that because of the ephemeral and unconsolidated nature of their 'presence' and the strong sense of connectivities with 'elsewhere', these contact zones are differently inflected compared to the more permanent, stable, often historically rooted presences forged by longer term migrants, or even by more recent lower-skilled migrants who arrive in much larger numbers and therefore constitute a stronger bodily presence.

This creation of spatial divisions within cities is nothing new of course. King (1990) describes the dual city in colonial space, in which 'separate European cantonments and native quarters were devised to inscribe the absolute cultural distinctions essential in supporting a rationale for colonialism' (Kothari 2006: 237). As we have seen, such constructions were accompanied by ideas that native spaces were potentially dangerous and disordered, and in the ways in which contemporary local spaces are today being obliterated by corporate space, the postcolonial landscape of the city can still be seen to be the site of transnational power relations. However, the ways in which the might of the cosmopolitan corporate intersects with other aspects of city life often means that some of the divisions between spaces are now becoming blurred and confused. Rather than have clearly demarcated spaces, transnational corporate space may *spill over* into social space, creating a sort of 'ambivalent space' (Cuthbert and McKinnell 1997). In Hong Kong for example, there has been a gradual extinction of the 'public domain', as urban social space has been gradually transferred to the private sector. The result has been that much of the public realm has become incorporated into the footprint of large new building complexes, usually owned by multinational corporations, banks, insurance, property companies and other manifestations of finance capital. Pedestrian movement is designed to reinforce monopoly land holdings by channelling pedestrians *through* these corporate spaces, which often encourage consumption through their simultaneous occupation by shopping centres. In this way *transnational* corporate space is able to change the character of *local* social space, and everyday life is framed by the global and capital connections of the city.

Within these transnational spaces however, white expatriates still tend to co-habit within very tightly bounded spaces. Their offices are often located in the business/financial/governmental zones of the city, and it is to these to which they appear to take refuge. As one respondent in Kothari's research with development consultants commented:

> So many [consultants] sit in government buildings or local headquarters and don't get out. Goodness knows colonialism had to stop but it was better from a rural point of view (2006: 249).

Coles (2007) also notes how DFID (Department for International Development) field offices were often co-located in British Embassies or High Commissions for security reasons, meaning that not only were expatriates enclaved, but local partners had to run the gauntlet of the guards before being admitted. Among the reasons claimed for this sort of geographical boundedness are the need for face to face meetings and the desire of senior personnel to restrict the length of their travel, for even a trip of as much as 15 minutes for a meeting can be resented (Gad 1991). As both Gad (1991) and Ley (2004) argue, in a contact-intensive sub-culture in which 'anxiety seems to be a constant companion of hubris' (Ley 2004: 157), the picture that emerges here is of behaviour which is much more local than global:

> But the speed of circulation is not the only factor that keeps these men and women tied to a small area. They worry a great deal about the threat of being out of touch, about not keeping up with news, about not keeping up with peers, about missing a deal, about not being available when a demanding customer calls (Gad 1991: 207).

The foreshortened time and space of expatriate life create a circumscribed lifeworld around work, bars, sporting and expatriate clubs (Ley 2004). Expatriates meet each other regularly and 'bond together' in these well established 'meeting places', social arenas and knowledge networks. Here information and intelligence is shared, whether between colleagues or competitors. In Singapore and Hong Kong, for example, expatriates from diverse organizations coagulate into the 'expaty' bars and restaurants near the financial districts in order to network: tending to avoid contact with locals, unless they are clients, potential clients or useful contacts (Beaverstock 2002). As one of the participants in Yeoh and Willis's research in China explains:

> The Chinese and Western groups keep very separate. I don't think it's deliberate, I don't want to socialize with them. But it's a very, very different way of behaving ... and way of socializing. I mean, going out to bars, well we go out to bars, party and get very drunk. The Chinese will go out and sing karaoake and have one beer ... I have Chinese friends here, and I invite them on various occasions but they don't come. They're either intimidated by gweilos or it's just not their thing. I personally think the Brits are very separate, lifestyles as well as culture. Which is a shame in a way there's probably a hell of a lot to learn (Eleanor, in Yeoh and Willis 2005b: 276).

As I discussed in Chapter 5, another popular and important expatriate space is that of the Club, and in Singapore, Beaverstock (2002) found that most of his respondents were members of clubs based around predominantly expatriate sports such as fitness, tennis, rugby, cricket, and, especially, golf. These spaces are used extensively for entertaining global, regional or local clients as well as other expatriates. The 'club scene' is usually a vital part of expatriate life, 'where they could "fancy a taste of home"' (p. 535). If not in the clubs or actually playing these sports, expatriates are watching them being played by home teams whilst drinking in bars with satellite TV: places which in the main are avoided by the locals. Less privileged expatriates, such as recently arrived university graduates, may move within different and less powerful transnational circuits and social networks however, lacking the capital to gain immediate access to the club scene. These more peripheral circuits still confer (white) distinction, but the capital amassed is less likely to be directly transferable to the corporate sphere (Scott 2006). There is a thus a complex social morphology: raced, classed and aged, which exists within expatriate space. However a constant is the degree of detachment from the outside world of the city, as Meier vividly describes:

> Working in an isolated business park or in an office building with controlled access, driving in a car, living in a separated condominium, or spending leisure time in clubs: all these places have formal entrance controls. The smell of the city, its sounds, and its climate are outside the window (2006: 129).

The extent of disembeddedness from the material space of the city may vary according to the perception of its 'foreignness'. Expatriates in Hong Kong, for example, comment on its 'Chineseness'; an aspect which sometimes comes as a surprise, as the city is often imagined in Britain as a British space:

> There's so few colonial buildings left or elements of colonialism here. ... I think it's very, very Chinese. You walk around any area of town and you're surrounded by Chinese people, Chinese architecture, Chinese shops, language ... (Eleanor, single in her 20s) (quoted in Yeoh and Willis 2005b).

Many white expatriates respond by avoiding the crowded streets, travelling from one space to another by air conditioned taxis. A recent popular form of transport for expatriates is the 'escalator': an enclosed Perspex bubble by which expats can safely flee the business district of Central at the end of the day, making it back to the rarefied tranquillity of the white residential enclaves of the Peak without having to negotiate the full reality of the physical and social landscape.

However, as already discussed, a competing discourse of whiteness is about being heroic and having no fear when travelling abroad: '*being a brave discoverer of the foreign land*' (Meier 2006: 130). Meier (2006) shows how, in the Singapore context, this is played out through the German expatriates' positioning of themselves as different to the locals, who they describe as 'anxious' and 'insular', a people who like to keep to their own company and traditions, and who avoid areas of the city which are seen to be 'dangerous'. In comparison, many of Meier's (2006) respondents attempted to position themselves as *comfortable* in their engagement with the foreign cultures of the city. However, the discourse of the '*brave explorer*' is clearly contradicted by the segregated and constrained spatial performances of whiteness in actuality. When interviewing German expatriates in London, Meier (2007) found that whilst they were happy to take on the (predominantly white) image of the (predominately white) City district in their personal and work identities, and travel through it on foot in their daily working lives, the suburb of Brixton was viewed with some terror. Although in fact only 26 per cent of Brixton residents are black, it was perceived by the German expatriates as 'a black area', and imagined as 'dangerous':

> Where I rarely go is Brixton in South London. There are I believe 70 to 80 per cent blacks there, I feel in a minority.

> I only drive through with locked doors. Especially when you pass by at night or in the evening: that's Brixton, that's East London, that's not nice and that's not safe (Meier 2007: 129–130).

Expatriates' use of the city may thus in practice be the opposite of the expansive and deterritorialized networks argued by some of the research on transnational elites which I discussed in Chapter 1 (Sklair 2001). Instead, the social geography of expatriate life may be highly localized, and restricted to a few very specific territories (Scott 2006). In their use of space, expatriates can reveal how their everyday lives are imbued with a partiality and a vulnerability (Ley 2004: 162) which they try and contain through a confinement to the familiarity of white/ national cultural reproductions:

> As they are dispatched internationally from city to city, the transnational capitalist class are [merely] island hopping from one expatriate enclave to another (Ley 2004: 157).

Constructing the Expatriate Workspace

Although much of the interaction and 'knowledge transfer' between expatriates takes place outside the workplace, in the bars and restaurants in close proximity to the business districts in which they are located, the spaces within the organization itself are also integral to the production of identities, race and gender. The evidence here suggests that a similar sort of spatial segregation exists along the axes and intersections of race, ethnicity and nation. Whilst a few of the more 'western educated and experienced' locals might be included in network formation, Beaverstock's (2002) research reveals little 'mixing' between expatriates and local employees in the actual spaces of the workplace. Spatially, whiteness keeps itself to itself: a fact that was reinforced in my own research.

Charles is a top manager within one of the largest, longest established and most powerful British *Hongs*.[1] Established in the early days of colonialism, it is now a highly diversified organization, specializing in shipping, transport and construction. Charles spends his days in what is generally acclaimed to be one of the most desirable new buildings in the Region: a twin towered skyscraper which is a wonder of the sort of contemporary design currently dominating the globe – sheet glass walling supported by immense shiny chrome pillars, marble floors and vast internal atriums filled with foliage and even birds. It is situated close to the Central business district, with all its connections to other major global cities, and for this brief moment in time, it is accepted as *the* most modern, cosmopolitan building in Hong Kong: one that allows its occupants to be seen as key players not only in this global city, but across the world. I visited Charles at his workplace, as my field notes describe:

> The escalator speeds me up to the 65th floor. As I step out, it is like going back fifty years or more: the resolutely contemporary architecture of the ground floor has been replaced by the trappings of the British Colonial hey day. Thick cream carpets, huge glass chandeliers, wood panelling on the walls, on which hang

---

1   A *Hong* is the term used for the major businesses in Hong Kong including those established by the British in the colonial period. The name itself reveals the interplay of Chinese and British cultures.

Turner-esque oil paintings depicting scenes of eighteenth century sea battles and English rural life. It is immensely quiet and cool: a shock compared with the teeming, baking streets below. At the end of the corridor, behind a western-made antique desk, is a white British woman secretary: an almost unique sight in itself. She offers me coffee, and asks me to wait. Few Chinese people can be seen: through another door, white men (no women) in shirt sleeves pad quietly round a semi-open plan office.

The secretary ushers me into her boss's office. Charles is a distinguished looking British expatriate, grey haired, be-suited, in his late fifties. He too sits behind a large western antique desk and apart from the map of the Asia Pacific region behind him we could be situated in London itself, as long as one was careful not to look out of the windows. On the wall next to him is an oil painting of a Victorian gentleman: all sideburned and black frock coated (my field notes, September 2002).

Charles' personal office comes as somewhat of a surprise in the ways it contrasts with the minimalist modernist shell in which it sits. A resolutely British organizational space of a bygone era has been fabricated here, by which Charles surrounds himself and conducts his working life. Crucially, it contains the symbolic imagery of a *colonial* space: nineteenth century in style, it represents a sense of timelessness, and the notion that little has changed – Britain *is* still a major player in the world. Working in this organizational setting offers the opportunity to live a classed, raced and gendered version of Britishness in which colonialist values have still not fully retreated. Charles spends his working life in this office, gazing over the Harbour as he chats on the phone. His talk reveals that he seeks to craft himself as a mobile, global citizen, but this contrasts with his actual use of space in his working life as well as in the city of Hong Kong, where he is to be found *only* in spaces constructed in or through the hey-day of colonialism. His daily movements through the spaces of the organization limit him to his office and his secretary's desk. People come to him, and most of his immediate colleagues and subordinates are also white and male: recruited in Britain straight from university. His domestic life is conducted in a large flat in a heavily gated community in the expatriate haven of The Peak, from which he travels by the containment of the escalator which connects to his office in Central. His leisure time is passed in a limited range of spaces: primarily the Club, the sailing waters of Aberdeen and following a book of walking trails in the Outlying Islands 'discovered' by a past Governor. Although his narrative reveals some acknowledgement of changing race relations in the organizational contexts of Hong Kong, particularly as regards employment law, his use and fabrication of space does not: it seems he is comfortable only in the spaces of whiteness, and in an old-fashioned version of white expatriate Britishness. Further, it is through the spatialization of this that he draws on in the construction and performance of his work identity and relations.

Charles' use of space reveals that his identity has been crafted primarily through the distinctive *habitus* (Bourdieu 1972) of the colonial British, marked as this is by both race and gender. His Britishness, whiteness, class and masculinity have provided him with the cultural capital to enjoy the benefits of colonialism, and engaging with Hong Kong in the most privileged of terms. The long history and immense size and power of the organization for which he works sustains this: whether this office design was provided for him, or whether he was instrumental in its design is not clear. However what it does mean is that Charles is offered both the discursive *and* material space in which the changing racial climate of Hong Kong can be resisted, and as such, Charles and his white colleagues are able to remain '*still colonial after all these years*' (Steyn 2001: 59). Although there is no animosity towards the Chinese, there is no engagement either. The master discourse of Charles' talk and use of space is 'you live your life and I will live mine', revealing the extent to which the continued imagining of being white, British and colonial is integral to his identity and lifestyle. His notion of citizenship in Hong Kong therefore appears to have been touched by neither the events following the handover nor the debates about multiculturalism in Britain; his is still a world of parallel lives.

This denial of the contemporaneousness of global space is also observed in Leggett's study of expatriates in Jakarta, Indonesia (2005). He notes that in certain spaces, the colonial imagination still appears, as a mythical discourse constructed out of historical encounters, through which 'a union is forged between Western populations and a divide created between East and West, as transnational economic processes become situated within a genealogy of empire' (p. 272). Leggett's study of the office space of BCB-Jakarta[2] reveals that whilst the international workforce shared a common office space, relied on shared communication and research technologies, and operated within a shared and promoted corporate culture, there still remained persistent and sharp social and structural divides. Subjectivity was often negotiated through the binary of 'expatriates' ('Western-born, largely American, mostly male, predominantly white, often single' (p. 273)) and 'nationals'. And whilst other identity markers such as gender, race, nationality and religion were also pertinent to social relations and social positions within the office, this was the dominant discourse by which people were positioned. This divide was played out spatially. Within the shared space of the office there was little interaction between these two groups, and the interior design of the office reinforced the social partitions:

> the individual offices of the various Directors (all "expatriates") lined the outer walls of the square space, whilst all the supervisors and support staff (all Indonesian "national" employees) occupied cubicles within the middle of an open floor plan. The Directors' offices were fronted with glass walls and venetian blinds. One could look, out but one could not necessarily look in. At first glance, BCB appeared to be an office designed with separation and surveillance in mind (Leggett 2005: 274).

---

2   Not its real name.

Leggett notes how Indonesian nationals rarely ventured into expatriate offices, and nor did expatriates move through the maze of 'national' occupied cubicles. Indeed, entering a superior's office was equated with punishment and extra work. To overcome the desire to restrict physical encounters, email was used. This was seen to be 'easier' and 'more efficient' as well as useful in terms of 'saving face' when a subordinate had made a mistake. However at the same time, this mechanism of communication also avoids the possibility of challenge to the presumed superiority of expatriates. As Leggett notes, 'it is perhaps an irony of the modern transnational corporate office that a technology believed to connect distant peoples has become instead a tool in the maintenance of social distance' (2005: 274). Leggett argues that the space of the workplace was constituted by the ideas about Indonesian nationals that the American expatriates held, formulated as these were through colonialism. Place is thus constituted both through the use of space *and* time: in this case a past time. 'To walk from the office of the American expatriate to the cubicle of an Indonesian national was, for many, a trip back in time' (Leggett 2005: 276): a trip that many tried to avoid. In short, the intentionally limited interactions of employees at BCB demonstrates 'the continued evidence of a corporate organizational map bifurcated by a grid of temporal distance' (Leggett 2005: 276).

Hybrid Spaces

In some other contexts, however, these processes of territorialization can be seen to be in a state of some challenge, as space is used to unsettle the binaries on which identities and race/national relations have been forged (Papastergiadis 2000). This may be as much about challenging identities *within* the expatriate community of an organization as about changing relations with local colleagues, thus reminding us of the important differences which exist *between* white people. In Hong Kong, the arrival of 'new' migrants to work alongside the old style expatriates has underscored the growing interconnection of the Region with the global forces and ideologies of multiculturalism at play in the contemporary world: and in particular with the hybrid, mixed community that 'home' now is for expatriates such as the British. The English Schools Foundation (ESF) is an example of an organization in which new diversities in identities and desired relations are clearly emerging, and where the old expatriate ways are no longer unquestioningly adopted by all.

ESF schools were originally built for the children of (white) British expatriates, and in the heydays of colonialism, white British teachers were brought out in force, so that the British curriculum and examination system could be followed, albeit under the hot skies of South East China. However, in order to survive after the handover, the mix of their student populations has changed dramatically. The schools are now predominantly populated by wealthy Chinese and other international migrants desirous of an English-speaking education. The teaching staff is gradually changing to reflect this new mix: whilst many of those recruited in the 1980s and 1990s still remain, other staff, from Hong Kong itself, as well as Britain, Canada, the United States, Australia and mainland China are now starting to appear.

> The school building overlooks a steep valley of cemeteries and graveyards: something no Chinese builder would have agreed to. However inside the space is a hybridity of cultures: whilst the staffroom could be that of any British school, other areas are bedecked with dragons, Chinese lanterns, and Chinese script posters. This is a lively working space, teeming with people. Whilst the majority of the teachers are white, the student population is completely multi-cultural, intermingling noisily and happily (field notes, May 2003).

Amanda and Bernard, a British couple in their 30s, have been teaching at an ESF secondary school for five years. Their interview narratives reveal far more ambivalence than those of Rob and Jim about the traditional versions of the British expatriate discourse and the colonialist racialized and classed subjectivities these offer, although constructing alternatives is difficult. Most of their waking lives are spent in the institution, but they try and avoid the 'white spaces' of the school: the staffroom, the directorate, and the staff social spaces. Amanda tends to remain up on the fifth floor in the Languages Department, where the members of staff are mainly Chinese: Mandarin is central to the curriculum. As a Department, they tend not to mix with the other staff. Bernard accuses them of being isolationist, but Amanda chooses to spend her time here, enjoying the opportunity to mix with Chinese colleagues, and avoid the upper echelons of the expatriate class structure which dominate other parts of the school. Coming from a Languages background, during which she has often lived abroad, she has found:

> There's a separation between the expatriate community and the Chinese community, which I found really strange when I came here.

Whilst Amanda is trying to challenge relations by remaining firmly within the Languages department, Bernard, who runs the lesser-valued Social Sciences Department, is located (rather symbolically) down in the basement classrooms. He rarely uses the staff room either, as the old guard have colonized it: '*you get looked at as to say why are you sat there? ... have you got nothing to do at lunchtime?*'

In contrast to the 'white space' of the staffroom, the teaching and student-based social spaces of the school are more hybrid in appearance. In deference to the mainly Chinese student population, the classroom walls reflect symbolic attempts to channel the British-based curriculum through a Chinese lens, and the student common rooms display a lively array of Hong Kong's translations of global youth culture. The differential use of space by the staff: from the powerful long termers' dominance of the staffroom to the relegation of newer staff to the (more multi-cultural) spaces of the classrooms, reveals the existence of strong and deep divisions between them. This is mainly due to differences in age and *length of service*, reflected in the different *terms and conditions* of employment which the staff receives. The 'long termers' are on the more prestigious contracts which were commonplace for government employees in the 1980s and 1990s: as with Rob the policeman, these include secure employment, accommodation, long leaves home and termly bonuses. More recent expatriate staff employed after 1997 are on 'local conditions' however, and do not receive any additional perks. More critically, their contracts are temporary and performance related: tied to examination successes and parental feedback. The long termers use this instability to position themselves as more powerful: *they* are the top tier, and others are 'second best'. The school is *their* space and newcomers must abide by *their* rules.

Different contracts fragment the organization, structurally and spatially, producing a classed and raced hierarchy which constructs different identities and different ways of living expatriate lives. Amanda and Bernard's local terms mean they are not housed in the school's prestigious (white) housing, but have to find their own accommodation in cheaper, Chinese areas. However, although the range of occupational and social spaces they inhabit are hybrid in nature, used by both expatriate and Chinese, it is clear in Bernard's talk in particular that he still feels acutely and uncomfortably positioned in both. At school, he feels proletarianized, marginalized by his unstable relationship with the powerful old guard, which is further augmented by his sense of difference along religious and ethnic grounds: being Jewish, the couple do not fit in with the dominant discourses of Christianity which prevail amongst the white expatriate staff. In contrast, out of school, he is conscious of powerful racialized discourses, and these have made him very aware of his white male body, and the privileges it accrues:

> I'm more aware on racial grounds ... How they won't sit next to you on a bus, many will stand up rather than sit next to you on a bus, and it's not because I'm too big and there's no space ... Taxis, if two people want a taxi one's a Gweilo[3] and one isn't, they'll take the Gweilo ... we've actually had that happen ... He got out and threw the Chinese lady out in the pouring rain and reversed back to us.

Both Bernard and Amanda are disappointed with such experiences of being white and British in Hong Kong, although small dark Amanda feels her body is less observed than Bernard's large and fair one. However although both feel an acute sense of difference from their expatriate colleagues, they reveal a sense of frustrated powerlessness at their inability to negotiate successfully the powerful discourses by which they are positioned. In particular, in spite of their attempts to challenge racialized divisions, they feel they are being gradually weakened by the powerful discourses which dominate expatriate life, and they are aware that in some respects they are starting to conform to the racially separatist expectations of their British colleagues through what seems to be inevitability about the form of life here. Bernard admits that he feels his identity is slowly being crafted for

---

3   Cantonese term meaning 'white devil' also adopted by expatriates to describe themselves.

him, and, although somewhat remorsefully, he can feel his resistance to this slowly ebbing away:

> It's a rhythm of life and you have to find a rhythm wherever you are. My only regret is that I can't find it with the local population, I do regret that, we could live here for fifty years and I would still never really move in Chinese circles, I think it's a missed opportunity. You can find a rhythm – the ex-pat community has its own rhythm and once you find it you accept it. This is true wherever you go isn't it? And I think once you take that on board I think you stop struggling and it becomes much easier.

Although Bernard and Amanda are attempting to subvert dominant racialized positionings in their spatial interactions, the highly structured cultures of their working lives in which social aspects of identity such as race are still treated as meaningful makes this difficult to achieve successfully. Their personal biographies (both worked previously in multi-cultural schools) mean that ideologically they are happy to 'let go' of social divisions and identities laid down in colonialism, but their lack of expatriate capital means they also lack the empowerment to 'take on' the system more fully (Steyn 2001). Their age and religious background, combined with their temporary status and even the subjects they teach, mean they are proletarianized within the workplace. They thus hug to the hybrid spaces of the institution, feeling uneasy about mixing with the stakeholders. Their making of more oppositional identities is further attempted through drawing on the spatial resources outside work, where they try to live as locals in a Chinese quarter, go to the market and beach, and use public transport. It is in these small spatial performances of everyday living lie their postcolonial challenges to the lingering legacy of colonialist raced relations.

Local Spaces

> As I wend my way through the bustling streets of Wanchai, I pass the odd British style pub in which I can see seasoned Old China Hands[4] propping up the bar with seemingly no sense of agenda. Otherwise this is a thoroughly Chinese quarter. I enter a dirty run down tenement by the tramline to meet Andrew, who runs his own small import export company. He has a scruffy, cramped one-room office on the second floor, which he shares with another long term expatriate and a Chinese secretary. It has cheap old-fashioned furniture and bits of paper are pinned all over the walls, along with pictures of motorbikes. The building is crammed with other small one-office businesses, and the lack of English signs informs me that these are mainly locally owned. Later I visit the small outlying island where Andrew

---

4   Term used to describe long term expatriates thoroughly familiar with Chinese life and culture.

lives: an hour's ferry journey away, it is inhabited by generations of Chinese families and expatriates without packages enjoying a hippy life-style. Here there is cheap low-rise accommodation as well as a sense of space and rurality unusual in Hong Kong. At night Andrew drinks in the bars on the island, whilst his wife Tina networks her way through business functions (fieldnotes 2003).

Andrew works in one of the poorer business districts of Hong Kong in which hundreds of one-roomed small businesses compete for space with clothing outlets, topless bars and downmarket pubs. He has lived in Hong Kong for about 15 years, and his working life and identity is constructed through a more obvious attempt at engagement with local people and local spaces. He is the owner of a small import-export business: a low-prestige organization which does not provide the same identity resources of Britishness, whiteness and class that Charles or even Amanda and Bernard can enjoy. Neither however does he share Amanda and Bernard's ambivalent positionings: whilst to some extent he can be seen to be successful in constructing his working life outside of the dominant subject positions of expatriates, if being white is useful to him, he will draw on this without guilt.

Andrew's role as sole manager in his own business means he mixes with few other expatriates in his business life however: his contacts are primarily with other similar outfits all over the Pacific Basin. He spends his day sitting in his small office, chatting on the phone. He is happy with his downbeat working space, explaining:

> A lot of Europeans more than Chinese fall into the glamour of a large office. [I have] a very, very small office in an elderly building and that is perfectly acceptable, especially to the Chinese guys who visit you, that's how they started twenty or thirty years ago, so it's nothing disparaging to the business.

Andrew, together with his wife Tina (who we met in Chapter 6), seek to distance themselves from the dominant expatriate identities of their compatriots, preferring to construct themselves as locals, thoroughly engaging with local spaces as well as politics and debates. Living in a Chinese village on one of the outlying islands, they draw on the local spaces in which they spend the bulk of their daily lives to reinforce these senses of self. Indeed, their use of the local spaces of work and home are *integral* to the identities they are attempting to craft for themselves – hating Britain, their narrative is generally one of the '*local Hong Konger*', in which whites are just part of the melting pot of local identities. However, their relatively 'poor white' lifestyle, combined with a hefty sprinkling of British political conservatism, means they are less burdened by the angst of Bernard and Amanda. As they attempt to get on with the hard business of cutting a living, they are happy to draw on whiteness and/or Britishness, and the networks they offer, if it brings them material and social advantage. The locality of their spatial performances and the level ground on which they construct their working lives with Chinese colleagues means that their whiteness lacks some of the power and coherence of their compatriots. However, as we saw in the last chapter, when occasion demands they *are* able and willing to enter some of the hallowed and privileged spaces of whiteness, such as the British Chamber of Commerce, by virtue of their race and nationality, if it is perceived to be useful to them.

This chapter has explored the ways in which place and space provide important resources for expatriates in their performances of whiteness and in the negotiation of their identities. Across a full range of spatial scales, place and space are drawn upon to define and constitute expatriate life. Spatial frameworks are the result of a legacy of global and colonial activity, and the norms and values which have been developed and contested through history. As Shohat and Stam have shown, it is essential to make visible the form of 'vestigial thinking which permeates and structures contemporary practices and representations even after the formal end of colonialism' (1994: 2). We have seen how the structuring of place through race is still an important and ongoing practice of expatriate working life: from the level of the global to the organizational and the local, space is drawn upon in the making, confirming or challenging of raced relations. At all of these levels, expatriates attempt to manipulate the 'poetics of space' (Said 1994).

However this is not to say that these attempts are always successful. As we saw at the beginning of the chapter, space and place are not static and fixed entities, but are highly mobile and ever in construction. In actuality the mapping of space by expatriates may be contested and resisted by others who also occupy it, and alternative 'poetics' will be always at play in any space. Distances and segregations are impossible to maintain (Mills 2005), such that, rather than seeing expatriates spaces as safely demarcated, it may be more useful to conceptualize these as 'contact zones' (Pratt 1992; Yeoh and Willis 2005b). Pratt (1992) used the term 'contact zones' to describe the ways in which the colonized and colonizing cultures *mutually* influence each other, a notion which was taken up in Yeoh and Willis's (2005b) discussion of expatriates in China. As they point out, we must not ignore the co-presence of others in place. 'A contact perspective' attempts to invoke the spatial and temporal co-presence of subjects previously separated by geographic and historical disjunctures whose trajectories now intersect, and emphasizes how subjects are constituted in and by their relations to each other (Pratt 1992). It treats these relations 'not in terms of separateness or apartheid, but in terms of co-presence, interaction, interlocking understandings and practices, often within radically asymmetrical relations of power' (Pratt 1992: 7). Rather than seeing the places and spaces discussed in this chapter as successfully and unilaterally appropriated by expatriates in the construction of whiteness and privilege therefore, the presence of other competing identities should be acknowledged. However at the same time, the often superior economic resources and powerful social capital of expatriates and expatriate organizations ensures that they are usually in a strong position by which to manage these.

Chapter 8
Returning Home

The transience of expatriate life means that as migrants come towards the end of a posting or contract, decisions will need to be made as to *what next?* Whilst the talk and activities of many expatriates reveal deep and strong connections to the places of home, at the same time these links are also often constructed with some ambivalence. Some dread the thought of actually returning home, and would rather try and seek another job elsewhere. A few hope *never* to return: desiring to retire and live out their final days in a place where the expatriate lifestyle, and perhaps the privileges of whiteness, might in some ways be maintained. Spain, Thailand or Australia are typically mentioned by my respondents in Hong Kong as attractive options for example. Whilst a *sense* of belonging to a national community can be intensified by migration, this is perhaps more likely to be animated in the new 'foreign' context than in the actual landscape of home:

> I'm very British, your sense of Britishness or Englishness, goes up remarkably as soon as you're away, suddenly you're very patriotic. What a bunch of hypocrites, what a bunch of hypocrites! I think ... it is because suddenly you're a minority, I'm an ethnic minority and I'm white ... therefore your identity becomes that much more important, because you're surrounded by 1.3 billion Chinese, suddenly you stand out a bit, and suddenly who you are and what you are becomes a little more important to you as a person ... expatriates are just so much closer I find, very strong community spirit (Adrian, mid-30s, working in the hotel industry in Beijing, quoted in Yeoh and Willis 2005b: 278).

In my own research, I found that many expatriates were now moving away from this nationality-based identity, even in migratory contexts. Becoming more mobile, and more involved in a new social environment, can bring new perspectives on home, and distance from it. For example Tina, who we met in Chapter 6, explains that she *no longer* 'feels British':

> I'm moving very much away from that, whereas I used to still be patriotic, you know I'd support the British at the Olympics or whatever. I'm actually moving away from that ... not because I've been away for so long, but I don't like who's running the country, I don't like what's happening. So far as I'm concerned – no thanks!

Tina has no intention of returning home, preferring to make plans to move on to Shanghai or Australia – both places where she feels they will be treated well.

Charles, who we met in Chapter 7, agrees with her, but also shows how *the working life* of the expatriate can itself weaken notions of nationality and attachments to the places of home:

> I've got property in the UK and I've got family in Cheshire but the longer we're out, the less we want to go back. I'm British – English – and I support the appropriate team – but it's not by far. Again the world is a much smaller place – people move around a lot, and that's the thing with working for a Group like ours, it's quite a significant amount of travelling when you put it together over the years. I suppose you get used to that sort of mobility and I've seen so much more of the rest of the world than what's in Britain.

Clearly, given the importance of work in the identities and lives of many expatriates, contracts coming to an end and the leaving of jobs may be bound up with the perceived loss of important aspects of personal identity which it is feared may not be sustained at home. This can not only make it problematic to return home, but may also make it seem untenable to carry on in the host country after the job has finished, where identities and relationships may have been constructed *entirely* through work. As Charles continues:

> Having been here for twenty-five years, it's become home to me, but having said that there is a very strong tie between work and the place. I can't see myself retiring in Hong Kong. There' s still very much a sort of "you come to Hong Kong to make money" and a lot of the social life is not who you are it's what you are. And once you leave and you no longer have a little office, suddenly attitudes change. Hong Kong's always been like that and it's still like that.

> **So where would you like to retire?**

> Good question! Somewhere in Europe – maybe the Mediterranean – and we're thinking quite seriously about Thailand. My wife has even less desire to go to the UK than I do. It's just sort of attitudes, certainly outside London I find it very parochial, whenever we go back to London we don't feel we're part of it.

> **You don't feel British?**

> I certainly don't have any pride in the British put it that way. I still go to London and I think it a very cool city, but the crime rate is something that is pretty worrying and crime round Britain is generally something that puts one off. The other thing is the service and that lies actually with Europe and America – they are the same thing, the service in comparison to Asia is just dreadful. I suppose we've been spoilt and we've got used to the service in this part of the world.

Indeed, few of my respondents claimed that they wished to return to the United Kingdom in the short term: stereotypical complaints about the country abounded. These were usually about perceived levels of crime, back-biting politics, parochial attitudes, appalling levels of 'service', cold weather and bad food: '*I'd be dead within a month!*' as one respondent put it. In spite of this, and unlike Charles, many of those who are now facing *retirement* feel that returning home is the right thing to do. Thus whilst white mobilities and identities are bound up with the doing of work, during which there may be a loosening of the importance of nationality, non-work is seen by most to be something to be enjoyed back at home, surrounded by a familiar culture and people. Nationality is thus constructed as a highly *flexible* aspect of identity, taken on in a new migratory context if it brings a sense of community and belonging, perhaps jettisoned if the work context itself can offer an alternative source for these social relationships, and reaffirmed as being once again of importance on returning home for good. As Vanessa, an academic at a University in Hong Kong explained:

> You want to die in your own language! I want to listen to [names a famous British broadcaster], watch the BBC and read *The Times*. I do like it here, but I know I don't want to retire here. I don't want to become the ghost of Christmas Past. I need to make a life for myself in the UK.

Richard, an architect who has been working in Hong Kong for seven years was typical in his response to this question:

> No, I would never move back to the UK for work, but like most people I would consider retiring there. For work, it is far, far better here. There is far more work, and of course it is a British model because all the contracts are based on British law so it is easy for me to work here.

Vanessa confirms that there is an interesting adjustment period in the time leading up to leaving. Identities can be seen to shift in terms of allegiance and senses of belonging. In the making of these shifts, and in the reconstruction of identities based on the landscapes of home, whiteness and nationality can again be important resources:

> When people know they are going they start to say "Hong Kong is dreadful" and start to negate it: it makes it easier for them to go. They switch themselves into believing it's the armpit of the universe. They've lived here for many years – and done very well out of it – it's not the way to behave! It's not a sinking ship – it's a ship taking a different course!

Returning home will bring with it new and different demands for identity negotiation. The resources of whiteness, nationality, gender and race may be more ambiguous in the home context than the expatriate one. Indeed, upon returning home, expatriates can experience a sort of 'reverse culture shock' and other problems of adaption (Forster 1994, Kohonen 2008). Whilst organizations might be very effective at managing the processes of out-migration, less care or interest might be taken over their return. Indeed, Moore (2002) found that expatriates are most critical of the support available for their partner and family during repatriation. Time emerges as a key issue: many expatriates are given very little notice of their return, which can prove challenging in terms of beginning new job searches and finding schools for children. For accompanying partners returning home (who, as we have seen, are usually women), many find that their career has 'slipped back' in promotion terms and that problems are encountered in re-entering the labour market. As we saw in the case of Conor in Chapter 1, in times of recession, returning home may even mean redundancy and so many couples will be reluctant to put themselves in that position, and may try very hard for another overseas posting (Hardill and MacDonald 1998). It has, however, been suggested that after five years as an expatriate, re-entry is problematical; and after ten years it becomes almost impossible (Salt 1988). Many repatriates will find that their work and social environments have totally changed, and they will have changed too. Whilst whiteness, ethnicity, nationality, gender and class may bring privileges on foreign soil, at home they may stand for much less.

Conclusions

In Chapter 1, I explained that the starting point for this book was a desire to contribute to three strands of research and debate. First, the book aimed to contribute to the burgeoning qualitative and quantative research on labour migrants by taking a specifically ethnographic focus to white, privileged labour migrants. Whilst research on the 'transnational capitalist class' (Sklair 1998) is now growing more generally, there is still a gap in detailed research which deconstructs the sites of their work, and questions the role and meaning of these in their migration experience and the making of their identities. This book has argued however that the specific contexts of work are central to these, as well as a critical means by which their more elite social status *vis-à-vis* other migrants is propagated and preserved. Work is also the means therefore by which *racial* boundaries can be produced: within the workplace, between the skilled expatriates and local members of staff, as well as in the city, between expatriates and the local community.

Second, this project would also help to broaden the ethnographic literature on expatriates and identity-making, which has traditionally prioritized domestic and family lives, to include a focus on work and organizational contexts, as well as the place of race within these. Work should not be relegated to an abstract backdrop to expatriate lives, but rather should be seen as critical in framing expatriate identities and understandings of their relationship to the new host country and its peoples. This whilst most global organizations present themselves as modern, bureaucratic, socially neutral places, their role in the organization of expatriation has been shown in actuality to contribute to the making of difference and augment the raced/ national aspects of identity. A range of evidence has been presented here to show how the practices, routines and spaces of work are critical in these processes of race/identity making. Historical accounts, ethnographic data and interview material have been drawn upon to enable a deconstruction of the everyday work contexts of skilled white migrants and to reveal how identities are negotiated within these. In particular I have explored what might be considered to be abstract organizational procedures and routines, such as recruitment and selection policies, acculturation activities, terms and conditions, meetings, arrangement of office space and so on to explore how these are deployed in very concrete ways to institute and maintain boundaries.

However what has also been revealed is the diversity which exists *between* white migrants working in different contexts. Not all of them can be accused of retreating completely to the binaristic epistemologies (white/other) which underpin (neo-) colonial subject positions. The evidence presented in the book suggests that for today's expatriate, a range of contemporary discursive locations exist by which to position oneself, from the more traditional versions of colonialism to more contemporary creolizations.

Third, the book has aimed to open up the research on workplace diversity to include an exploration of the impact of migration on race (specifically whiteness) making within organizations and organizational life (Proudford and Nkomo 2006). As globalization and changes in labour market mobilities are bringing together different nationalities, ethnicities and cultures, our taken for granted notions about organizational and national boundaries and cultural space are being questioned (Pringle et al. 2006). Research on workplace diversity thus needs to adjust with the times and start to fill the gap which exists in the literature, making links between workplaces and the full range of historical and socio-political contexts of the countries within which they are situated. As Pringle et al. (2006) argue:

> We ... advocate that research into workplace diversity attends to the politics of location, including history, culture and societal concerns, to develop a more critical discourse on the dynamic and reciprocal impacts of diverse social identity on and in workplaces (p. 533).

The three aims of the book have been pursued within a broad framework of poststructuralism. Poststructuralist epistemologies have been seen to be particularly useful as they acknowledge the ways in which identities and experiences are produced in specific social and interactional contexts, and consider that lived experience is contingent, partial, fragmented and contradictory, as people constantly shift between different allegiances (Baxter 2008, Leonard 2003). I have argued that this approach is valuable in exploring the ever-changing, on-going construction of identity making, the multiplicity of positions that may be situated simultaneously, and the ways in which competing, and sometimes even contradictory positions may be held in tension (Baxter 2003, Leonard 2008). In other words, it is a valuable method to approach the '*how*?' of whiteness as well as the '*what*?', a question which is central to the current project of 'third wave whiteness' as outlined recently by Twine and Gallagher (2007). In their discussion of future directions within whiteness studies, Twine and Gallagher urge a 'focus on emerging empirical accounts of how whiteness is deployed and the discursive strategies used to maintain and destabilize white identity and privilege' (2007: 6).

The poststructuralist perspective is therefore particularly suited to this project, as it provides a methodology by which to the interrogate discursive strategies, and the complex ways in which these are drawn upon to construct and maintain identities (Mills 2003, Baxter 2003, Leonard 2008). Foucault's formulations of discourse, power and subjectivity (Foucault 1980) offer one theoretical strand by which to approach analysis. A Foucauldian approach focuses on how discourses evolve historically, how they become part of common sense culture and how they provide the structure for the operation of institutions. The historical explorations in Chapter 2 provided insight into the ways in which discourses of work have long positioned white/other differently and how this positioning has been built into work and organizational understandings, operations and routines. The approach thus foregrounds an analysis of power, and the ways in which powerful discursive positionings develop through processes of 'normalization': 'through defining what is usual and habitual and to be expected, as opposed to the deviant and the exceptional' (Wetherall and Potter 1992: 84). In colonialism, white discourses were established as the norm, and those by which others were judged. In postcolonial contexts, whilst versions of these discourses continue, these are constantly being challenged and contested by a broad range of alternative discourses, such as those of multiculturalism, localization and social democracy, all of which are working to fragment the hegemony of white privilege. The Foucauldian approach thus emphasizes how power operates *through* discourses: the 'knowledge', social practices and 'administrative procedures' produced by institutions, as well as the interplay of power *between* these institutions. This is a form of power that is understood as *producing* subjects, and can be recognized when 'a subject willingly says 'yes' to some mode of behaviour, or sees this mode as particularly expressive of their real identity' (ibid: 84). Foucauldian discourse analysis thus also helps us to analyse speech and texts to reveal how subjects are constituted and formed, as well as how they construct themselves and their social world.

The approach is useful therefore in showing how people may position themselves within different sets of power relations, and in this process, how these may be shaped and reshaped by individual acts of support or resistance (Baxter 2008). Indeed it is particularly interesting to explore acts of conflict and contestation, as a Foucauldian analysis sees that there are no simple divisions between homogeneous power *for* and homogeneous power *against* (Wetherall and Potter 1992). Thus whilst we have seen how white expatriates are positioned as different to their local colleagues, and how they themselves are active in positioning themselves as 'Other', we have also seen that speakers can shift between different discourses and subject positions in their narratives, and as such construct themselves in ways which are uneven, fragmented and contradictory. Expatriates do not have a seamless relationship to power: certainly at times they construct themselves as relatively power*ful*, but at other times they are relatively power*less* (Wetherall and Potter 1992, Baxter 2003). This is illustrated in Chapter 6, in the discussion of Penny. Although Penny certainly enjoyed some of the privileges of expatriate whiteness: nice accommodation and a comfortable lifestyle, she felt powerless and humbled in the face of the substantial wealth and status of some Chinese business people.

This sense of mutuality is echoed in a second theoretical strand upon which it is productive to draw: Derrida's deconstructionist analysis and questioning of dualisms (Derrida 1972). Deconstruction encourages a critical focus on centres, or the organizing principles of structures:

> Centers carry with them a number of qualities consistent with the structuralist enterprise, including an either/or epistemology, an apparently noncontingent, natural and enduring nature, and a seemingly independent, self-positing and self-defining presence. To deconstruct one must therefore first recognize the existence of a center, and with it, both a marginalized periphery (the "other") and a boundary that produces and maintains – as opposed to merely "indicates" – the difference (Dixon and Jones III 2008: 92).

That work and organizations are critical discursive sites of centring and marginalization has been well documented in the organizational literature, particularly as regards to gender (Halford and Leonard 2001, Konrad et al. 2006). It is through the rules, regulations, practices and discourses of institutions and groups of persons that centres and margins are reproduced and policed, as well as become available for the further exercise of social power (Dixon and Jones III 2008). This book has explored the ways in which, in migratory contexts, work and organizations, and the people employed by them, may construct unequal relations between people, designating some people as more central than others. The invocation of race, and in particular of *white* identities, has been shown to be particularly powerful here: often used by both contemporary organizations and expatriates themselves to suspend other social divisions such as class and nationality and link people who share whiteness to dominant organizational and social locations, even though the expatriates themselves may have come from positions of relative powerlessness (Garner 2007). However, it has also revealed the ways in which employees themselves are implicit in this process and that positioning and repositioning oneself and others is an ongoing and continual activity. As such whiteness is by no means a self-sufficient category, but one that has to be continuously made and reasserted. Further, the ways in which it relates to, and is dependent upon, other (marginalized) races is highly contingent upon the particular context, as well as ambivalent within this. The time when whites could position themselves without question (if ever only to themselves!) as the 'foundational' race has long disappeared, and to a greater or lesser extent, their subjectivities now have to be accounted for. The grounds by which white privileges were once claimed and asserted are now far more contested, and even by (some) white people themselves.

The second step to deconstruction therefore is to explore the processes by which 'the centre' is maintained and by which it may be possible to be subverted (Dixon and Jones III 2008). We have seen how the 'doing' of particular forms of work have been integral to definitions of whiteness, although these have varied across time and space according to socio-historical contexts. In many work contexts, whites position themselves as central to the discourses of professional/skilled/'experts' and therefore necessary for effective international competitiveness. Further, spatial mobility is increasingly being built into discourses of professionalism, which is 'identified with constant motion and a disembedding of work roles from other social relationships, modelling carefully calculated footlooseness as a standard of successful adaptation to high modernity' (Amit 2002: 146). By being (able to be) hypermobile, white migrants are further solidifying their position within these discourses and central positionings. Whilst these discourses emanate from a range of discursive sites, we have seen how organizations themselves form critical locations. From selection and recruitment, decisions about postings, compensation packages and accommodation to the conduct of meetings, speech-acts, bodily comportment and appearance, larger discourses about race, nationality and gender are tapped into and sustained. In this way organizational power is not only independent of the particular individuals they employ, but also becomes vested in and through them, such that through the enunciations and practices of particular raced and gendered individuals organizational power becomes further animated and represented. However it is here that opportunities for contestation and challenge also exist. In my discussion of different sites of expatriate work, I have shown how both men and women may shift quite pragmatically between corporate/racialized discourses in the construction and maintenance of their identities, and that, in the ways in which these interplay with other discourses existing within their personal biographies, hegemonies may be resisted.

However whilst the voices, experiences and identities of expatriates reveal diversities, they also simultaneously reveal the sustainability of the colonialist legacy within contemporary discourses. The book has explored the ways in which some expatriate subject positions may continue to draw upon and connect with the discourses of whiteness established in the past, whilst others are attempting to challenge these and the foundations on which these are based. Although the evidence is piecemeal and uneven, some 'new identities' are appearing. This point about identity diversity is picked up nicely by one of the respondents in Yeoh and Willis's (2007b) research in China. In explaining the different ways expatriates could interact with and experience Chinese society, Nicholas (a British engineer in his 50s) draws on language which is shaped by his colonial heritage to explain that there are three broad ranges of expatriates: the 'culturalists', the 'colonialists' and the 'imperialists'. Culturalists are people who enjoy integrating into Chinese society, making friendships and enjoying the new culture. On the other hand,

> The imperialists are the ones who want to impose their will on all of us, and have an arrogant style ... it's the one thing that you must avoid at all costs. To patiently listen, to learn and to understand is probably the first step in integration in China, of course not only from a personal point of view but also from a professional point of view, it's much appreciated. So imperialists find that pretty difficult to do, because they keep bouncing against a brick wall. ... If you're young you're adaptable, and you have that tendency to listen, and you probably won't fit into this category. If you're older ... and slightly arrogant, you fit into the imperialist category, especially when you get to my age, over 50, that age you're pretty difficult and of course it depends on whether you've had any expatriate postings or not ... if you're a colonialist you come in and out without having felt a difference because you tend to build a colonial barrier around yourself.

Expatriates such as Nicholas are, arguably, attempting to affirm more of a 'creole' identity through elective processes. Cohen and Toninato (2010) argue that the word 'creole' should *not* be understood as racially bound, but should be a term which is opened up to people of all colours:

> Speaking a creole language, through friendships and relationships, or simply by identifying with the many expressions of creole popular culture (music, art, dancing, food, syncretic religion and forms of material culture that are prevalent in their region). Creole is thus not a "hard" racial category with strongly policed edges defined by "blood" or colour, but a "fuzzy" or "soft" identity with highly permeable frontiers (p. 9).

In reference to white privileged migrants however the term needs to be used with great caution. Taking into account the critiques of authors such as Palmie (2007), Mintz (1998) and Sheller (2003), the term can perhaps be usefully used to *imagine* new ways of being an expatriate.

A further and third step in the deconstruction process is to show the significance of space and place, and the built environment (Dixon and Jones III 2008). We have seen how these can also be vested with power by virtue of the meanings people associate with particular places, spatial usages and designs. Taking the physicality of space and place into account helps to reiterate the importance of 'the local' even when talking about global migrants. Whereas some aspects of expatriate life might be shared across global contexts: terms and conditions, or a structured career path for example, these must play themselves out within and against the particular local context. The example of expatriates in Hong Kong have shown how specific these are in place. This 'located-ness' of expatriates within a specific context can thus serve as a metaphor for particularity and complexity as well as the *inter-relatedness* of the global and the local (Dyb and Halford 2009). In this book, then, rather than seeing the debate about the 'placelessness' of transnational elites in terms of a mutually exclusive either/or – are they above and beyond attachments to place or not? – I want to draw further on Derrida's deconstructionist approach to reframe the very concept of 'placelessness' itself.

Derrida (1978) argues that meaning is inherently unstable, continually deferred and supplemented. This continual supplementarity of meaning, the constant substitution and adding of meanings through the play of signifiers, challenges any notion of fixed meanings (Barker and Galasinski 2003), for example in terms of opposition such as colonial/postcolonial, white/non-white. Rather, the approach reveals how one term in any pair of oppositions inhabits and interpenetrates the other, producing a supplementarity or *double movement*, between the two. 'By juggling with both meanings simultaneously, by keeping one's options always open, a richer, more nuanced range of meanings comes into play. It is not a question of *either/or* but *both/and*' (Baxter 2008: 204).

Applying this analysis to placelessness allows us to acknowledge the *presence* of place as well as its *absence* in the term, as well as the fact that that expatriates are *simultaneously* place*less and* placed. Whilst loss of direct involvement in national citizenship matters might on the one hand render expatriates the ability to be 'placeless', to act beyond the parochiality of their home nation states and enjoy the opportunities of the global stage; at the same time, their new lives are also conducted *in place*; within the particularity of the local context, and their ongoing connections with the spaces of home. It is to a specific, grounded place that the migrant arrives, transporting their (raced/gendered/classed) senses of self and entitlement, and memories of home, along with their baggage.

Further, Massey (2005: 140) has also demonstrated the ways in which 'place' can also be conceptualized in terms of supplementarity. Place is not an inert physical landscape, but an 'event': an ongoing 'throwntogetherness', a coming together of the previously unrelated. This 'constellation' involves a range of social, economic and cultural processes from the very local to the global. 'This is place as open and internally multiple' (p. 141), and, as such, ever incoherent, as the meanings of place are constantly substituted and added to by the ebb and flow of arrivals and departures. Drawing on the work of Low and Barnett (2000), Massey argues for working with the term 'conjuncture': 'thinking conjuncturally' suggests a shuttling back and forth between different temporal and spatial frames or scales to capture the distinctive character of processes which appear to inhabit the same moment in time and space (Massey 2005: 141). In this continual supplementarity, we gain a *mobile* sense of 'place': one which not only demands negotiation by the migrant, and poses a sense of challenge, but which in turn is changed by the migrant as they bring their experiences and senses of other places – places of home and other aways – and other times. We also gain a *specific* sense of place: we cannot speak about places in abstract or general terms, but must acknowledge their own particular complexity.

This mobile *and* specific conception of 'place' can also be extended to the organization or workplace (Lefebrve 1991, Halford and Leonard 2006). Massey (2005) reminds us how organizations too can be conceptualized at a range of spatial scales and relationships, through the links which exist locally, regionally, nationally and globally. By migrating, expatriates are not only animating these links, but are also contributing to the ongoing and dynamic making of the (work)*place*. Thinking conjuncturally allows us to see the specific intersections which exist between their individual temporally and spatially raced, gendered, classed and nationalized biographies and memories and those already at play in the workplace. It is through this iterative productive process that the senses of self and place are continuously negotiated and reconfigured.

However the discussion also reveals that in the reworking of colonial discourses and practices, and their interplay with global debates, important opportunities may exist to recast white identities and power relations. It is clear that individual biographies of expatriates shape the subjective effects of organizational contexts, and it is this individuality and agency in response which may be productive in challenging white privilege.

Bibliography

Achbar, M., Abbot, J. and Bakan, J. (dirs) (2004) *The Corporation*. In2Film and Metrodome.

Acker, J. (1990) 'Hierarchies, jobs, bodies: a theory of gendered organizations', *Gender and Society* 4(2): 139–158.

Adas, M. (1986) 'From foot dragging to flight: the evasive history of peasant avoidance protest in South and Southeast Asia', *Journal of Peasant Studies* 13: 64–86.

Adler, N. (1994) 'Competitive frontiers: women managers across borders', *Journal of Management Development* 13: 24–41.

Adler, N. and Izraeli, D.N. (1994) *Competitive Frontiers: Women Managers in a Global Economy*. Cambridge, MA: Blackwell.

Ahmed, S. (2000) *Strange Encounters, Embodied Others in Postcoloniality*. London: Routledge.

Alexander, C. (2004) 'Writing race: ethnography and the imagination of *The Asian Gang*', in Bulmer, M. and Solomos, J. (eds) *Researching Race and Racism* London: Routledge.

Alexander, C. (2006) 'Introduction: mapping the issues', *Ethnic and Racial Studies* 29(3) May: 397–410.

Allen, T.W. (1994) *The Invention of the White Race Vol. 1: Racial Oppression and Social Control*. London: Verso.

Allen, T.W. (1997) *The Invention of the White Race Vol. 2: The Origin of Racial Oppression in Anglo-America*. London: Verso.

Amit, V. (2002) 'The moving "expert": a study of mobile professionals in the Cayman Islands and North America', in Sørenson, N.N. and Olwig, K.F. *Work and Migration: Life and Livelihoods in a Globalizing World*. London: Routledge.

Appadurai, A. (1996) *Modernity at Large*. Minneapolis: University of Minnesota Press.

Aveling, N. (2004) 'Being the descendant of colonialists: white identity in context', *Race, Ethnicity and Education* 7(1): 57–71.

Back, L. (2002) 'Guess who's coming to dinner? The political morality of investigating whiteness in the gray zone', in Ware, V. and Back, L. (eds) *Out of Whiteness: Color, Politics and Culture*. Chicago: University of Chicago Press.

Back, L. (2004) 'Writing in and against time', in Bulmer, M. and Solomos, J. (eds) *Researching Race and Racism*. London: Routledge.

Barker, C. and Galasinski, D. (2001) *Cultural Studies and Discourse Analysis.* London: Sage.

Barnes, W. (2006) 'FT Careers Asia: women executives poised to enter the male storm', *The Financial Times*, 26 October 2006.

Basch, L., Glick Schiller, N. and Blanc, C.S. (1994) *Nations Unbound: Transnational Projects, Postcolonial Predicaments and Deterritorialized Nation-States.* London: Routledge.

Bauman, Z. (1989) *Legislators and Interpreters: On Modernity, Post Modernity and the Intellectuals.* Cambridge: Polity Press.

Baxter, J. (2003) *Positioning Gender in Discourse: A Feminist Methodology.* Basingstoke: Palgrave.

Baxter, J. (2008) 'Is it all tough talking at the top?: A post-structuralist analysis of the construction of gendered speaker identities of British business leaders within interview narratives', *Gender and Language* 2(2): 197–222.

Beaverstock, J.V. (1994) 'Re-thinking skilled international labour migration: world cities and banking organisations', *Geoforum* 125(3): 323–338.

Beaverstock, J.V. (1996) 'Migration: knowledge and social interaction: expatriate labour within investment banks', *Area* 28(4): 459–470.

Beaverstock, J.V. (2002) 'Transnational elites in global cities: British expatriates in Singapore's financial district', *Geoforum* 33(4): 525–538.

Beaverstock, J.V. (2005) 'Transnational elites in the City: British highly-skilled inter-company transferees in New York City's financial district', *Journal of Ethnic and Migration Studies* 31(2): 245–268.

Beaverstock, J.V. and Boardwell, J.T. (2000) 'Negotiating globalisation, transnational corporations and global city financial centres in transient migration studies', *Applied Geography* 20: 227–304.

Beaverstock, J.V., Smith, R. and Gand Taylor, P.J. (2000) 'World city network: a new metageography of the future?', *Annals of the Association of American Geographers* 90(1): 123–134.

Belloc, H. (1929) 'Introduction', in Dutton, E. *Kenya Mountain.* London: Jonathan Cape, pp. i–ix.

Bergsten, C.F., Horst, T. and Moran, T.H. (1978) *American Multinationals and American Interests.* Washington: The Brookings Institute.

Bhabha, H. (1994) *The Location of Culture.* London: Routledge.

Billig, M. (1992) *Talking of the Royal Family.* London: Routledge.

Billig, M. (1995) *Banal Nationalism.* London: Sage.

Black, J.S. and Porter, L.W. (1991) 'Managerial behaviours and job performance: a successful manager in Los Angeles may not succeed in Hong Kong', *Journal of International Business Studies* 22(1): 99–113.

Boden, D. (1994) *The Business of Talk: Organizations in Action.* Cambridge: Polity Press.

Bonnett, A. (1998) 'How the British working class became white: the symbolic reformation of racialized capitalism', *Journal of Historical Sociology* 11(3): 316–340.

Bonnett, A. (2000) *White Identities: Historical and International Perspectives.* Harlow: Pearson Prentice Hall.

Bourdieu, P. (1977) *Outline of a Theory of Practice.* Cambridge: Cambridge University Press.

Bourdieu, P. (1984) *Distinction.* London: Routledge.

Bourgois. P. (2000) 'Violating Apartheid in the United States: on the streets and in academia', in Twine, F.W. and Warren, J.W. (eds) *Race-ing Research and Researching Race.* New York: New York University Press.

Boyle, P., Halfacree, K. and Robinson, V. (1998) *Exploring Contemporary Migration.* Harlow: Pearson Prentice Hall.

Brah, A. (1996) *Cartographies of Diaspora: Contesting Identities.* London: Routledge.

Brewer, J. (2000) *Ethnography.* Buckingham: Open University Press.

Brewster, C. and Scullion, H. (1997) 'A review and agenda for expatriate HRM', *Human Resource Management Journal* 7(3): 32–41.

Brodkin, K. (1998) *How Jews became White Folks and What That Says about Race in America.* New Brunswick: Rutgers University Press.

Burawoy, M., Blum, J.A., George, S., Gille, Z., Gowan, T., Haney, L., Klawiter, M., Lopez, S.H., O'Rianin, S. and Thayer, M. (2000) *Global Ethnography: Forces, Connections and Imaginations in a Postmodern World.* Berkeley: University of California Press.

Byrne, B. (2006) *White Lives: the Interplay of 'Race', Class and Gender in Everyday Life.* London: Routledge.

Callan, H. and Ardener, S. (eds) (1984) *The Incorporated Wife.* Beckenham: Croom Helm.

Cameron, D. (2001) *Working with Spoken Discourse.* London: Sage.

Campbell, J. (1968) *Hero with a Thousand Faces.* New York: Doubleday.

Cannandine, D. (2001) *Ornamentalism: How the British Saw their Empire.* London: Allen Lane.

Castells, M. (1996) *The Rise of the Network Society.* Oxford: Blackwell.

Castells, M. (2000) *The Rise of the Network Society.* (2nd edn) Oxford: Blackwell.

Chambers, I. (1994) *Migrancy, Culture, Identity.* London: Routledge.

Chambers, R. (2005) 'Critical reflections of a development nomad', in Kothari, U. (ed.) *A Radical History of Development Studies: Individuals, Institutions and Ideologies.* Cape Town: Zed Books.

Chen, H.H. (2006) 'Imagining the Other: The construction of whiteness in Taiwan', unpublished PhD thesis Arizona State University.

Chun, A. (2000) 'Introduction: (Post) colonialism and its discontents, or the future of practice', *Cultural Studies* 14(3/4): 379–384.

Clifford, J. (1988) *The Predicament of Culture: Twentieth Century Ethnography, Literature and Art.* Cambridge: Harvard University Press.

Clifford, J. and Marcus, G.E. (eds) (1986) *Writing Culture: The Poetics and Politics of Ethnography.* Berkeley: University of California Press.

Cohen, D. (1996) 'In the wake of the wife', *The Independent* 12 September 1996 http://www.independent.co.uk/life-style/in-the-wake-of-the-wife-1362882. html accessed 28 April 2009.

Cohen, R. (2000) 'The incredible vagueness of being British/English', *International Affairs* 76(3): 575–582.

Connerton, P. (1989) *How Societies Remember.* Cambridge: Cambridge University Press.

Conradson, D. and Latham, A. (2005a) 'Friendship, networks and transnationality in a world city: Antipodean transmigrants in London', *Journal of Ethnic and Migration Studies* 31(2) March: 287–305.

Conradson, D. and Latham, A. (2005b) 'Transnational urbanism: attending to everyday practices and mobilities', *Journal of Ethnic and Migration Studies* 31(2) March: 227–233.

Cormode, L. (1994) 'Japanese foreign direct investment and the circulation of personnel from Japan to Canada', in Gould, W.T.S. and Findlay, A.M. (eds) *Population Migration and the Changing World Order.* Chichester: Wiley.

Cresswell, T. (2004) *Place: A Short Introduction.* Oxford: Blackwell.

Cuthbert, A.R. and McKinnell, K.G. (1997) 'Ambiguous space, ambiguous rights-corporate power and social control in Hong Kong', *Cities* 14(5): 295–311.

Cyert, R.M. and March, J.G. (1992) *A Behavioural Theory of the Firm.* Oxford: Blackwell.

Davis, O.I., Nakayama, T.K. and Martin, J.N. (2000) 'Current and future directions in ethnicity and methodology', *International Journal of Intercultural Relations* 24(5): 525–539.

Dawson, G. (1994) *Soldier Heroes: British Adventure, Empire and the Imagining of Masculinities.* London: Routledge.

Deal, T.E. and Kennedy, A. (1982) *Corporate Cultures: The Rites and Rituals of Corporate Life.* Reading, MA: Addison-Wesley.

Derr, C.B. and Oddu, G. (1993) 'Internationalizing managers: speeding up the process', *European Management Journal* 11(4): 435–442.

Derrida, J. (1978) *Writing and Difference.* London: Routledge and Kegan Paul.

Deutsche, R. (1996) *Evictions: Art and Spatial Politics.* Cambridge: MIT Press.

Dirks, N. (1992) *Colonialism and Culture.* Ann Arbor: University of Michigan Press.

Dixon. D.P. and Jones III, J.P. (2008) 'Poststructuralism', in Duncan J.S., Johnson N.C. and Schein R.H (eds) *A Companion to Cultural Geography.* Oxford: Blackwell.

Doel, M. (2000) 'Un-glunking geography', in Crang, M. and Thrift, N. (eds) *Thinking Space.* London: Routledge.

Doyle, J. and Nathan, M. (2001) *Wherever Next: Work in a Mobile World.* London: The Industrial Society.

Du Bois, W.E.B. (1977) *Black Reconstruction in the United States 1860–1880.* New York: Free Press.

Duncan, J.S. (2000) 'The struggle to be temperate: climate and "moral masculinity" in mid-nineteenth century Ceylon', *Singapore Journal of Tropical Geography* 21(1): 34–47.

Duncan, J.S. (2002) 'Embodying colonialism? Domination and resistance in nineteenth century Ceylonese coffee plantations', *Journal of Historical Geography* 28(3): 317–338.

Duruz, J. (2005) 'Eating at the border: culinary journeys', *Environment and Planning D: Society and Space* 23: 51–69.

Dutt, R.P. (1970) *India Today.* New Delhi: Najivan Press.

Dwyer, O.J. and Jones III, J.P. (2000) 'White socio-spatial epistemology', *Social and Cultural Geography* 1(2): 209–222.

Dyb, K. and Halford, S. (2009) 'Placing globalizing technologies: telemedicine and the making of difference', *Sociology* 43(2): 232–249.

Edwards, J. (1991) *Banzai You Bastards!* London: Sovereign Press.

Elder, C. (2007) *Being Australian: Narratives of National Identity.* Crows Nest NSW: Allen and Unwin.

Eyben, R. (2008) 'Becoming a feminist in Aidland', in Coles, A. and Fechter, A-M. (eds) *Gender and Family among Transnational Professionals.* London: Routledge.

Featherstone, D., Phillips, R. and Waters, J. (2007) 'Introduction: spatialities of transnational networks', *Global Networks* 7(4): 383–391.

Fechter, A-M. (2007) *Transnational Lives: Expatriates in Indonesia.* Aldershot: Ashgate.

Fechter, A-M. (2008) 'From incorporated wives to "Expat Girls": a new generation of expatriate women?', in Coles, A. and Fechter, A-M. (eds) *Gender and Family among Transnational Professionals.* London: Routledge.

Fielden, S.L. and Davidson. M.J. (1996) 'Sources of stress in unemployed female managers: an exploratory study', *International Review of Women and Leadership* 2(2): 73–97.

Fielding, A.J. (1991) 'Migration and social mobility: southeast England as an escalator region', *Regional Studies* 26(1): 1–15.

Findlay, A.M. (1990) 'A migration channels approach to the study of high level manpower movements', *International Migration* 28: 15–22.

Findlay, A.M. and Garrick, L. (1990) 'Scottish emigration in the 1990s', *Transactions of the Institute of British Geographers* 15: 177–192.

Findlay, A.M. and Gould, W.T.S. (1989) 'Skilled international migration: a research agenda', *Area* 21: 3–11.

Findlay, A.M., Li, F.L.N., Jowett, A.J. and Skeldon, R. (1996) 'Skilled international migration and the global city: a study of expatriates in Hong Kong', *Transactions of the Institute of British Geographers* 21(1): 49–61.

Findlay, A.M. and Li, F.L.N. (1998) 'A migration channels approach to the study of professionals moving to and from Hong Kong', *International Migration Review* 32(3) Autumn: 682–703.

Forster, N. (1994) 'The forgotten employees? The experience of expatriate returning staff returning to the UK', *International Journal of Human Resource Management* 5: 405–423.

Forster, N. (1996) *A Report on the Management of Expatriates in 36 UK Companies.* Cardiff: Cardiff Business School.

Forster, N. (2000) 'The myth of the international manager', *International Journal of Human Resource Management* 11(1) February: 126–142.

Forster, N. and Johnsen, M. (1996) 'Expatriate management policies in UK companies new to the international scene', *International Journal of Human Resource Management* 7: 179–205.

Fortier, A-M. (2000) *Migrant Belongings: Memory, Space, Identity.* Oxford: Berg.

Foucault, M. (1972) *The Archaeology of Knowledge and the Discourse on Language.* New York: Pantheon.

Foucault, M. (1979) 'Governmentality', *Ideology and Consciousness* 6: 5–22.

Foucault, M. (1980) *Power/Knowledge.* New York: Pantheon.

Frankenberg, R. (1993) *White Women, Race Matters: The Social Construction of Whiteness.* London: Routledge.

Freeman, M. (1993) *Rewriting the Self: History, Memory, Narrative.* London: Routledge.

Friedmann, J. (1986) 'The world city hypothesis', *Development and Change* 17: 69–83.

Furnham, A. and Bochner, S. (1986) *Culture Shock: Psychological Reactions to Unfamiliar Environments.* London: Methuen.

Gad, G. (1991) 'Toronto's financial district', *The Canadian Geographer* 35: 203–207.

Gallagher, C.A. (2000) 'White like me? Methods, meaning and manipulation in the field of white studies', in *Racing Research Researching Race: Methodological Dilemmas in Critical Race Studies.* New York: New York University Press.

Garner, S. (2006) 'The uses of whiteness: what sociologists working on Europe can draw from US research on whiteness', *Sociology* 40(2): 257–275.

Garner, S. (2007) *Whiteness: An Introduction.* London: Routledge.

Gartrell, B. (1984) 'Colonial wives: villains or victims?', in Callan, H. and Ardener, S. (eds) *The Incorporated Wife.* Beckenham: Croom Helm.

Ghoshal, S. and Nohria, N. (1989) 'Internal Differentiation within Multinational Corporations', *Strategic Management Journal* 10: 323–332.

Glick Schiller, N., Basch, L. and Szanton-Blanc, C. (eds) (1992) *Towards a Transnational Perspective on Migration: Race, Class, Ethnicity and Nationalism Reconsidered.* New York: New York Academy of Sciences.

Glick Schiller, N. (1997) 'Cultural politics and the politics of culture', *Identities* 4: 1–8.

Gordon, L. (2008) 'The shell ladies' project: making and remaking home', in Coles, A. and Fechter, A.-M. (eds) *Gender and Family Among Transnational Professionals.* London: Routledge.

Green, M. (1980) *Dreams of Adventure, Deeds of Empire*. London: Routledge, Kegan Paul.

Gregory, D. and Urry, J. (1985) *Social Relations and Spatial Structures*. New York: St Martin's Press.

Guarnizo, L.E. and Smith, M.P. (1998) 'The locations of transnationalism', in Smith, M.P and Guarnizo, L.E. (eds) *Transnationalism from Below*. New Brunswick: Transaction, pp. 3–34.

Gubrium, J.F. and Holstein, J.A. (1995) 'Biographical work and new ethnography', in Josselson, R. and Lieblich, A. (eds) *Interpreting Experience: The Narrative Study of Lives*. Thousand Oaks: Sage.

Gunaratnam, Y. (2003) *Researching Race and Ethnicity: Methods, Knowledge and Power*. London: Sage.

Gutting, D. (1996) 'Narrative identity and residential history', *Area* 28: 482–490.

Hacking, I. (1986) 'Making up people', in Heller, T., Sosan, M. and Wellbery, D. (eds) *Reconstructing Individualism: Autonomy, Individuality and the Self in Western Thought*. Stanford: Stanford University Press.

Halford, S. and Leonard, P. (2001) *Gender, Power and Organisations*. Basingstoke: Palgrave.

Halford, S. and Leonard, P. (2006) *Negotiating Gendered Identities at Work: Place, Space and Time*. Basingstoke: Palgrave.

Hall, S. (1994) 'Cultural identity and diaspora', in Williams, P. and Christman, L. (eds) *Colonial Discourse and Post-Colonial Theory: A Reader*. New York: Columbia University Press.

Hall, S. (1996) 'Introduction: who needs identity?', in Hall, S. and du Gay, P. (eds) *Questions of Cultural Identity*. London: Sage, pp. 1–17.

Hannerz, U. (1992) 'The global ecumene as a network of networks', in Kuper, A. (ed.) *Conceptualizing Society*. London: Routledge.

Hannerz, U. (1996) *Transnational Connections*. London: Routledge.

Hardill, I. (1998) 'Gender perspectives on British expatriate work', *Geoforum* 29(3): 257–268.

Hardill, I. (2002) *Gender, Migration and the Dual Career Household*. London: Routledge.

Hardill, I. and MacDonald, S. (1998) 'Choosing to relocate: an examination of the impact of expatriate work on dual career households', *Women's Studies International Forum* 21(1): 21–29.

Hardy, C., Palmer, I. and Phillips, N. (2000) 'Discourse as a strategic resource', *Human Relations* 53(9): 1227–1248.

Harper, D. (1998) 'An argument for visual sociology', in Prosser, J. (ed.) *Image-based Research: A Sourcebook for Qualitative Researchers*. London: Falmer Press.

Harper, D., Knowles, C. and Leonard, P. (2005) 'Visually narrating postcolonial lives: ghosts of war and empire', *Visual Studies* 20(1): 4–15.

Hartl, K. (2003) *Expatriate Women Managers: Gender, Culture and Career*. Mering: Hampp Verlag.

Hartl, K. (2004) 'The expatriate career transition and women managers' experiences', *Women in Management Review* 19(1): 40–51.

Henry, N. and Massey, D. (1995) 'Competitive time space in high technology', *Geoforum* 26: 49–64.

Hindman, H. (2007) 'Outsourcing difference: expatriate training and the disciplining of culture', in Sassen, S. (ed.) *Deciphering the Global: Its Scales, Spaces and Subjects*. New York: Routledge.

Hindman, H. (2008) 'Shopping for a hypernational home: how expatriate women in Kathmandu labour to assuage fear', in Coles, A. and Fechter, A-M. (eds) *Gender and Family among Transnational Professionals*. New York: Routledge.

Hirst, P.Q. and Thompson, G. (1996) *Globalisation in Question: The International Economy and the Possibilities of Governance*. Cambridge: Polity Press.

Holdsworth, M. (2002) *Foreign Devils: Expatriates in Hong Kong*. Oxford: Oxford University Press.

Holloway, S.R. (2007) 'Identity, contingency and the urban geography of "race"', *Social and Cultural Geography* 1(2): 197–208.

Hugo, G. (1994) *Economic Implications of Emigration from Australia*. Canberra: Bureau of Immigration and Population Research.

Hunter, S. (2009) 'Subversive attachments? Gendered, raced and professional realignments in the "new" NHS', in Barnes, M. and Prior, D. (eds) *Subversive Citizens: Power, Agency and Resistance among Public Service Users and Workers*. Bristol: Policy.

Ignatiev, N. (1995) *How the Irish Became White*. New York: Routledge.

Iredale, R. (2001) 'The migration of professionals: theories and typologies', *International Migration* 39: 7–24.

Jackson, P. (1998) 'Constructions of "whiteness" in the geographical imagination', *Area* 30(2): 99–106.

Jacobson, M.F. (1998) *Whiteness of a Different Color: European Immigrants and the Alchemy of Race*. Cambridge: Harvard University Press.

Jervis, S. (2008) 'Moving experiences: responses to relocation among British Military Wives', in Coles, A. and Fechter, A-M. (eds) *Gender and Family Among Transnational Professionals*. New York: Routledge.

Jones, A. (1993) 'Becoming a girl: poststructuralist suggestions for educational research', *Gender and Education* 5(2): 157–166.

Kapoor, P. (1999) 'Provincializing whiteness: deconstructing discourse(s) on international progress', in Nakayama, T.K. and Martin, J.N. (eds) *Whiteness: The Communication of Social Identity*. Thousand Oaks: Sage.

Kearney, M. (1995) 'The local and the global: the anthropology of globalization and transnationalism', *Annual Review of Anthropology* 24: 547–565.

Keenan, B. (2005) *Diplomatic Baggage: The Adventures of a Trailing Spouse*. London: John Murray Publishers.

Kenny, J.T. (1995) 'Climate, race and imperial authority: the symbolic landscape of the British hill station in India', *Annals of the Association of American Geographers* 85(4) (Dec): 694–714.

Kenny, K. (2008) '"Arrive bearing gifts...": Postcolonial insights for development management', in Dar, S. and Cooke, B. (eds) *The New Development Management*. London: Zed Books.

Kirkwood, D. (1984) 'Settler wives in Southern Rhodesia: a case study', in Callan, H. and Ardener, S. (eds) *The Incorporated Wife*. Beckenham: Croom Helm.

Knowles, C. (1999) 'Race, identities and lives', *Sociological Review* 47(1): 110–135.

Knowles, C. (2003) *Race and Social Analysis*. London: Sage.

Knowles, C. (2006) 'Seeing race through the lens', *Ethnic and Racial Studies* 29(3): 512–529.

Kofman, E. (2000) 'The invisibility of skilled female migrants and gender relations in studies of skilled migration in Europe', *International Journal of Population Geography* 6(1): 45–59.

Kofman, E. and Raghuran, P. (2005) 'Gender and skilled migrants: Into and beyond the work place', *Geoforum* 36: 149–154.

Kofman, E. and Raghuran, P. (2006) 'Gender and global labour migrations: incorporating skilled workers', *Antipode* 38(2): 282–303.

Kohonen, E. (2008) 'The impact of international assignments on expat's identity and career aspirations: reflections upon re-entry', *Scandinavian Journal of Management* 24: 320–329.

Konrad, A.M., Prasad, P. and Pringle, J.K. (eds) (2006) *Handbook of Workplace Diversity*. London: Sage.

Kothari, U. (2002) 'Feminist and postcolonial challenges to development', in Kothari, U. and Minogue, M. (eds) *Development Theory and Practice: Critical Perspectives*. Basingstoke: Palgrave.

Kothari, U. (2006) 'Spatial practices and imaginaries: Experiences of colonial officers and development professionals', *Singapore Journal of Tropical Geography* 27: 235–253.

Langlands, R. (1999) 'Britishness or Englishness? The historical problem of national identity in Britain', *Nations and Nationalism* 5(1): 53–69.

Lawson, V. (2000) 'Arguments within geographies of movement: the theoretical potential of migrants' stories', *Progress in Human Geography* 24(2): 173–189.

Lefebvre, H. (1991) *The Production of Space*. Oxford: Blackwell.

Leggett, W.H. (2005) 'Terror and the colonial imagination at work in the transnational corporate spaces of Jakarta, Indonesia', *Identities: Global Studies in Culture and Power* 12: 271–302.

Lemke, J. (1995) *Textual Politics: Discourse and Social Dynamics*. London: Taylor and Francis.

Leonard, P. (2003) '"Playing" doctors and nurses? Competing discourses of gender, power and identity in the British National Health Service', *The Sociological Review* 51(2): 218–237.

Leonard, P. (2008) 'Migrating identities: gender, whiteness and Britishness in post-colonial Hong Kong', *Gender, Place and Culture* 15(1): 45–60.

Leonard, P. (2010) 'Work, identity and change? Post/colonial encounters in Hong Kong', *Journal of Ethnic and Migration Studies* 36: 6.

Levine-Rasky, C. (2002) *Working through Whiteness: International Perspectives.* New York: State University of New York Press.

Ley, D. (2004) Transnational spaces and everyday lives', *Transactions of the Institute of British Geographers* 29: 151–64.

Li, F.L.N., Jowett, A.J., Findlay, A.M. and Skeldon, R. (1995) 'Discourse on migration and ethnic identity: interviews with professionals in Hong Kong', *Transactions of the Institute of British Geographers* 20: 342–356.

Linderman, P. and Hess, M.B. (2002) *Realities of Foreign Service.* San Jose, CA: Writer's Club Press.

Linehan, M. (2000) *Senior Female International Managers: Why so Few?* Aldershot: Ashgate.

Loomba, A. (1998) *Colonialism/Postcolonialism.* London: Routledge.

Low, M. and Barnett, C. (2000) 'After globalisation', *Environment and Planning D: Society and Space* 18: 53–61.

Lugard, F. (1922) *The Dual Mandate in British Tropical Africa.* London: Frank Cass.

Macauley, T.B. (1972) 'A minute on Indian education', in Macauley, T.B. *Selected Writings.* Chicago: University of Chicago Press.

McClaren, P. (1998) 'Whiteness is...the struggle for postcolonial hybridity', in Kincheloe, J.L., Steinberg, S.R., Rodriguez, N.M. and Chennault, R.E. (eds) *White Reign: Deploying Whiteness in America.* New York: St Martin's Press.

McDowell, L. (1992) 'Multiple voices: speaking from inside and outside "the project"', *Antipode* 24: 56–72.

McDowell, L. (2008) 'Thinking through work: complex inequalities, constructions of difference and transnational migrants', *Progress in Human Geography* 32(4): 491–507.

McSweeney, B. (2002) 'Fundamental flaws in Hofstede's research', *EBF* 9: 39–33.

Mahler, S.J. (2006) 'Theoretical and empirical contributions toward a research agenda for transnationalism', in Smith, L.E. and Guarnizo, L.E. (2006) *Transnationalism from Below.* New Brunswick: Transaction.

Martin, R. (1847) *China: Political, Commercial, Social – Official Report to Her Majesty's Government.* Vol 2. London: James Madden.

Massey, D. (1994) 'Double articulation: a place in the world', in Bammer, A. (ed.) *Displacements: Cultural Identities in Question.* Bloomington: Indiana University Press.

Massey, D. (2005) *For Space.* London: Sage.

Mathur-Helm, B. (2002) 'Expatriate women managers: at the crossroads of success, challenges and career goals', *Women in Management Review* 17(2): 18–28.

Meier, L. (2006) 'On the road to being white? The construction of whiteness in the everyday life of German high fliers in Singapore and London', in Berking, H., Frers, S., Low, L., Meier, M., Steets, L. and Stoetzer, S. (eds) *Negotiating Urban Conflicts*. New Brunswick and London: Transcript Veleg/Transaction Publishers.

Meier, L. (2007) 'Working in the skyline-images and everyday action', in Frers, L. and Meier, L. (eds) *Encountering Urban Spaces*. Aldershot: Ashgate.

Memmi, A. (1990) *The Colonizer and the Colonized*. London: Earthscan Publications.

Mervosh, E.M. (1997) 'Managing expatriate compensation', *Industry Week* 246(14): 13–18.

Metcalf, T. (1989) *An Imperial Vision: Indian Architecture and Britain's Raj*. Berkeley: University of California Press.

Michel, M. (1995) 'Positioning the subject: locating postcolonial studies', *Ariel* 26(1): 83–99.

Mickelthwait, J. and Wooldridge, A. (2001) *A Future Perfect: The Challenge and Hidden Promise of Globalisation*. London: Random House.

Miles, R. and Phizacklea, A. (1984) *White Man's Country: Racism in British Politics*. London: Pluto Press.

Miller, K. (1985) *Emigrants and Exiles: Ireland and the Irish Exodus to North America*. New York: Sage.

Mills, S. (2003) *Michel Foucault*. London: Routledge.

Mills, S. (2005) *Gender and Colonial Space*. Manchester: Manchester University Press.

Mohanty, S.P. (1991) 'Drawing the color line: Kipling and the culture of colonial rule', in La Capra, D. (ed.) *The Bounds of Race*. Ithaca: Cornell University Press.

Moore, F. (2005) *Transnational Business Cultures: Life and Work in a Multinational Corporation*. Aldershot: Ashgate.

Moore, F. (2007) 'Introduction: bridging business and bureaucracies', in Ardener, S. and Moore, F. (eds) *Professional Identities: Policy and Practice in Business and Bureaucracy*. New York: Berghahn Books.

Moore, H.L. (1986) *Space, Text and Gender: An Anthropological Study of the Marakwet of Kenya*. Cambridge: Cambridge University Press.

Moore, M.J. (2002) '"Same ticket, different trip" supporting dual-career couples on global assignments', *Women in Management Review* 17(2): 61–67.

Morgan, G. (1997) *Images of Organization*. London: Sage.

Mouffe, C. (1988) 'Radical democracy: modern or post modern?', in Ross, A. (ed.) *Universal Abandon? The Politics of Postmodernism*. Minneapolis: University of Minneapolis Press.

Mueller, F. (1994) 'Societal effect, organizational effect and globalization', *Organization Studies* 15(3): 407–428.

Myers, G.A. (2002) 'Colonial geography and masculinity in Eric Dutton's *Kenya Mountain*', *Gender, Place and Culture* 9(1): 23–38.

Nash, C. (1996) 'Men again: Irish masculinity, nature and manhood in the early twentieth century', *Ecumene* 3: 427–453.

Nayak, A. (2005) 'White lives', in Murji, K. and Solomos, J. (eds). *Racialization: Studies in Theory and Practice*. Oxford: Oxford University Press.

Nowicka, M. (2006) *Transnational Professionals and their Cosmopolitan Universes*. New York: Campus Verlag.

Oberg, K. (1960) 'Culture shock: adjustment to new cultural environments', *Practical Anthropology* 7: 177–182.

Oliver, C. (2007) 'Imagined communities: older migrants and aspirational mobility', in Vered, A. (ed.) *Going First Class? New Approaches to Privileged Travel and Movement*. New York: Berghahn Books.

Ong, A. (1999) *Flexible Citizenship: The Cultural Logics of Transnationality*. Durham, NC and London: Duke University Press.

O'Reilly, K. (2000) *The British on the Costa del Sol: Transnational Identities and Local Communities*. London: Routledge.

Parker, D. (2000) 'The Chinese takeaway and the diasporic habitus: space, time and power-geometries', in Hesse, B. (ed.) *Un/settled Multiculturalisms: Diasporas, Entanglements, Transcriptions*. London: Routledge.

Patten, C. (2008) *What Next? Surviving the Twenty-first Century*. London: Allen Lane.

Pederson, P. (1995) *The Five Stages of Culture Shock: Critical Incidents Around the World*. London: Greenwood.

Prasad, A. (1997) 'The colonizing consciousness and representations of the other: a postcolonial critique of the discourse of oil', in Prasad, P., Mills, A., Elmes, M. and Prasad, A. (eds) *Managing the Organizational Melting Pot: Dilemmas of Workplace Diversity*. Thousand Oaks: Sage.

Prasad, A. (2003) 'The gaze of the other: postcolonial theory and organizational analysis', in Prasad, A. (ed.) *Postcolonial Theory and Organizational Analysis: A Critical Engagement*. Basingstoke: Palgrave.

Prasad, A. (2006) 'The jewel in the crown: postcolonial theory and workplace diversity', in Konrad, A.M., Prasad, P. and Pringle, J.K. (eds) *Handbook of Workplace Diversity*. London: Sage.

Prasad, P. (2005) *Crafting Qualitative Research: Working in the Postpositivist Traditions*. Armonk: M.E. Sharpe.

Pratt, G. (1997) '"Stereotypes and ambivalence" nanny agents' stereotypes of domestic workers in Vancouver, British Columbia', *Gender, Place and Culture* 4: 159–177.

Pratt, M.L. (1992) *Imperial Eyes: Travel Writing and Transculturation*. London: Routledge.

Price, F. (1909) *Ootacamund: A History*. Madras: Madras Government Publishing Press.

Pries, L. (2001) *New Transnational Social Spaces*. London: Routledge.

Proceedings of the Planters' Association, Kandy (1869–70) Colombo: E.H. Peterson.

Proudford, K.L. and Nkomo. S. (2006) 'Race and ethnicity in organizations', in Konrad, A.M., Prasad, P. and Pringle, J.K. (eds) *Handbook of Workplace Diversity.* London: Sage.

Pugliese, J. (2002) 'Race as category crisis: whiteness and the topical assignation of race', *Social Semiotics* 12(2): 149–168.

Raban, J. (1999) *Passage to Juneau: A Sea and its Meanings.* New York: Pantheon Books.

Rapport, N. and Dawson, A. (1998) *Migrants of Identity: Perceptions of Home in a World of Movement.* Oxford: Berg.

Reynolds, C. and Bennett, R. (1991) 'The career couple challenge', *Personnel Journal* 70: 46–49.

Richards, T. (1994) *The Imperial Archive: Knowledge and the Fantasy of Empire.* London: Verso.

Ritzer, G. (1993) *The McDonaldization of Society.* Thousand Oaks: Pine Forge Press.

Robertson, R. (1992) *Globalization: Social Theory and Global Culture.* London: Sage.

Roediger, D.R. (1991) *The Wages of Whiteness: Race and the Making of the American Working Class.* London: Verso.

Roediger, D.R. (1994) *Towards the Abolition of Whiteness: Essays on Race, Politics and Working Class History.* London: Verso.

Rose, N. (1999) *Governing the Soul: The Shaping of the Private Self.* London: Free Associations Books.

Royal College of Nursing (2002) *Internationally Recruited Nurses: Good Practice Guidance for Health Care Employers and RCN Negotiators.* London: RCN.

Rutherford, J. (1997) *Forever England: Reflections on Race, Masculinity and Empire.* London: Lawrence & Wishart.

Said, E. (1978) *Orientalism.* London: Penguin.

Said, E. (1993) *Culture and Imperialism.* London: Verso.

Salt, J. (1988) 'Highly skilled migrants, careers and international labour markets', *Geoforum* 19: 387–399.

Salt, J. (1993) *Migration and Population Change in Europe.* Geneva: UNDIR.

Salt, J. (1997) 'International movements of the highly-skilled', Paris: OECD, International Migration Unit Occasional Paper No 3.

Salt, J., Clark, J. and Schmidt, S. (2001) *Patterns and Trends in International Migration in Western Europe.* London: Eurostat.

Sassen, S. (1988) *The Mobility of Capital and Labour.* Cambridge: Cambridge University Press.

Sassen, S. (1991) *The Global Cities: New York, London, Tokyo.* Princeton: Princeton University Press.

Sassen, S. (1994) *Cities in a World Economy.* Thousand Oaks: Pine Forge Press.

Sassen, S. (ed.) (2002) *Global Networks, Linked Cities.* New York: Routledge.

Sassen, S. (2003) 'Women's burden: counter geographies of globalization and the feminization of survival', *Journal of International Affairs* 53(2): 503–524.

Sassen, S. (ed.) (2007) *Deciphering the Global: Its Scales, Spaces and Subjects.* New York: Routledge.

Savage, M., Bagnall, G. and Longhurst, B. (2005) *Globalization and Belonging.* London: Sage.

Saxton, A. (1990) *The Rise and Fall of the White Republic: Class Politics and Mass Culture in Nineteenth-Century America.* London: Verso.

Scott, J. (1985) *Weapons of the Weak: Everyday Forms of Peasant Resistance.* New Haven: Yale University Press.

Scott, S. (2006) 'The social morphology of skilled migration: The case of the British middle class in Paris', *Journal of Ethnic and Migration Studies* 32(7): 1105–1129.

Scullion, H. (1994) 'Staffing policies and strategic control in British multinationals', *International Studies of Management and Organisation* 24(3): 86–104.

Selmer, J. (2001) 'Expatriate selection: back to basics?', *International Journal of Human Resource Management* 12(8): 1219–1233.

Selmer, J. (2001b) 'Coping and adjustment of Western expatriate managers in Hong Kong', *Scandinavian Journal of Management* 17: 167–185.

Sharma, S., Hutnyk, J. and Sharma, A. (eds) *1996 DisOrienting Rhythms: The Politics of the New Asian Dance Music.* London: Zed Books.

Shohat, E. and Stam, R. (1994) *Unthinking Eurocentrism: Multiculturalism and the Media.* London: Routledge.

Shome, R. (1999) 'Whiteness and the politics of location: postcolonial reflections', in Nakayama, T.K. and Martin, J.N. (eds) *Whiteness: The Communication of Social Identity.* Thousand Oaks: Sage.

Shome, R. (2000) 'Outing whiteness', *Critical Studies in Media Communication* 17(3): 366–371.

Shome, R. (2003) 'Space matters: the power and practice of space', *Communication Theory* 13(1): 39–56.

Simpson, J. (1996) 'Easy talk, white talk, talk back: some reflections on the meanings of our words', *Journal of Contemporary Ethnography* 25(3): 372–389.

Sinha, M. (2001) 'Britishness, clubbability, and the colonial sphere: the genealogy of an imperial institution in colonial India', *The Journal of British Studies* 40(4): 489–521.

Sklair, L. (2001) *The Transnational Capitalist Class.* Oxford: Blackwell.

Smith, A.D. (1990) 'Towards a global culture?', in Featherstone, M. (ed.) *Global Culture: Nationalism, Globalization and Modernity.* London: Sage.

Smith, A.D. (1995) *Nations and Nationalism in a Global Era.* Cambridge: Polity Press.

Smith, M.P. (1992) 'Postmodernism, urban ethnography and the new social space of ethnic identity', *Theory and Society* 21: 493–531.

Smith, M.P. (1999) 'Transnationalism and the city', in Beauregard, R. and Body-Gendrot, S. (eds) *The Urban Movement*. London: Sage, pp. 119–139.

Smith, M.P. (2005) *Transnational Urbanism: Locating Globalisation*. Oxford: Blackwell.

Smith, M.P. (2005) 'Transnational urbanism revisited', *Journal of Ethnic and Migration Studies* 31(2) March: 235–244.

Soja, E.W. (1996) *Thirdspace: Journeys to Los Angeles and Other Real-and-Imagined Places*. Malden: Blackwell.

Soloman, C.M. (1998) 'Women expats: shattering the myths', *Workforce* 5(10): 10–12.

Song, M. (2005) 'Global and local articulations of Asian identity', in Alexander, C. and Knowles, C. (eds) *Making Race Matter: Bodies, Space and Identity*. Basingstoke: Palgrave.

Sørensen, N.N. and Olwig, K.F. (2002) *Work and Migration: Life and Livelihoods in a Globalizing World*. London: Routledge.

Spurr, D. (1993) *The Rhetoric of Empire: Colonial Discourse in Journalism, Travel Writing and Imperial Administration*. Durham: Duke University Press.

Sriskandarajah, D. and Drew, C. (2006) *Brits Abroad: Mapping the Scale and Nature of British Emigration*. London: IPPR.

Stahl, G.K., Miller, E.L. and Tung, R.L. (2002) 'Towards the boundaryless career: a closer look at the expatriate career concept and the perceived implications of an international assignment', *Journal of World Business* 37: 216–227.

Stanley, H.M. (1885) *The Congo and the Founding of its Free State*. New York: Harper and Row.

Steyn, M. (1999) 'White identity in context: a personal narrative', in Nakayama, T.K. and Martin, J.N. (eds) *Whiteness: The Communication of Social Identity*. Thousand Oaks: Sage.

Steyn, M. (2001) *Whiteness Just Isn't What it Used to Be: White Identity in a Changing South Africa*. Albany: State University of New York Press.

Stoler, L.A. (1991) 'The struggle to be temperate: climate and "moral masculinity" in mid-nineteenth century Ceylon', *Singapore Journal of Tropical Geography* 21(1): 34–47.

Taylor Jr, H.L. (1995) 'The hidden face of racism', *American Quarterly* 47(3): 395–408.

Townsend, A. (1997) *Making a Living in Europe: Human Geographies of Economic Change*. London: Routledge.

Trollope, J. (1983). *Britannia's Daughters: Women of the British Empire*. London: Hutchinson.

Tuan, Y. (1977) *Space and Place: The Perspectives of Experience*. Minneapolis: University of Minnesota Press.

Tully, J. (2008) *Public Philosophy in a New Key: Volume 2, Imperialism and Civic Freedom*. Cambridge: Cambridge University Press.

Twine, F.W. (2000) 'Racial ideologies and racial methodologies', in Twine, F.W. and Warren, J. (eds) *Racing Research, Researching Race: Methodological Dilemmas in Critical Race Studies*. New York: New York University Press.

Twine, F.W. and Gallagher, C. (2007) 'The future of whiteness: a map of the "third wave"', *Ethnic and Racial Studies* 31(1): 4–24.

Urry, J. (2002) *Global Complexity*. Cambridge: Polity.

Valentine, G. (2001) *Social Geographies; Space and Society*. Harlow: Pearson Education Ltd.

Vandsemb, B. (1995) 'The place of narrative in the study of Third World migration: the case of spontaneous rural migration in Sri Lanka', *Professional Geographer* 47: 411–25.

Wacquant, L. (2003) 'Ethnografeast: a progress report on the practice and promise of ethnography', *Ethnography* 4(1): 5–14.

Wai, K.C. (1991) *The Making of Hong Kong Society: Three Studies of Class Formation in Early Hong Kong*. Oxford: Clarendon Press.

Walsh, K. (2005) 'British expatriate belonging in Dubai: foreignness, domesticity, intimacy', unpublished PhD Royal Holloway, University of London.

Walsh, K. (2006) 'Dad says I'm tied to a shooting star! Grounding (research on) British expatriate belonging', *Area* 38(3): 268–278.

Walsh, K. (2008) 'Travelling together? Work, intimacy and home amongst British expatriate couples in Dubai', in Coles, A. and Fechter, A-M. (eds) *Gender and Family among Transnational Professionals*. New York: Routledge.

Weedon, C. (1997) *Feminist Practice and Poststructuralist Theory*. 2nd edn Oxford: Blackwell.

Weiss, A. (2005) 'The transnationalization of social inequality: conceptualizing social positions on a world scale', *Current Sociology* 53(4): 707–728.

Westwood, S. and Phizacklea, A. (2000) *Transnationalism and the Politics of Belonging*. London: Routledge.

Wetherall, M. and Potter, J. (1992) *Mapping the Language of Racism:Discourse and the Legitimation of Exploitation*. New York: Columbia University Press.

White, S. (1980) 'A philosophical dichotomy in migration research', *Professional Geographer* 32: 6–13.

Willis, K. and Yeoh, B. (2000) 'Gender and transnational migration strategies: Singaporean migration to China', *Regional Studies* 34(3): 253–264.

Willis, K. and Yeoh, B. (2002) 'Gendering transnational communities: a comparison of Singaporean and British migrants in China', *Geoforum* 33(4): 553–565.

Wu, Y. (1999) 'Prelude to culture: interrogating colonial rule in early British Hong Kong', *Dialectical Anthropology* 24: 141–170.

Wuthnow, J. (2002) 'Deleuze in the postcolonial: on nomads and indigenous politics', *Feminist Theory* 3(2): 183–200.

Yeoh, B. and Khoo, L-M. (1998) 'Home, work and community: skilled international migration and expatriate women in Singapore', *International Migration* 36(2): 159–186.

Yeoh, B. and Willis, K. (2005a) 'Singaporean in China: transnational women elites and the negotiation of gendered identities', *Geoforum* 36: 211–222.

Yeoh, B. and Willis, K. (2005b) 'Singaporean and British transmigrants in China and the cultural politics of "contact zones"', *Journal of Ethnic and Migration Studies* 31(2): 269–285.

Yeoh, B., Willis, K. and Abdul Khader Fakhri, S.M. (2003) 'Introduction: transnationalism and its edges', *Ethnic and Racial Studies* 26(2) March: 207–217.

Zickmund, S. (1997) 'Approaching the radical other: the discursive culture of cyberhate', in Jones, S.G. (ed.) *Virtual Culture: Identity and Communication in Cybersociety*. London: Sage.

Index